Resilient
RUIN

Also by Laura McHale Holland

Reversible Skirt: a Memoir
http://amzn.to/2bDBNwB

The Ice Cream Vendor's Song: Flash Fiction
http://amzn.to/2bCDQTd

Resilient Ruin

*A memoir of hopes
dashed and reclaimed*

Laura McHale Holland

WordForest
Rohnert Park, California 94928

Resilient Ruin
© 2016 by Laura McHale Holland

ISBN: 978-0-9829365-7-3 (paperback)
ISBN 978-0-9829365-8-0 (epub)
ASIN: B01KP5AMZ2 (.mobi)

Library of Congress Control Number: 2016910032

Cover design
Stefanie Fontecha, http://stefaniefontecha.com

Interior design
Jo-Anne Rosen, www.wordrunner.com

Ebook formatting
BB eBooks
http://bbebooksthailand.com

Note: To respect privacy, the names and identifying characteristics of most
people mentioned in this book have been changed, author's close family
members excepted.

For Kathy and Mary Ruth,

with infinite gratitude.

In the midst of winter, I found there was,

within me, an invincible summer.

Albert Camus, *Retour to Tipasa, L'Eté, 1954*

ONE

June 1963

A DIAMOND NEEDLE MEETS VINYL AND CRACKLES the air; electric guitar licks resonate ceiling to floor; and, like divers slicing water after flawless somersaults, The Beach Boys rock into *Surfin' USA*. A late arrival, I merge into a ring of students watching the more confident graduates of our eighth grade class partner up. In perfect sync, they are masters of the Swim, Twist, Jitterbug, Mashed Potatoes.

Dead center, with taps on her flats and charm bracelets jingling on her wrists, is Becky, one of my best friends. My other best friend, Jillie, is mortified because her latest diet backfired: instead of losing five pounds she gained six; she's nowhere to be seen. Becky never even bothers to weigh herself. She's not a cheerleader, well dressed, or especially popular, but she twirls about with abandon. I'm sure she'd be unbeatable on *American Bandstand*, a show I watch at her house since I'm not allowed to see it at home.

Chet, whose eyes are level with my chin, saunters up, extends his hand. "How about it?" he asks.

I'd wished for a young version of Steve McQueen as my very first dance partner, but I'm not anybody's dream partner either. Dominating my face are two-toned brown-and-white glasses with fins like a 1959 Cadillac. I've dropped them so often they are cracked, crooked and prone to sliding down my nose. My loose cotton shift with attached white eyelet vest was picked from racks of castoffs at a second-hand store. My naturally ebony locks are frizzy and orange from the last perm Mommy, my stepmom, forced me to get from her friend Florence. She does hair at a discount in her kitchen as her drooling son, who was dropped on his head as a baby, rocks on a wobbly chair, grunts unintelligibly, and slices his skin with any sharp object inadvertently left within his grasp.

I accept Chet's offer. He takes my arm and escorts me to a spot on the now crowded dance floor. Copying my classmates' moves, I pretend this isn't new to me. We dance through The Beach Boys' last lines and through the Four Seasons' *Sherry,* but when Bobby Vinton's *Roses Are Red* serenade begins, tall, tan, slightly bucktoothed Todd taps Chet's shoulder to cut in. Chet backs away; Todd takes my hand.

Todd and I have never spoken, but we both attend youth group meetings at a church across the street from the junior high. My sisters, Kathy and Mary Ruth, and I joined the congregation after our father, on his deathbed, asked that we return to the church. I was eleven, Mary Ruth twelve, and Kathy thirteen. I'd always felt guilty about attending mass only on holidays and for weddings and funerals. I was eager to study the Catechism, but Mommy doesn't like the local Catholic parish, so we didn't just join another parish; we switched religions.

I thought I'd go to Hell for going along with this and felt way out of place—until last year, when Becky moved to Hinsdale, one of Chicago's most affluent suburbs, from a small blue collar town in southern Illinois. The day she showed up at Sunday school I was drawn in by her Pepsodent smile, azure eyes and heart-shaped face framed by dark brown curls that bounce like mini Slinkys. I still feel like an impostor every time I veer from the Catholic version of *The Lord's Prayer* and ask the Lord to forgive my "debts" instead of my "trespasses," but I keep my anxiety in check because this church has brought friends to me.

Becky says folks in her hometown are more easygoing than people here, and they're super proud of their roller rink. Roller-skating indoors isn't popular in Hinsdale. So her mom found a rink in a town not too far away, and her whole family skates together there. Becky has an inner glow so strong, no gossip or chiding from girls at school ever causes her to go pale and slip away unnoticed. I feel protected by that glow. If it weren't for her, I probably would never have come to this dance.

I smile tentatively at Todd, hoping he knows what to do. He's several inches taller than I am, slim and wiry. His blue-green eyes sparkle in the dimly lit auditorium as we fumble, trying to get properly positioned for a slow dance. We settle down, inches apart.

"Ready?" He grins.

"Sure," I beam back. He moves to the side. I try to follow, and instead step on his pristine dress shoes. We break apart laughing.

"I'm just gonna move in a square," he says. "It's easy; you'll see." He demonstrates. Step with one foot, slide with the other, repeat around a square. It seems simple enough. We come together again, and I follow him, never quite relaxing into the music, but without further damage to his shoes.

Chet tries to cut in when the dance is over, but Todd won't budge. "Tough luck, buddy," Todd says.

Later, we spill out of the auditorium with the rest of the Hinsdale Junior High School class of 1963, officially released from the eighth grade. Todd and I stand about a foot apart on the sidewalk, the warm, humid air between us pressing like a caress.

Becky rushes up with a gaggle of girl friends, wraps her arms around me and kisses my cheek. "Are you sure you can't come with?"

"Yeah, you're invited, you know," says Deb, a perfectly proportioned brunette with a ponytail that swings down below her waist.

3

She's hosting a slumber party to celebrate our graduation.

Gloom invades me like Martians in *War of the Worlds*. Becky and Deb don't know I wasn't even supposed to attend the dance, let alone go to a sleepover afterward. "Nah, I have to get home."

"Well, call me tomorrow. We'll go swimming, or something." Becky rushes off, giggling and whooping with the other girls.

Todd and I wait in silence as cars, clean and polished, line up at the curb, graduates pile in, and cars pull away. It isn't long before his mom arrives in a green Dodge Polara wagon. "I've got to go. Um, do you want to ride bikes tomorrow?" he asks.

"Sure. Where?" My glasses slide down my nose; I push them up.

"The church parking lot, around one o'clock?"

"Okay."

He sprints toward his mom. I slip out of the thinning clumps of students waiting for parents and head home. Thrilled to have come through my very first dance unscathed, I break into a run. Soon, I'm leaping and soaring over the sidewalk squares. I catch my glasses as they bump down my nose and hold them in a fist. I feel as though I've stepped into someone else's life, not like the girl who fears her slip is showing, even when she's not wearing one. Not like the one whose parents, long dead, will never pick her up at the curb.

Soon I'm at the corner of our front yard. I run across the lawn, leap over the three concrete steps leading to the porch, put my glasses back on and try the door. It's locked. My punishment. I disobeyed, went to a dance, tried to be normal.

Mommy's voice blasts through the open dining room windows. "It's none of your beeswax when I let her in, the two of you all high and mighty, thinkin' you can tell me what to do," she bellows at my sisters.

I settle onto the porch and break into song. I know the words to every hit played at the dance, and I'm going to sing them all. Mommy will let me in eventually; the neighbors, already peeking from curtained windows, would talk if she didn't.

TWO

December 1963

OUTSIDE IT'S STORMY. INSIDE PETE AND I are steamy in the church's bell tower. He's my second boyfriend, but that's a secret because Mommy says Pete, a junior, is too old for me. I think that's just an excuse to keep me down. She didn't approve of my first crush, Todd, either—and he's my own age. Plus we never really dated; we just rode bikes together.

All summer long, we pedaled to every corner of our tree-lined suburb. We often stopped for ice cream at a spot near his home. The stout man behind the counter always greeted Todd by name when he ordered vanilla for himself, chocolate for me. I basked in the kindness, which permeated the air like fine perfume. Then we'd push off. He rode swiftly, one hand on the handlebar of his Schwinn, the other gripping his cone, which he consumed with nary a drip.

I couldn't get the hang of eating ice cream one-handed while wheeling through sweltering summer days. My bike, a dented contraption that has been repainted so many times its brand is a mystery, would wobble as ice cream dripped down my hand and splattered the handlebars, my glasses, arms, and sleeveless blouse. Feeling gooey inside and out, I would pause at the curb. Todd would double back, chortling as he reached into the pocket of his cutoffs for a paper napkin.

We didn't make other stops. We didn't stroll into the library to check out books, buy candy at the five and dime, park our bikes and find a quiet path where we could walk hand in hand. We didn't kiss, not even a peck on the cheek, when we said goodbye. I was looking forward to a goodnight kiss after our first real date to a dance or the movies, which I was sure was coming in the fall.

But that never happened. My first kiss turned out to be with Pete, the boy I'm melted into right now, the boy who is with me even when we're not together because I'm always daydreaming about the taste of his lips, the smell of his skin. I get woozy at the thought of him being near.

I sometimes think that if Becky hadn't come biking with Todd and me shortly before summer's end, I probably would never have spoken to Pete. I would have been with Todd instead. At the church barbeque where Pete and I met, Todd was lurking in a corner of the yard with his buddies. I hadn't seen him since he and Becky had gotten into a big fight during our ride. It began when the three of us stopped for a Burlington Northern train racing along the tracks toward Chicago. Becky said her family was moving to a town that has a roller rink. She wound a ringlet of hair around her finger and tried not to smile. She broke into a grin anyway, unable to hide that she was excited to be going to a place more like her hometown in southern Illinois.

After that, Todd and Becky argued about everything, from whether to sit or stand while pedaling uphill to whether her new school is as good as ours. They spat out insult after insult. Then she pulled a marble from her pocket, aimed and hit him in the neck. He rode up alongside and shoved her, almost knocking her down. She caught her balance and sped away. Rattled by the fight, I followed Becky, leaving Todd fuming in the street.

I didn't see Becky again till the day she moved. She'd been busy packing. I'd wanted no part of helping her leave me behind.

"It's only a few towns over—ten, twelve miles," she said before sliding next to her brother in the back seat of her family's Woody wagon. "We'll still see each other."

"We won't be going to the same school. You might as well be moving to Siberia," I grumbled, as the wagon backed out of the driveway.

Sorely missing Becky at the barbeque a few days later, I saw Todd with his friends and wondered if he expected me to join him or whether he was about to come over and say hello. Then it occurred to me that he might not like me anymore because I'd left with Becky after their argument. While those thoughts preoccupied me, Pete sidled up with a mischievous look in his brown eyes and an open bottle of Coke in each hand.

"It seems I've got an extra here. Do you want it?" He sipped one drink and extended the other toward me.

I was drawn to his gap-toothed grin. "Yeah, sure." The cold, moist surface felt good in my hand.

Pete and I moved to the buffet table, where we hovered like humming birds at salvia until the barbecue ended. Pete offered me a ride home. I glanced at Todd; he scowled back. I hadn't noticed before how bony he was, how stiff, like the Tin Man from *The Wizard of Oz*. Pete took my hand. I felt a surge of warmth, a sense of possibility.

I still feel that way when I'm with Pete. The best thing is being held so close I can feel his heart beat. My mind quiets down and everything except Pete and me fades far away. It's like when I learned to float on my back for the first time, only it's not water caressing me; it's Pete.

I wish we could walk the school halls together and go to parties and movies like a real couple, but Mommy put the kibosh on that.

"All Pete wants to do is get into your pants," Mommy said when Pete asked me to the movies the day after the barbeque. "You can only go to school events—with boys your own age."

It's impossible to reason with Mommy once she has her mind set on something. Plus, Kathy took Mommy's side. When she heard Pete had asked me out, she said it wouldn't be fair for me to date boys in her class since she couldn't date boys in mine, and if anybody in our family should date Pete, it ought to be her.

I can't remember the last time Kathy agreed with our step-mother on anything. She, Mary Ruth and I came up with Plan X last year to force Mommy to make changes. It is an us-against-her kind of thing that has led to a few improvements—one being able to bathe weekly instead of monthly. Mommy insisted baths wasted water. With all three of us arguing against her, she finally relented. But she holds tight like she's playing Crack the Whip. When she gives in, it's often only a tactic to shut us up. A day or so later, she'll say she never agreed to let us go to a basketball game, bake a cake or do any number of ordinary things girls enjoy. As far as Pete went, there was no Plan X, no "us." I was on my own.

Now, with lips red from too much kissing, Pete and I lie side by side on the bare wooden floor and listen to sleet pound the roof. It feels a little creepy that for months we've been climbing up a rickety, built-in ladder just to make out, because the rest of the time, we pretend we barely know each other so nobody gets wind of what we're up to. But everything seems off now that John F. Kennedy is embalmed underground, a flame burning perpetually above, and Lyndon B. Johnson, who looks like a cross between a gnarled elm and the Jolly Green Giant, is occupying the Oval Office.

Pete checks his watch. "Jeez, it's four o'clock already." He reaches for his glasses on the floor, puts them on and stands up.

While wind rattles the tower's only window, I straighten my cranberry and blue polka dot blouse, and don my glasses. The tortoise shell frames looked so good when I put them on layaway four months ago. But last week, when I tried them on with lenses in, they didn't look much better than the cheap frames they'd replaced.

"Do you like these glasses?" I stand and brush creases from my navy wool skirt. "I wish I'd gotten those mosaic-style ones, you know, like the ones Gayle has."

"Glasses are glasses. No big deal." He tucks in his green-and-white pinstriped shirt and walks to the corner where we'd peeled off our jackets and sweaters in a rush. He shakes our clothes apart and hands me my blue cardigan and jacket. The room is damp and pungent as we tug on our outer layers in the waning afternoon light.

A few minutes ago, I let Pete feel my breasts through my bra. Before, I'd always put my hand on his to stop it from inching up my ribs. But today, as soon as I would relax, his hand would creep up again. I finally just let go, and his touch on my bra felt thrilling—but now I feel awkward as an ostrich stuffed into a chicken coop as I wrap my coat tightly around myself. I'm embarrassed both that I didn't stop him and that my breasts are so small. It's not like he didn't know before, but now he's felt them, felt how flat they really are.

I follow Pete down the ladder and into the bright light of the hallway. "See ya," I say, as we step out the door.

He pulls his collar up and hunches his shoulders against the ice pellets bombing everything in their path. "Do you want a ride? It's really coming down hard."

"No thanks. I'm going to the record store to listen to the Beatles. It's only a couple of blocks." Like everybody I know, except for grownups, I love rock and roll, and this new band from England gave me a jolt of joy when I heard them for the first time at the end of swim class today. I can't wait to learn all their songs.

"Running through the sleet to listen to a band called the Beatles? Suit yourself, silly." He gives me a you're-too-lame-for-words look before darting to his car.

I leap over patches of ice in the parking lot and imagine he's already dreaming of a girl with bigger breasts.

THREE

February 1964

MOMMY IS UP AGAINST THE COOL PINK sink, robe open, bare breasts hanging, brown eyes fierce. I edge away from the powder room and toward the dining room table where my schoolbooks are stacked, a leaning tower balanced on vinyl plaid with scribbled formulas, timelines, verb conjugations and love notes protruding like broken wings. Growls from the basement furnace rumble up the stairs.

"Don't back away from me," Mommy snaps. She juts out her chin and raises her eyes to meet mine. She's indignant that I'm taller than her 4'11" frame by a good four inches, and growing—a reminder that she did not give birth to me.

I reverse directions and step to the powder room threshold. Less than two feet from her now, I glance at the toothpaste splattered on the medicine cabinet mirror, the wallpaper's pink roses climbing verdigris stems, the pink and beige tiles, her pink-painted toenails, chipped at the edges. If only I hadn't dawdled at the closet door, moving my handful of skirts and blouses back and forth across the rod, hoping to see a new way of putting them together.

Kathy, my willowy sister, and Mary Ruth, the svelte one, are probably halfway to school by now. Both 5'8", they easily march in step while they argue about which of them is smarter, a contest that began before I could talk, a contest I will never enter. What would they say if they were here?

"So, you can't stand to look at me, can you," Mommy snarls. "It's written all over your stupid face. You can't hide anything from me. And you can't hide from this either. Look!" She pulls down her baggy underpants and rips off a thick gauze bandage to expose a wound so raw it appears to have a pulse all its own, like Edgar Allen Poe's telltale heart. But this is a scar beating, beating on its own. I can hear it, I swear.

I hold my breath. No clue what to do. I knew she'd need help after her hysterectomy. But I thought it would be getting things down from shelves she can't reach, keeping her comfortable and warm, making her bed, fetching water for her pills, cooking supper. Not this.

"Take a look. Take a good look, missy," she spews. "This is pain. This is real pain, and you don't know what that is. You don't care about anybody but yourself. But mark my words, oh yes, mark my words. Your time is coming. Just you wait. Your time is coming. You'll see, oh yes, you'll see."

She reminds me of a jack-in-the box sprung loose, but I can't stuff her back inside, snap the cover closed and go back to fastening the stupid straps on the stupid clear plastic boots I had just slipped over my stupid loafers before she called me to her powder room lair.

"I suppose you think I'm all washed up now. Deformed. A good for nothing freak, don't you."

"Why? Why would I think that?"

"Don't you lie to me."

She points to the incision, belly button to pubic hair, thick and oozing and pink and punctuated with black stitches top to bottom. It's a railroad track, a railroad track leading somewhere I never want to go. Screaming now, she raises her raw-knuckled fist and shakes her arm, a metronome set faster than I could ever play. She lurches toward me. It looks like she'll pop straight into the air any minute. I'd like to see that: her head cracking against the ceiling.

I spin around, grab my books and rush outside. Coat

unbuttoned, I barely notice the bitter cold as I kick off my five-and-dime substitute for winter boots, which are thick, black marks in the high school fashion game my sisters and I play handicapped. I stuff the boots in my coat pockets, one bulging on each side.

Since Daddy died, three years ago now, I've been fighting for focus like a prizefighter against the ropes. Each morning I get dressed, hoping this will be the day that someone, somewhere will ring the bell, end the round. So the assault can end. So we can all staunch the bleeding. So my stepmother can rise up and become the mother she never was even before Daddy eased out of this world, the mother she promised him she would be when she married him, a man with three girls all under the age of five. But the bell never rings. She goes on and on, punching, jabbing, punching, and Kathy, Mary Ruth and I are the ones she wants to knock out.

But this time she has pushed me past an edge I didn't know was there. I feel assaulted, slapped breathless just because I'm here, just because I'm me. I don't know how I'll do it, but I must starve any trace of love I have for her until there is none left. I will not join her battles. She will fight alone. This is it. This is really it. She will be nothing to me. Nothing. She's not my real mother anyway. No more calling her Mommy, Mom or even Helen, her given name. She's a witch, yes, Wanda the Witch, Wanda the Wicked Witch of the Western Suburbs. That is who she will be to me from now on.

I suck in the biting air, roll up my skirt a couple inches and trudge forward, determined to have a smile on my face before I enter my first class. I arrive just as the bell signals all students should be in their seats, quiet and ready to learn.

Mr. Gardner struts up and down the aisles between desks, returning our Western Civilization semester exams. It irks me that he is balding, though my own grandfather has only a thin fringe of white hair running temple to temple around the back of his head, and that has never bothered me. Perhaps it is the air of confidence Mr. Gardner exudes, like he's Yul Brenner dancing with Deborah Kerr in *The King and I*. My grandfather is a quiet, humble man, like I imagine the shoemaker in Grimm's *Shoemaker and the Elves* fairy tale would be.

When he hands me my exam, Mr. Gardner says, "Laura, I want to see you after class." I look down at my paper. I'd scored 93 percent, which is a solid B—about what I'd expected. I can't imagine what he wants to see me about.

Our school doesn't grade on the curve. To receive an A, you have to score a 95 percent or above. I score in the 93 to 96 percent range in most of my classes, except for French, where I score in the high 90s. I had expected to do better in Mr. Gardner's class. I'd always done well in history and social studies. I'd aced every question on my eighth grade American history final, plus some extra credit questions. But try as I might, the mid-90s is where I land on almost every test in freshman Western Civ. It's more often in the B+ than A- range. Maybe I'm just not that interested in Attila the Hun or Cyrus the Great, or the distinction between a trebuchet and an ordinary catapult.

The bell rings, signaling the end of first period. As my classmates file out, I stand at the bulletin board where Mr. Gardner has just posted all our grades. It looks like my 93 was among the higher marks in the class.

"Well, Laura, how do you think you're doing in class?" Mr. Gardner says, hovering over me.

"Okay, I guess."

"Really?"

"Yeah, I think so."

"Well, kiddo, the fact is that you're not working hard enough. You're just getting by."

I wonder how he could really know how hard I'm working. "What do you mean?"

"You've got to step up like your sisters. They earned A's on every test. Mary Ruth often earned perfect scores. And their homework was impeccable."

"Um, yeah, well, I've never been as smart as they are." I tuck stray strands of my almost black hair behind my ears. A striking contrast to my sisters' subtle shades of brown, my mane seems only to broadcast that I am our family's black sheep.

"You're just lazy," he says. "And I'm going to help you get over that."

"You think I'm lazy because I don't get perfect grades?"

"What do you think you've earned this grading period?"

"Same as last time, a B." I'm certain that I am correct.

"No, you haven't. Your test and quiz average might be a B, but you haven't earned a B. I'm going to give you what you've earned." He leans over me, a smiling vulture.

My mouth is suddenly dry. "What do you think I've earned?" I squeak out.

"You, my dear, have earned a D."

"You're giving me a D? But I got B's on all my tests, even got a couple of A's." My face heats up. I know my cheeks are turning red, and I have no way to stop it.

"You're putting in a D's worth of effort." He smiles, smug.

"I don't think that's true."

"You can do better."

I know this is unfair. I don't talk with friends during class. I pay attention. I turn in all my homework. I take all the tests. I hardly ever miss class. I am speechless. In all the years I've followed one year behind Mary Ruth—who gets A's in every class except for

P.E., which isn't figured into anybody's GPA—no teacher has ever compared me to her, not to my face anyway. They have seemed to accept that academic geniuses like Mary Ruth don't come along that often, nor do those with brilliant creativity like Kathy, who excels academically and whose artwork is out of this world. Now Mr. Gardner is comparing me negatively to both of them. I suddenly appreciate how kind my former teachers have been about my inability to reach the very top. I don't know what to say to Mr. Gardner. I just want to escape his smirk.

"So, are you going to do better?" he asks.

"I don't know." I wonder whether this is God's way of punishing me for thinking Mr. Gardner's shiny dome is repulsive. But then I think about the semester exam, which has as much weight as a regular grading period. "Are you giving me a D for the exam, too?"

"No, that'll still be a B."

I realize then that as long as he doesn't give me another arbitrary D and if I keep earning B's, I'll still get a B for the year. And if somehow, miraculously, I were to grow some new brain cells and earn all A's for the second semester, the D averaged in for this grading period would ensure I'd get a B for the year anyway. I wonder what the point of even trying to get A's would be now. I think he is just messing with me, because he can.

FOUR

March 1964

THE SMELL OF HOT, SALTED FRENCH FRIES permeates the cafeteria. I suck chocolate milk through a straw and thumb through *Lord of the Flies*, one of the assigned books for English class. It was an easy read, unlike the historical novel *Ivanhoe*, where each paragraph was like a street full of potholes slowing traffic down. Yet *Lord of the Flies* unsettles me. I don't think the savagery of the stranded boys featured in the novel is a true reflection of human nature, but I'm not sure; the author must know a lot more about the ways of the world than I do.

"Hey there, Laura." Carleton's voice seems to float above my head. I look over my shoulder. He and his best friend, Jay, loom over me, peering down at the book. I know them from the youth group. Like Pete, they're in the junior class, so I'm not allowed to date them, not that I'm drawn to them that way.

Carleton is flabby, with black hair and skin so fair it looks snowflake-white against his dark green, horn-rimmed glasses. Jay is tall and skinny with hair so devoid of highlights it's the color of a dirty mop, and his hooknose irritates like an itch on your back you want to scratch but can't quite reach. Even so, the duo manages to exude a nonchalance that garners them a fair amount of respect in school.

"We've got a better book for you than that," Carleton says.

"Much better," Jay adds.

Carleton holds up a weathered copy of *Stranger in a Strange Land* by Robert Heinlein. "Ever heard of it?"

"Nope," I reply. I ask Shelby, who sits to my left, "You ever heard of *Stranger in a Strange Land*?" Shelby and I met the first day of school in P.E. Class when I told her that her shoulder-length red hair was to die for. We've been friends ever since.

"Yeah," she says. "Some kind of science fiction thing." She brushes her lush locks away from her face.

"It's way more than that," Carleton sniffs. He tosses the book onto the table in front of me. "Just read it, and tell us what you think. We've had our eye on you. We think you could be one of us."

Shelby snorts, rolls her light-brown eyes. "Are you done?" she asks me. Shelby is a girl who leaps off the high dive with abandon, one who likes to go to the speedway on dates, who sneaks cigarettes between classes in bathroom stalls and drinks sloe gin after school. Reading is low on her to-do list. Plenty of other students would rather goof off than read, but unlike most of us, Shelby antagonizes our teachers during class by blurting out what she really thinks. This often lands her in detention after school.

I draw in the last of my milk, "Yeah, I'm done."

"Let's split," she says. We each maneuver our nylon-stockinged legs from under the table's attached bench, stand and pick up our books. I leave *Stranger in a Strange Land* behind.

"Just take it." Carleton grabs the book and slaps it on the stack I'm already carrying. "Meet us at the church after school Friday. We have a lot to talk about."

The paperback slides to the side of my armload. I pause to steady it so it won't fall to the floor. "I'll think about it." I run to catch up with Shelby. We pass Pete on our way to class. He is walking with Gayle, the girl with the mosaic-style glasses. They are looking into each other's eyes, making small talk and laughing. He is smitten with someone new, someone he can take to the movies and to parties, someone who has breasts that protrude like apples instead of mini pancakes

"That Pete, what a dork," Shelby says. "I don't see what she sees in him."

"Me neither," I say, afraid to admit that I pine for him.

In English class, Leland passes me a note. I went to one dance with him, only because I couldn't go with Pete. I haven't been on a date with Leland since. I unfold the note near the end of class, when the teacher turns her back to write our assignment on the board. His message is a scathing, penciled screed. I read that I am calculating, unkind, manipulative, and that I'd deliberately set out to win his heart and then stuff him on a shelf just like some other girl did last year. It doesn't seem to me that I've won anything. I like Leland, sure, but I haven't fallen for him. The way his hands tremble and sweat when he's near me gives me the creeps, and it seems he's always after my attention, not the other way around. What am I supposed to do? Ignore him?

I slip out of class, stunned and silenced by Leland's accusations. What if it's all true? What if I've been worse to Leland than Kathy and Mary Ruth were to me when we shared a room not much bigger than a 9 by 12 rug? Kathy, with lips pursed as though she'd just been forced to drink vinegar, and Mary Ruth, with dream-curdling disdain in her eyes, taunted me about almost everything I did. They even complained if I didn't have enough knickknacks on my dresser. I didn't mean to treat Leland badly; maybe my sisters never meant to be bad to me either. This has never occurred to me before. Maybe I dashed some of their hopes, too, by withholding a heart that's been on the defensive ever since I can remember. I look down at *Stranger in a Strange Land* and think reading it this week might help get my mind off of what a bad person Leland thinks I am. I track down Carleton after school and tell him I'll meet him and Jay on Friday.

By the end of the week, I haven't finished the book, but I hope it doesn't matter as Jay and I scrunch into pint-sized chairs at a table where kids in the primary grades draw pictures of Jesus during Sunday worship services. Carleton lifts a Mason jar from a cabinet shelf at the far side of the room and saunters over. He places the jar in the center of the table. It's filled with a clear liquid. White labels with "Grok" printed in blue ballpoint ink are taped to the lid and the sides.

Carleton settles into a chair to my right. Jay is to my left. "What do you think of the book?" Carleton asks.

"Yeah, Lur, what do you think of the book?" Jay asks.

"What did you call me?" I wonder if he has a slight speech impediment.

"Lur. L-u-r," Jay says. "You have to have a secret name, one that nobody knows except us. One that's like your name, but not. Something ordinary people would never guess. Carleton is Cal, I'm Jy, Jodie is Ode and you're Lur."

"You might be Jy, but I'll never be Lur," I insist. Being named Laura is one of the good things that's happened to me. I won't answer to a bizarre substitution. I don't even answer to Laurie. Whenever my father used to hear someone call me Laurie, he'd say, "Her name is Laura. If I wanted her to be called Laurie, I'd have named her Laurie." I don't know why this was so important to him, but since it was, I keep my name intact as a way of honoring his memory.

"Oh, come on. Be a good sport, like Jodie. She never complained about Ode," Jay snorts.

"Is she the girl Carleton used to go with who moved to Pennsylvania?"

"She moved, but not completely. She's here, too. She sits in the chair across from you," Jay says.

I stare at the empty chair. "You really think she's in that chair?"

"You're jumping way ahead, Jy. Let's just talk about the book, shall we?" Carleton says. "What do you think about it?" he asks me.

"It's interesting, as far as I've gotten."

"You haven't read it yet?" Carlton stiffens his back, leans toward me.

"I have other things to do, you know, like homework."

"Oh, but this is serious. You have to finish the book. It could be the most important thing you ever do," Carleton says.

"Yes, most important," Jay echoes.

"Why is that?" I ask.

Carleton leans back, almost tipping over his chair, steadies himself, and offers his explanation: "We know you know how idiotic everything going on here is. All the adults work so they can have more and more things. And we're supposed to grow up and do the same. We're sick of all this buying, buying, buying and all those shallow people at school."

"Yeah, all that popularity nonsense," Jay adds.

Carleton stabs the book with his index finger and continues, "We're strangers in a strange land, just like Valentine here. It's like we came from another planet, a better, more intelligent place. And we think it's the same for you, so you can 'grok' with us. You've read far enough to know what grok is, haven't you?"

"Well, yeah, it's a kind of understanding."

"That's exactly right," Carleton says. "I knew you'd get it, that it's not exactly understanding as we usually know it, but a kind of understanding. That's a good way to put it. I knew you were the right choice."

"I knew it before you," Jay says to Carleton.

"The right choice for what?" I ask.

"See that jar?" Carleton raises a bushy eyebrow above his horn rims.

"Of course, I see the jar." I think for two guys who are rumored to have IQs in the 140 range, they're acting very stupid.

"Yes, of course, you do. I just meant to direct your attention to something vital," Carleton says.

"Why is that jar so important?" I ask, although I can guess, based on the importance of sharing water in the book.

"That's sacred water. We each sipped from it before Ode's parents forced her to move. Just her body though. She's here now. I can feel her," Carleton says. "It's okay with her for you to join our group, to become our water sister. In fact, she's almost demanding it. She wants you to be one of us as much as we do."

"I feel her, too," Jay says. He smiles and his cornflower blue eyes light up. I think he might be a little bit cute.

"How do you know Jodie would want me to be part of this group?"

"I called her last night and told her all about you," Carleton says. "She said you're the perfect choice. She wants us to bring you in today."

"Bring me in?"

"Today is the best day to grok. We'll each take a sip from the jar and then in June, when Ode's back in physical form, we'll do it again, make it official."

"So it wouldn't really be official until Jodie's back?" I say.

"Right," Carleton says.

"Okay, guys, I'll grok with you." I'm curious and figure I can always back out before June comes along if it gets too weird. Besides, nobody's ever asked me to be part of a secret group before.

"There's just one other thing," Carleton says.

"What's that?" I ask.

"Ode and I are soul mates, and we think you are destined to be Jy's, for now. Eventually, all four of us will be equal soul mates."

"I'm not into this whole soul mate thing. Maybe you've got the wrong girl."

"I don't think so," Carleton says. "I think it's just that Jy and I keep forgetting how young you are."

"So we don't have to do the soul mate thing?"

"No, you just have to join us in creating a better world," Carleton says.

"Well, okay then."

Carleton picks up the Mason jar, unscrews the lid and takes a sip. Next, he tilts it slightly over the table where Jodie's seat is and pretends she is imbibing. Then he passes it to Jay, who takes a swig and hands it to me. I grasp the thick jar with both hands, put it to my lips and hope something new will happen, something I've never experienced, though I know how improbable that is. I swallow the water. It tastes like good old Hinsdale water, and I feel exactly as I did before I took a sip.

Over the next few months, I meet with Jay at the church after school a couple of afternoons a week. Sometimes Carleton joins us, but usually it's Jay and me in the Sunday school classroom, sitting a few couple of feet apart in miniature chairs. He complains incessantly about his sister, who is in eighth grade. He describes with contempt her obsession with clothes and sleepovers and being popular. Obsessed with the same things, I realize I have more in common with her than with him. But I keep quiet, having nothing else going on socially in my life, until May, when Jay and Carleton and I are in the cafeteria after school. They mention how much they're looking forward to Jodie's return and how significant that will be for all of us.

"Having Ode back will mean we'll be complete for the first time," Carleton says. "Then we can really grok, make some plans, true soul mates all the way."

"Complete, yes, grok, yes, full steam ahead," Jay says."

I'm not sure exactly what they have in mind, but I don't want to find out. Being with them has been like drinking the powdered orange juice substitute Tang when I desperately want the real thing. I know it's time to bow out before I get in deeper. "Guys, I think I need a break. This is all too much for me," I say.

Carleton's face reddens. "You've made a commitment; you can't just back away," he says.

"It's not that you aren't important to me," I say, trying to ease them down slowly. "It's more like I'm not ready for this, you know. I'm just a freshman. I haven't lived yet."

Carleton puts both of his hands on my shoulders and smiles. I think my argument has impressed him. "Okay, then," he says. "We'll be back for you in two years. But if you need anything in the meantime, just let us know."

"Yeah, just let us know," Jay says. "Anything you need, we'll be there."

Carlton lowers his arms and backs away. Jay grabs my hand, presses something into my palm and wraps my fingers around it. Then he and Carleton nod to each other, turn and march out of the cafeteria. As I watch this Mutt and Jeff team walking away, I realize that if I continue to go to youth group events, they'll be there eyeing me, so my days in that group are over, too.

I uncurl my fingers and see a plastic troll with orange hair in my palm. I'm surprised Jay has given me something so popular with all the girls at school. Then I see it on the bottom of one of the troll's feet: Lur printed in blue ballpoint ink.

FIVE

July 1964

JILLIE LICKS A SPRINKLE OF CRUMBS from her lips and sets the oven to 350. It's still warm from a batch of blond brownies we polished off with her mom, Mrs. Keenan. We were supposed to save some for her dad, but the platter, crammed with gooey squares just minutes ago, now soaks in sudsy water in the kitchen sink. In the living room, ominous chords seep from the TV as a male voiceover declares, *The Edge of Night*.

A sweet chocolate-vanilla scent lingers as Jillie's little brother, Joey, wiggles in his chair, swings his legs under the table, and hums *Three Blind Mice* between nibbles of a peanut butter and jelly sandwich. That's all he eats—breakfast, lunch and supper. If he were my kid, I'd put an end to that straight away. Eating nothing but PBJ isn't right. But then, Jillie and her mom's eating habits are even worse.

I've seen how they eat nonstop because I've been here almost every day this summer. I expected to spend time at Shelby's, too, but two weeks before school got out, she stormed into the girls' locker room, threw her books down, started peeling off her clothes and wouldn't speak to me, wouldn't even say hello. I thought something terrible must have happened if she couldn't even talk about it. Our lockers were a few spaces apart. We'd always goof off while getting ready for freshman PE, and we'd barely make it to class in time for roll call.

I asked Shelby, "What's wrong?" She wouldn't look at me. "Are you okay?" No answer. I inched toward her. She turned her back and pulled her shining red locks into a ponytail. I felt Brillo pads sprouting up my throat and under my tongue. I creaked out, "Did I do something to upset you?" She tugged on her PF Flyers and tied the laces, concentrating as though she were mastering a new skill.

Girls changing clothes nearby stole glances at us. Feeling on display, I made a dash for the double doors leading to the gym and blasted through. My classmates were lining up against a wall, each in a one-piece navy blue gym suit. I pulled on the legs of the same suit I've worn since seventh grade when it fit me like a Roman legionary tunic. There was still ample room in the bust, but the short shorts barely covered burgeoning thighs I hoped were just borrowing me and would soon move on to their rightful owner.

Shelby strolled in, arm in arm with two other girls. I stood alone staring at the glossy wooden floor, the space between the nearest girls and me too immense to bridge. Finally, the teacher blew her whistle, and we raced to the track outside. After class, Shelby looked away when she passed by. She needn't have worried; I'd gotten her message. I've been practically living at Jillie's ever since.

Jillie scrapes her front teeth against her lower lip before declaring, "Now, for the peach toast!" She pulls a loaf of Butternut from the breadbox. Peach toast is a low-rent version of peach dumplings, which I've had exactly once at Shelby's. Her mom subscribes to *Gourmet* magazine. She never cooks anything normal like meatloaf or tuna casserole. I used to eat soufflés and marinades and pâtés at Shelby's.

"Peach toast? Right after brownies?" I ask. "We're going to the carnival later, remember? You have to leave room for cotton candy and stuff."

"That's hours away. Besides carnival food can't compare to peach toast. It's sooooo good."

Jillie's mom heaves herself out of the kitchen chair, where she'd plopped for "just one" brownie while headed to the basement with a load of laundry. "I'd better get moving or I'll miss the latest from Monticello," she says, referring to her favorite soap opera. She grips the basket of dirty clothes with hands flawless enough for an Ivory commercial. But the tops of her feet bulge over the edges of her black flats, reminding me of the Blob from that scary movie, except her feet aren't red and gooey.

"Save some bread for tomorrow, girls," she says. A smile spreads across her wide, but perfectly symmetrical face as she walks away. Elizabeth Taylor's eyes have nothing on Mrs. Keenan's. They bathe her surroundings like moonlight, splashing love on her kids nonstop. And when I'm around, some of it lands on me. Wanda never telegraphs love like Mrs. Keenan, who could be the prettiest mom in all of Hinsdale if she were normal size. And Jillie probably wouldn't be the butt of so many jokes if she didn't have a double chin, a waist wider than her hips and wavy blonde hair that looks like a dented helmet no matter how she tries to style it.

Jillie works fast. She's got three baking pans on the counter and is spreading Imperial margarine on the slices. I grab the can opener and tackle a cafeteria-sized can of peaches, enjoying the crinkle of metal piercing metal as I work my way around the lid. Together, we finish the preparations: half a peach on each piece, a bit of thick syrup from the can, and a sprinkle of cinnamon. I pull down the oven door; Jillie crams the trays inside.

"I want another one." Joey pushes his plate in Jillie's direction.

"Do I look like Mom?" Jillie snaps.

Joey's face, streaked with mud-pie dirt from earlier in the day, puckers up. He slumps in his chair, starts kicking the table.

"Okay, okay. Don't have a cow. I'll make your stupid sandwich."

Jillie pulls out two more slices of bread.

Soon, a cinnamon smell envelops the room like a warm hug. I rub my fingers over the tabletop. It is flecked, white Formica, just like the one at my grandmother's home. Gramma told me her table belonged to my mother—my real mother—once upon a time. It was a whispered secret, just between Gramma and me, shared in passing while I helped spoon coffee grounds into her electric percolator one Sunday afternoon. That was back when Daddy was alive and used to drive Kathy, Mary Ruth and me, along with our stepmom, to visit Gramma every Sunday. In an untidy row in the back seat, we three did our usual jockeying for a window seat, but we put aside our typical snide remarks and dirty looks because our father was relatively relaxed, leading us in song all the way to Gramma's. I never dreamed those long, lazy Sundays would end. But they were just one of all kinds of things lost since his death, things I so easily took for granted way back when.

I wait with Jillie in this roomy kitchen with frayed blue gingham framing the windows and linoleum worn almost to the wood in a path from the refrigerator to the table. When the peach toast is ready, Jillie devours several servings. I can fit in only a couple of bites. This is why she's 150 pounds and I'm 116. I wish she'd eat like a normal person, but I'm happy she's my friend and grateful to have a place where I'm always welcome no matter how long I stay.

At suppertime, Jillie and I forego the burgers sizzling on the stove, and leave Joey howling in Mrs. Keenan's arms because he's too young to come along. Melding into a cacophony of clicks, whirrs, screams and laughter at the annual Fourth of July carnival, we zip past the Tilt-O-Whirl, the Scrambler, the Ferris wheel, and game booths until we reach the biggest tent in the field. My heart thumps from running all the way to the canvas behemoth, where a local garage band is pulling off a good rendition of the Dave Clark Five's *Glad All Over*. I brush flecks of straw from my Wrangler cutoffs and make sure my red-and-white checked blouse is buttoned straight. Jillie opens the flap. We both step in, and her friend Alice rushes over. "Gosh, you guys, it took you long enough," she says.

"You didn't tell me she'd be here," I whisper to Jillie. When Alice's name comes up at school, people tend to let out *eews* and *ughs* and *icks*. I was leery of being seen with her.

"She's around when you're not," Jillie whispers back. "Besides, if you got to know her, you'd like her."

Realizing there's nothing I can do about Alice, I shrug and run my fingers through my hair, making sure no locks are tucked under my collar. Last week, I cut off all the orange ends, remnants of a perm gone awry. Now my nearly black hair falls just below my shoulders, and it's straight and shiny, which is in style these days. I look better than I ever have, especially since I now wear glasses only to see the chalkboards at school. And lately, some cool boys have noticed me—the ones girls sigh over at night while they hold their pillows and drift off to sleep, the ones whose pictures girls pull out from between textbook pages to peek at during class. I'm feeling like a new girl in town, not the same sad sack orphan who's been chewing her pencils at school since first grade.

Some cute boys I don't recognize are near the stage in front of the lead singer, whose hair is in a Beatle cut just like half the guys in the tent. Alice says the boys are from La Grange, Hinsdale's biggest rival in football. It seems every girl in the tent is looking at them. I glance their way just as a boy in the group checks me out. He has black hair and black eyes, and he dances through the crowd, maintaining eye contact with me all the way. His friends follow. When he reaches me, he asks, "Dance with me?"

"Sure." I shift away from Jillie to face him.

Then, right by his side, Shelby appears, pigtails bouncing against skin aglow from the first weeks of summer sun. "Hey," she says. She starts dancing with a real heartthrob with sandy bangs that keep falling into his blue eyes. She smiles at me like we're fast friends.

I ignore her. I can't believe she's pretending everything's just fine. I focus on the black-eyed boy. We do the Swim, hips wiggling, arms circling around. We even pretend to take breaths over our shoulders, and we both laugh. I can't be upset when dancing. The rhythm lifts my spirits; the harmony quickens my pulse.

When the song ends, Shelby pulls me aside and says, "I'm fuckin' sorry, okay?"

"That's supposed to mean something to me?" I refuse to engage her prodding toffee-colored eyes.

"I know you're mad, but Trish said to stay away from you, said you're fuckin' bad news."

Trish Carlisle sat behind me way back in sixth grade English. I haven't had one class with her since then. I got A's on our tests; she got D's. She always said, "I hate you" when our teacher returned our papers. I didn't know she really meant it. It floors me that after all this time Trish is telling people I'm bad news. I wonder who else might be holding grudges for unspoken rules broken when most of us still wore undershirts, not bras.

"You dumped me because Trish told you to?"

The band begins Peter and Gordon's *A World Without Love*. The boys start dancing in front of us, and we join them.

"Trish *is* my neighbor," Shelby says, bopping in time with the blond guy. "She bugged me about you every day, every fuckin' day."

"Why don't you just go be with her then?" I move to my partner's other side.

"I've missed you," she calls to me.

After a few more dances, the boys ask if we'd like to take a ride. They are clean, polite and silly, much like our classmates. They seem safe. I check in with Jillie, who has been dancing with Alice.

"So, I'm thinking of taking a ride with these guys," I say.

"And Shelby?" she says.

"It's not like I invited her."

"She only came over because those boys were paying attention to you."

I look over at my dance partner. He has a devilish smile. "So, I'm gonna go, then. See you tomorrow?"

"Alice's coming over, too, in case you flake," Jillie says. She waves me away and resumes dancing with Alice.

Knowing Jillie will be too curious about the rest of my evening to stay angry for long, I leave the tent with Shelby and the boys from La Grange. They lead us to an old Buick convertible parked nearby. I climb into the front seat next to the raven-haired lad, who is driving. He puts his arm around me, and we ride through the hot summer night, the warm wind soothing salty, suntanned skin as we head for a diner that sells giant sodas.

A couple hours later, the black-eyed boy clings to my side as we mosey toward my stepmom's front door. He reminds me of a bloodhound drooling for Purina's Gravy Train. Absent a dance floor, I feel no magic between us. On the porch, he leans in for a good-night kiss. I turn my head and call to Shelby, "I've missed you, too."

SIX

February 1965

GLIDING THROUGH FRESHLY FALLEN SNOW ON my way to visit Kathy at Hinsdale Sanitarium and Hospital, I imagine I'm an Olympic contender. I get a running start and then slide down the sidewalk, leaving marks like ski tracks in my wake. Roy Orbison's *Pretty Woman* blasts through the transistor radio in my hand. Whenever I hear it, I imagine some cute guy admiring me as I walk by, even though I'm not a woman yet. Well, in the physical sense, I guess I am.

My first period leaked out just two weeks before I started high school and three weeks before my fourteenth birthday. I welcomed it with about as much enthusiasm as I would a quart of Penzoil poured into my underpants. I was one of the last girls from our neighborhood to menstruate. That's what Jillie said anyway. She finds out stuff like that from her mom, who actually has friends in town, unlike Wanda the Wicked Witch of the Western Suburbs. She acts as though everyone in Hinsdale thinks she's a leper. There's some truth in that. She's different than other parents, and not just in the way she treats Kathy, Mary Ruth and me. Take her clothes. She wears only floral patterned, synthetic house dresses that zip up the front. Even when the temperature plunges below zero. That's all she'll wear under a ratty car coat my sisters and I outgrew ages ago. The dresses were cartoonish when new; they get worse with wear. Threads stick out at the seams like legs on a centipede. The only footwear she puts on her tiny feet are sandals with wedged heels

33

and black canvas straps crisscrossed over her toes and behind her ankles. She calls them "wedgies." In winter, she wears white bobby socks with her wedgies, making them look even more bizarre.

A couple of years ago, I accompanied Wanda to Ben Franklin, which is not far from the junior high. The store was having a half-price sale on wedgies. While I was helping her search a bin of shoes for size 4-1/2, two girls from school sauntered in. I slinked to another aisle. Head down, I pretended to be absorbed by a jewelry display. But then Wanda yelled, "Laura!" The girls approached me, their faces aglow with a devilish mirth.

"Is that your *mother*?" one of them asked. The other snickered.

"Uh, no, she's just somebody I know." I backed away and returned to the wedgie aisle.

"Where were you?" Wanda snapped as we walked to the cashier.

"Just over looking at some circle pins."

"Liar. You wanted to get away from me, didn't you. You're just like everybody else in this town. You think you're too good for me."

I kept quiet, feeling guilty as Peter when he denied knowing Jesus. I also feared Wanda might raise her voice and make a scene before we were safely inside her Chevy Bel Air, where nobody else would be able to hear her rant.

Classmates used to taunt me about Kathy and Mary Ruth, too. "She's not your sister, is she?" they'd say when one of my sisters passed by. When I'd answer in the affirmative, their laughter would hit like a basketball aimed at my gut. That was in junior high, when, despite everything our teachers said to the contrary, the only thing that seemed to matter was how you looked, not who you were on the inside. As the eldest, Kathy had to face this scrutiny first, wearing second-hand outfits that looked like they'd been swiped from the set of *Oklahoma*.

These days, we babysit, clean houses and do other odd jobs, and we buy our own clothes. The ribbing has subsided. It seems, overall, things are going well this year for all three of us, that is, if you don't include Kathy's fall, which broke her back.

Snowflakes land and melt on the sidewalk as I approach the hospital and open the door. I rush through the lobby, to the elevators and up to Kathy's room. Soon, I'm perched on the edge of her bed, concentrating as a ball of yarn rolls on the floor. Under, over, under, over—I finish a row of knitting and pass the half-completed scarf to her.

"That's very good, Laur, nice and even." She runs her nimble fingers along my stitches. "See, you can do it." I'm not used to Kathy encouraging me. I wonder if she might be setting me up for some king of ridicule like when we were younger and I was the butt of all the family jokes.

Kathy hands the project back to me. "Do another row. You'll be knitting a sweater soon."

I doubt that. I tried knitting once before back in Brownie Scouts. Each girl was supposed to make a scarf to give to her mother for Christmas. I stuffed my twisted disaster in the back of my closet, where it sat like contraband for months, until Wanda did one of her routine purges of all possessions she deems useless or unnecessary.

I start on the next row. Under over, under over. How I envy Kathy's fortitude. She's been here for two months and has kept up with all of her schoolwork, and she's teaching me how to knit to boot. She's always up to something productive, like theater, where she works magic backstage. That's what led to her broken back, though. She was painting scenery for a play when she fell fourteen feet from a scaffold. Friends on the scene helped her up and asked if she was okay. She said she was fine and even walked around for several minutes. Then the stabbing pain hit. She asked Lainie, her closest friend on the crew, to take her to the emergency room.

"Should we call your mom?" Lainie asked.

"No. Take me to the hospital first, otherwise I'll never make it there." Kathy knew too well that, without intervention, Wanda would give her an aspirin, send her off to bed and tell her to be in school the next day.

Lainie drove Kathy to the emergency room, where Wanda was notified after Lainie made sure the doctor on duty saw Kathy and knew she was badly hurt.

I'm finishing another row when Mary Ruth tromps in, the lenses of her brown tortoise-shell glasses still a little steamed up at the edges, her cheeks rosy from the cold outside air. She's just finished a study session with her calculus buddies.

"Ready for a ride?" Mary Ruth asks. She unbuttons her coat and lays it across an upholstered chair by the window.

"Sure thing," Kathy says. Earlier today, her doctor gave her the okay to use a wheel chair, and we intend to take full advantage of that development. The three of us giggle as we ease Kathy out of the bed and into the chair. And we're off. Mary Ruth and I walk her down the hallway to a window. Then we spin her around and push her to the other end of the hall. Up and down we go, one end to the other. Mary Ruth and I take turns pushing the chair, and with each switch at the helm, we increase our speed until we're running so fast, we can barely stop at the windows on either end of the hall. All three of us find this hilarious.

"Watch it, girls," a nurse calls. "You know you're not supposed to run in the halls." We slow down, stop at the elevators and move our frivolity to another floor, until a nurse there tells us to slow down too. "Think of the other patients here," she scolds.

Feeling guilty, we return to Kathy's floor, where aides are bringing dinner trays to all the patients. It's time for Mary Ruth and me to go.

Mary Ruth hugs Kathy. Then it's my turn. "See ya tomorrow," I say. Mary Ruth and I back out the door and then shuffle, arm in arm, toward the elevators. I'm sorry Kathy got busted up, but I enjoy seeing my sisters every day at the hospital, a place where Wanda never visits, a place where we are safe from her rage, safe to let our armor down, safe to dream of love washing bitterness from our home like showers flushing away decay and awakening the earth in spring.

SEVEN

July 1965

JILLIE AND I PAW THROUGH A RACK of Bermuda shorts at Patty Page boutique. I touch the silky interior of a seersucker pair and wonder what it would be like to wear shorts that are lined. Alice is trying on a wrap-around skirt in one of the dressing rooms. I can't believe I'm in downtown Hinsdale with Alice.

"Of all the girls in our class, why did you pick Alice to pal around with? It's like she has kooties or something." I speak softly so my voice doesn't carry to the dressing room.

"What do you care? You're always on a date or off somewhere with Shelby," Jillie snaps.

"That's not true," I say, but I know she has a point. Boys who never made eye contact with me freshman year flirted with me sophomore year, invited me to parties, asked me to the movies. I even went steady for three months with Doug, whose sly eyes and gruff edge reminded me of Charles Bronson, but his grace when dancing made me think of a gazelle. Doug took me to my first and only make-out party. It was in his best friend Wayne's basement. We pretzeled-up in a corner while other couples throbbed on the couch, chairs and floor, and the air heaved with grunts, giggles, sighs and heavy breathing, that is, until Wayne's parents and younger brother came home from the movies. We all had to break apart and start dancing fast.

The group make-out thing wasn't my cup of tea, but I did enjoy the novelty of going steady, walking down the hall hand in hand, the peaceful glow inside my body at the light touch of his bony fingers, the Brute aftershave on his face and neck. I was on cloud nine as far as romance goes. I never imagined ordinary guys, some of whom can barely write coherent sentences, could work such magic.

I let go of the shorts and shift my attention to a rack with matching skorts and tops. I think I still wear a size five. I weigh five more pounds than I did this time last year because in March I started earning $11 every Saturday for cleaning a wealthy family's house. I was able to buy a hot lunch at school instead of having a seven-cent carton of chocolate milk like I'd done since the start of freshman year. I think being 121 pounds is okay, though, because I've grown an inch and a half taller and my clothes aren't any tighter. And when Randy saw me in my two-piece bathing suit yesterday, he said I'm ravishing head to toe, so that's reassuring.

Jillie follows me to the skorts. "You've been with Randy nonstop since school got out, except for when you're with Shelby."

"I'm going swimming with Shelby tomorrow. Want to come with?"

"You and Shelby would probably dump me like you dumped Doug."

"I didn't dump Doug. He dumped me because I hung up on him, remember?"

Doug often teased me. He said it was because I was cutest when angry. One night we were talking on the phone, and he told me I looked like Olive Oyl in the long skirt I'd worn to school that day. More flustered than upset by that comparison, I slammed the receiver down on impulse, thinking if he could play with my feelings, why shouldn't I play with his? I thought he would call me right back, but he didn't. The next day Doug told Wayne I'd have to beg him to take me back. I didn't feel like begging, and over the next couple of days I didn't miss him, his jokes, his teasing, his bossy ways. Then, when I was rearranging books and papers in my locker, Randy, a graduating senior, approached me from behind and tapped my shoulder. I turned around and was dazzled by his sapphire eyes. He asked if he could walk me to my next class, and I said yes.

A salmon-colored shorts set catches my eye. I hold it up. "Hey, do you think they'll mark these clothes down in August, to make room for the fall stuff? I'd love to have this."

"That color would look good with your black hair," Jillie says.

"My hair's not black."

"Oh, come on. It's so dark you look like Snow White."

"Wanda used to say that about me, back in Chicago when I was really small."

"She probably had something nasty up her sleeve, even then." We both snicker at that. For me, laughing at the source of so much pain is like plunging into Lake Michigan on a ninety-nine-degree day.

Jillie points to a row of dresses at the back wall. "Oh, look at those." She strides over.

I put the salmon set back and join her in thumbing through the clothes. "About Alice," I say. "Why her?"

Jillie gnaws on her bottom lip before answering. "Because I like her, and I can be friends with whoever I want. It's a free country."

I know she's right; I can't tell her who can and can't be her friend, but I wish I could. "Well, just because she's your friend doesn't mean she has to be mine. I don't like her tagging along with us."

"I won't ditch her just because you call up and want to do something. If I already have plans with her, and you ask what I'm up to, I'll invite you to tag along with us."

"But everybody hates her."

"I don't and you don't either," Jillie says.

She's right about this, too. I've been enjoying Alice's company in spite of myself. "But doesn't it bother you that everybody finds her creepy?"

"The way I see it is that I'm such a wit, people can't help but be charmed by me, and your popularity with boys makes up for anything people might say about Alice."

"I don't know about that." Despite the recent attention from boys, I feel like the slightest mistake could get me shunned at school; hanging out with Alice could be it.

Alice steps out of the dressing room and saunters to the checkout counter, her dishwater blonde waves poking up at odd angles, giving her hair the look of a bird's nest that has crashed to the ground. She's chewing a big wad of Bazooka bubble gum and carrying a Madras plaid skirt.

"How did it look?" Jillie asks, joining Alice at the counter.

"Fabulous." Alice blows a little bubble, sucks it back in and pops it between her teeth. The sales clerk at the register twirls her index finger around a strand of blonde hair, worn in a flip. "Are you going to buy this one, dear? It's charming."

"Actually, I'd like you to hold it for me. I want my mom to see it first," Alice blurts through a new bubble.

"I can hold it until the end of the day. What's your name?"

Alice keeps blowing. She leans over the counter toward the clerk as the bubble grows.

The clerk backs away. "Watch it. You might pop that on this nice clean skirt. Then you'll have to buy it."

Alice blows harder. The bubble explodes all over her lips. She gathers the pink fragments with her tongue and fingertips.

The clerk pulls the skirt off the counter. "Your name?" She shakes the garment, then brushes it with her palm, though there is nothing on it.

"Mia Farrow," Alice says.

Jillie and I muffle our giggles and sidle toward a shelf full of soft suede purses near the door. I'm prepared for a quick getaway in case the clerk throws us out. As I run my fingers over a patch of particularly soft navy blue, I hear a boy's voice say hello. I don't look up.

Jillie pokes my arm and says, "Laura, it's that guy Kip Mercer. He's saying hello to you."

I glance up and see Kip in the doorway, a big grin on his face. Scraggly light-brown bangs hang in his eyes. "Hi," he says again. He backs out to the sidewalk, and his friend Dave Brown pops in and leans against the doorframe. His dangling arms look too long for his thick body as he squeaks out a hello.

"Hi," I say. Dave trips while backing up and bumps into Kip, who is just inches behind him. I put down the navy purse and pick up an olive green shoulder bag. When I look up again, the boys are gone.

Chomping her gum with gusto, Alice walks over from the counter. "What was that?" she asks.

"Stupid Dave Brown probably has a crush on Laura," Jillie says.

"Him and a hundred other guys." Alice picks up a patchwork bag in olive green, brown and cranberry.

"Yeah, Kip was probably egging Dave on," Jillie says.

"Hey, let's go back to my house and get out the Slip 'n Slide. It'll cool us off, and we can work on our tans," Alice offers.

"I'm up for it," Jillie says.

"Me too, since someone just told me I look like Snow White. I'll have to stop by Wanda's and get my suit first."

We slap the purses down, clatter out the door and race to Wanda's, where the doors are locked. I'm used to this. My sisters and I are always locked out when Wanda's not home and sometimes when she is.

"This way." I motion for Jillie and Alice toward the garage, which is never locked. Inside, I grab a screwdriver and put it in my back pocket. Then the three of us haul a ladder to the bathroom window. I unscrew the screen, lift the window and climb in. They follow because for them breaking in is a lark.

A few minutes later, with the screen replaced, and ladder and screwdriver back in the garage, we run three abreast to the street. I turn on my transistor radio, and the summer's biggest hit, *Satisfaction*, blasts out. I throw myself into the song. I know some shades of dissatisfaction, being the third girl born to a mother who hanged herself when I was still in diapers and a father who put off going to the doctor for so long he succumbed to ulcerative colitis, something people don't usually die of. And I surely "can't get no satisfaction" living with Wanda. But the kind of hot, growling dissatisfaction the song expresses seems far beyond my high school universe and the boys I've gotten to know lately. There's a sweetness to them that's nowhere to be found in that song. I would never trade them for Mick Jagger.

I wave my swimsuit as though I were Isadora Duncan whirling a scarf, and the three of us dance down the street. We chortle and guffaw until we stop to catch our breath. Bending over with my hands at my knees, heart beating fast, I look at my dear, hefty Jillie and Alice with her Medusa hair. They make no judgments about me, my family or the way I live. I accept that Alice will become a fixture in my life, probably even a friend.

EIGHT

July 1965

I STRADDLE KIP'S YAMAHA AND HOLD tight to his waist to keep from flying off as we speed along 55th Street toward La Grange. The warm wind blows through my hair, which has been growing like Jack's beanstalk this summer. Today I rinsed it black at Jillie's house, so all the warm highlights are gone, and my locks sparkle like they're loaded with tiny stars. Kip says my hair's so shiny it looks wet. I don't know if that's a compliment or not.

Ever since Kip and Dave bumbled their hellos at Patty Page boutique, Kip's been everywhere, splashing me at the pool, pestering me to dance with him at the youth center, asking to drive me home from parties, phoning me for dates. I've turned him down because I was going with Randy, but we broke up yesterday because Randy decided we should get married, and he wouldn't talk about anything else for two weeks straight. He's eighteen and headed to college soon. Maybe marriage is right for him, but I'm fifteen, and what girl in her right mind gets married at fifteen?

Randy was always so carefree, so certain of his basic okay-ness that I felt at times like I was dating a cartoon. And when I'm alone, I feel like I'm losing my balance at the edge of Alice's rabbit hole, except not really, because my hole is pitch black and so cold and empty it's terrifying. No dark holes lurk in Randy's universe. But it was his obsession with marriage that made me want to put a paper bag on his head and shove him out the door. I finally told him I didn't love him, and that was the end of my relationship with the cutest guy I've known.

Kip swerves to avoid a pothole, then dips us to the right and up again. The moves are smooth. I sense he is in control and relish the warm wind whipping over us. I'd planned to walk to Wanda's when the youth center closed tonight, but Kip rolled up, and it's hard to resist a motorcycle ride on a warm summer night, especially when you're eager to kill some time. Jillie's out of town, Shelby's on a date, and Alice's grounded for staying out past her 11 p.m. curfew. I have nowhere to go but home, and I dread walking through the door. Mary Ruth's away at some camp where she's helping little kids learn to read, and I haven't seen Kathy since the day after her senior prom.

Kathy stayed up all night with friends after the dance. They'd been outside around a campfire, and the songs, jokes and stories went on until sunrise. When Kathy came home, Wanda phoned her friend Florence and said, "I don't know what I'm going to do with Katherine. She just spent the night with a boy. Yes siree, she slept with a boy, the tramp."

"That's not true!" Kathy exclaimed. "Why are you saying that? A bunch of us were up all night, celebrating. That's all."

Wanda ignored her and finished her conversation with Florence. Then she called her cousins and every member of her Wednesday afternoon card club. She gleefully told each of them the same lie, leading them to believe Kathy had gone all the way with her prom date.

That was it for Kathy. No more living even part time with Wanda's distortions. She spends more nights than ever on her friend Lainie's living room couch. She probably won't return to Wanda's until it's time to pack her things and leave for MacMurray College. Who knows when I'll see her after that?

Kathy, who has such enthusiasm for life, is slipping away. Mary Ruth, who always knows what to do, will be next. Then what? My earliest memories of my sisters are of intense biting, hair pulling, kicking and punching. We were never a cuddly bunch. When we got older, our resentments came out in cutting remarks, constant scorn. We've become friends in the past few years, but with adulthood fast approaching, whether we're ready or not, I wonder if our chance to be the best of friends has already passed by. That thought has a Humpty Dumpty finality to it that gives me the quivers.

Kip and I are now on a stretch of open road, no other traffic in sight. He accelerates, and familiar surroundings blur as we roar by. I am thrilled with the extreme speed. When a traffic light comes into view, he slows to a more reasonable pace before stopping. My thoughts drift back to my sisters.

I wish we had a lifetime of happy memories, or at least a few more good times to balance out Wanda's rot before we go our separate ways. But that's about as pointless as pining for my father, which I do way too much. Almost five years after his passing, I still mark every birthday and holiday by the date of his death. When I think of my sixteenth birthday coming up in September, I don't think about presents or getting kissed; I note to no one but myself that it will be my fifth birthday without Daddy. I think it's morbid to mark the passing of time this way, but I can't stop. I dwell on these somber anniversaries, and foreboding burns my dreams like dry ice. My heart feels mummified no matter how much I wish it weren't so. I haven't shed one tear since the day my father was buried.

Tonight I'll be alone in bed, longing for Daddy to come home and fix things only he could fix, while Wanda mutters in the next room about what an ungrateful daughter I am. Riding around with Kip is a way of stretching out the normal side of my life for a while, the side where I feel safe from attack, safe from insanity.

Kip pulls into the McDonald's lot and parks at a curb. We dismount and enter our burger and French fries mecca.

"What'll you have?" Kip asks when we reach the counter.

"Coke and a small bag of greasies." I smile at the familiar aroma of frying junk food.

"That's what I'm having, too." Kip flashes an endearingly wide grin before he places our order. I reach into my cutoffs to pull out a twisted dollar bill.

"That's okay." Kip waves my hand away. "I've got it."

After he pays, we carry our snack outside and plunk down by his motorcycle at the curb.

"So, Laura, why won't you go out with me?" He gobbles a few warm fries.

I sip my Coke. "You've got a girlfriend, for one," I challenge. Until the school year ended in June, Kip and a girl named Claire were always goofing around at a row of lockers I passed on my way from geometry to P.E. He's over six feet tall, and she's half a foot shorter. Her Rapunzel hair flowed way down her back as she peered up at him, and he looked way down, hanging on her every whisper. They laughed often. I liked seeing them together, just as I like seeing every couple that stays together more than a few months. They prove that love is possible. It troubles me that Kip is showing so much interest in me now.

"Claire? She's not my girlfriend," Kip says.

"Sure seems like it to me; seems like it to everyone else, too." I nibble on the end of one of my fries. I wonder why there's a problem with every guy I get to know. Just when I think a boy shows promise, I'll notice there's always a dark ring of sweat on his shirt under his armpits, or he'll want to know where I am every second, or he'll invite

me to a party and then ignore me when I arrive. Or sometimes I'll
like a guy, but he'll dump me after one date. I'm hoping to find a cute
boy who's fun to be with who'll also understand me and won't go all
wimpy like Randy. Now there's Kip, who is one half of Kip and Claire.

"She was my girlfriend, but we broke up," Kip says.

"Really? Why?"

"She's mean to me." He sucks in about half of his Coke with one
long draw from his straw. His chocolate brown eyes look so sad he
reminds me of the stray dogs I visit at the Hinsdale Animal Shelter
every now and then. They look out from their cages, some friendly,
some not. I feel like they are kindred spirits looking into my soul.

"What does Claire do that's mean?" I ask.

"She just doesn't care about me at all."

"That's how my stepmother is."

"So you understand." He pours fries from the paper wrapper
into his mouth. I'm jealous of his ability to gobble greasies with
impunity. He's about the skinniest guy I've ever seen. I eat one more
fry and offer him the rest of mine. He devours them, too, and then
squints at me. "Will you go out with me?"

"I don't know." I haven't gotten used to thinking of him as dat-
able material. I stand up, gather our trash and walk it to a nearby
bin. Sensing Kip's gaze on me, I feel uncomfortable, like I'm slinking
to the chalkboard to work algebra problems I don't understand.

Kip mounts the motorcycle and starts the engine. I get on and
snuggle a little closer to him than before. He takes a roundabout
route through a forest preserve. Moonlight turns the landscape into
a fairy tale scene. Even Wanda's driveway seems touched with magic
in this light when we arrive. Kip parks the Yamaha, leans against it,
pulls out a box of Winstons and lights up with a Zippo.

"Can I have one?" I ask. I've practiced smoking with Shelby, so

I know how to inhale without choking.

"Girls shouldn't smoke; it's a dirty habit." He frowns. But he shakes a cigarette out, lights it and hands it to me. I inhale and wish we could spar like Humphrey Bogart and Lauren Bacall, but I am too tongue-tied. When we are done smoking, we throw our cigarettes on the blacktop, step on them and twist our feet to make sure they're out. He walks me to the door and we kiss goodnight. I drink in this feeling of togetherness, the taste of tobacco on his lips as his arms envelope me. I think if we did go out, being mean to him would be the last thing I would want to do. We end the kiss, but stay just inches apart.

"Are you going to invite me in?" he asks.

"I'm not allowed to bring boys inside. I can't even bring my girlfriends over. I don't know what Wanda would do if I walked in with you."

"Wanda?"

"My stepmom, Wanda the Wicked Witch of the Western Suburbs. Wanda's not her real name. It's just what I call her behind her back. I don't call her anything to her face anymore."

"Say what?"

"We don't talk."

"That's bad news," he says. "What about your dad?"

"He's dead."

"Where's your mother?"

"Dead, too."

"That must be rough," Kip says. He puts his hands on my shoulders and searches my eyes.

"I guess." I have a feeling he might be able to understand my life and maybe even care about what's going on with me underneath. With most of the boys I know, there are things in me they just don't get. It's like they're dancing through scenes from *Mary Poppins* while I'm gasping for air in *The Amphibian Man*. I adore them, but I'm disconnected.

We kiss again, and I feel a surge of feeling for him that's both emotional and physical. This enchants and frightens me. I say a quick goodnight and slip inside.

The next day, Kip calls and asks me to go with him to the 66 Drive-In. I say yes. A few minutes later his friend Dave calls and asks me out, too. I decline. It seems odd that Dave called me right after Kip, but I figure Kip just hasn't told him about our date yet.

NINE

September 1965

ABOUT AS HAPPY WITH THE LOOMING school year as a fish on a hook, I straighten stacks of brand new physics texts at a lunch table in the high school cafeteria. Last year I was beside a baby grand piano in a chorus room, a stash of geometry books behind me. The job of passing out textbooks before school begins is given to a select group of students each year. I joined the crew two years ago because my sisters shooed me in, not because of anything I did. I feel like a party crasher who should be thrown out the door.

Foot traffic is slow. I sit down, pull out my knitting and begin a new row. I've graduated from scarves to sweaters since Kathy taught me the trick to knitting is to make sure the stitches don't get too tight. My thoughts drift to an end-of-summer party coming up tonight. I had hoped Kip would ask me to go with him. Now I'm hoping just to see him there. Kip. I try to figure out what's going on with him as I stitch—under over, under over, under over—but no matter how many times I review what goes on between us, I remain confused.

He asks me out. I accept. We go to the drive-in, goof off with other kids in the snack bar line, return to his Mustang with buttery popcorn and Cokes in hand, then cover the area between the bucket seats with pillows. Our bodies tucked together, we nibble and sip, watch the movie (sort of), kiss (a lot). Then I don't hear from him, and I wait because, unless it's for the annual Sadie Hawkins dance, girls don't ask boys out.

Just as I'm about to give up on him, Kip invites me to a party. He takes me to a friend's crowded basement where Canoe, Brute, Ambush and Chantilly clash in the air. We dance to Sonny and Cher's big hit *I Got You Babe*, and then the Supremes' *Stop! In the Name of Love*, the Byrds' *Mr. Tambourine Man* and so many other songs I've memorized start to finish. Whenever Kip and I make eye contact, I grin like a grammar school kid who just won her first goldfish at a carnival. And when he takes me home, I don't think I'd be any happier if George Harrison himself were walking me to my door.

Kip bombards me with attention for a week or so. But then, the boy who has been doting on me is nowhere to be seen. After several days of silence, I figure he just isn't into me anymore, so I go out with another guy and have an American cheese sort of time, nothing punchy like Wisconsin sharp cheddar. Nevertheless, I vow to move on. But it seems Kip is psychic, because as soon as I decide I'm through with him, he pulls up to the curb while I'm ambling across town to Shelby's house.

"Want a ride?" he offers. "I got you some ice cream—chocolate, your favorite."

I slip into the Mustang. He puts an arm around me, and that feels so good, thoughts of other boys fade like bleached jeans. Then he hands me a wooden spoon and a whole quart of ice cream. It's softened but not drippy. I relish the treat, but after I've downed about half of it, he says, "You really shouldn't eat that, you know, you're getting fat."

Nobody has ever told me I'm fat before. I want to say, "Why buy me ice cream if you think I'm getting fat?" but the words won't come out. I toss the carton and spoon out the window, scrunch down in the seat and stare straight ahead all the way to Shelby's, where Kip parks and leans in to kiss me goodbye. I turn my head away, open the door and slide out of the car fast. A couple days later Kip pulls into Wanda's drive. I run out barefoot and famished because, for the first time in my life, I've started a diet. He asks if I want to go for a drive. I say yes. When it comes to Kip I have the willpower of a Ping Pong ball.

Under, over, under over, my needles click as I fret. I don't understand why Kip keeps coming back if he doesn't even like me. Why doesn't he just let me go? And if he does like me, why does he seem to forget I exist half the time and say mean things the rest of the time? Usually, a guy either wants to be with me or he doesn't and vice versa. Kip is like nothing I've ever experienced.

I look up from my knitting to greet a few stragglers who've come to my table. Thomas, a senior who looks like a young Gregory Peck only heavier, picks up a book and asks, "Hey, Laura, would you knit me a scarf when you finish that, whatever it is?"

"Why should I?" I'm flattered that one of our school's swim stars knows my name.

"'Cause I'm a really nice guy." His obsidian eyes look full of mischief.

"Sure." I think I may as well since Kip has expressed no interest in my knitting. I hold up my project. "This is going to be a sweater, by the way."

"Wow. That's cool."

"What colors do you want?"

"You're really going to knit me one?"

"I said I would, didn't I?"

"All right, then, green and white, I guess."

"Green and white it is." I extend my hand, and we shake on it.

He eases away from the table, but then steps right back. "Maybe we could go out sometime?" He smiles, showing off a row of beautifully straight teeth.

"Yeah, we could, I guess." I don't want to be too enthusiastic in case things work out with Kip.

"I'll call you, then. I mean, if you give me your number."

I scribble Wanda's number on a scrap of notebook paper and hand it to him. He stuffs it in his back pocket. I think it'll probably go through the wash, and that will be that. Or maybe he'll take it out and pin it on his bulletin board. Maybe we will go out. Maybe I'll end up liking him. Maybe life without Kip will be fine. Maybe.

I return to my needles—under, over, under over. I hear laughter and look up. Looming over my table is Claire, Kip's old girlfriend, with two other girls. All three are wearing light blue, sleeveless blouses and plaid shorts. Claire smiles and asks for a physics text.

I hand her a book and say, "You used to be Kip's girlfriend, didn't you?"

"Used to be? I thought I still was." She laughs an effervescent, husky laugh. Her friends scowl.

"That's not what he told me," I reply.

"We were very much still going together last night." She glances at her friends, who nod in agreement.

"He told me you broke up way back in June," I say.

"Well, yeah, we had a fight and split up for, oh, a day." She brushes a hand through her flaxen waves. She looks curious, friendly even.

"Let's get out of here," one of her companions says. She pulls on Claire's arm.

"Thanks for the book." Claire smiles briefly at me before walking off flanked by her posse, who glance over their shoulders, each giving me her interpretation of the evil eye. I turn away, thinking Claire and her friends were probably just messing with my head because Kip doesn't like her anymore. I try to put her out of my mind and focus on all the classmates I've seen today, and how just about everyone who stopped by my station looked laid back and sun-kissed after hanging loose all summer—a little excited too, because September brings the promise of a blank slate at school.

I start each year aiming to have the best year ever, be more disciplined with my homework, have the perfect boyfriend, wear beautiful clothes that will be given to me by an as yet unknown benefactor. But that lasts about a week, maybe two. Then I'm in my regular groove, averaging a B+, scrambling to look stylish in hand-me-downs and castoffs, and feeling frustrated instead of blissful in love. I hope this, my junior year, will be different, that at the very least, I'll rise to the year's academic challenges and earn more A's than B's.

Two minutes before closing time, I pull a cardboard box from under the table and place some of the leftover texts inside, and along comes Kip.

"Hey, Lau...ra." Kip drawls out my name. "Want a ride home?" Dave is right behind him, grinning like Bugs Bunny.

I have a Love Potion No. 9 kind of urge to rush up and hug Kip, but, thinking of Claire, keep my feet planted. "Nah, I've got to stay here and pack up. It'll be a while," I say.

"We can wait." Kip reaches across the table and runs his fingers through the ends of my hair.

"I don't think so." I pull away. "I saw Claire. She says she's still your girlfriend."

"Didn't I tell you she's crazy?"

"She didn't seem crazy to me."

"How would you know, squirt?" he teases. "Should we wait or what?"

"Don't bother."

"Okay." He turns to Dave. "Let's split, sports fan."

"'K man," Dave replies.

Kip saunters off with Dave. He turns at the exit, winks, puts his fingers to his lips and blows me a kiss. "See ya later," he calls. I wave back and immediately wish I hadn't. Then out the door he goes. I return to packing up my station, before pushing off to Jillie's to get ready for tonight's big, end-of-summer party.

Jillie and Alice are chowing down on ham sandwiches and Fritos when I arrive. Eager to primp for the party, we rush to Jillie's room, where Alice shuffles to the dresser and turns on the radio, and Jillie puts a half-eaten sandwich on her nightstand. I flop on the bed and sing along as *You Were on My Mind* by the We Five blasts from WLS AM. Jillie and Alice sing along, too, as they brush their hair in front of the dressing stand. Jillie pretends her brush is a microphone. I pick up an issue of *Seventeen* magazine and flip through an article I've already read several times. The author says she gets naked with her boyfriend and they snuggle in her bed but don't go all the way. She makes it sound so sweet and easy. Nobody I know has gotten naked with a boy or come close to going all the way.

I turned down a date for tonight, hoping Kip would ask me to the party that just about everyone in the junior and senior classes is going to. Terry, my most persistent would-be escort this week, is probably there right now. I imagine he's brushing his chestnut brown bangs out of his eyes as he sips beer or malt liquor purchased by someone's older brother or sister, or maybe some scotch or gin smuggled out of an unsuspecting parent's liquor cabinet. Instead of being with Terry, a nice guy I really ought to like, I'm singing sad songs of longing with Jillie and Alice.

Jillie unscrews the top of her Maybelline eyeliner, pulls out the slender brush and wipes off the excess liquid at the top of the tube.

Then she leans over Alice, who closes her eyes and tilts her face up. Jillie applies a thin line on each of Alice's upper lids. Alice opens her eyes, looks in the mirror. "Not bad," she says. Grabbing a soft eyeliner pencil, she begins applying liner below her eyes.

"Come on, Laura, put some on, too," Jillie says. She dips the brush in again. This time she runs a smooth line across one of her own eyelids.

"I may as well," I say.

When Jillie finishes her lids, I refresh the brush, and with a steady hand, paint a perfect line across one eyelid. It doesn't work so well with the other eye. A big black blob protrudes at the outer edge. I wipe the line away with mineral oil and tissue and start over. Jillie and Alice decide their liner needs improvement, too. They wipe all of theirs off and start again. Halfway through the job, Jillie stuffs the half of ham sandwich in her mouth and gulps it down. Then she clomps downstairs in search of more food. Remaining in front of the mirror, Alice and I and continue to paint and dab and wipe. Jillie's pink Princess extension rings. Alice and I don't budge, knowing someone will grab the wall phone in the kitchen. By the time Jillie comes back with a bag of potato chips and a bowl of dip she just made with onion soup mix and sour cream, Alice and I are adding the final swipes of Blush On to our already rosy cheeks.

"Hey, guess what?" Jillie says, wiping a few drops of dip from her chin.

"What?" Alice and I ask in unison.

"The Gordons' babysitter got the flu, and they're desperate to find a replacement tonight. It's for a couple of hours, and we could all do it together. I already asked Mrs. Gordon, and she said she'd even pay a bonus if we actually play with her kids."

"What kind of bonus?" Alice asks.

"$10, total, for two hours. What do you think?"

"That's a lot of money," I say.

"That could buy so many Cherry Cokes," Alice says.

"I'm up for it. We'll have plenty of time to get to the party afterward," I conclude.

We throw on our cutoffs and blouses, slip into our Keds and race to the Gordons' home, which is just a few blocks away.

Soon we're on duty, and Mr. and Mrs. Gordon are easing their LTD out of the drive. Their three kids are munching Jiffy Pop in front of the TV. Jillie and Alice are in the kitchen making Oscar Mayer liverwurst and Miracle Whip sandwiches on Wonder Bread. I'm on the phone with Terry, who wormed the Gordon's number out of Jillie's mom. He's drunk now and begging me to join him at the party. I listen, waiting for him to pause. Jillie walks in and hands me a sandwich. Terry continues to babble. I hang up the phone, thinking he probably won't notice for quite a while that I'm no longer on the line. I bite into the sandwich, breathe in the pungent smell of cold liver and spot the Gordon's liquor cabinet in a corner of the den.

Jillie, Sally and I sample every opened bottle in the well-stocked cabinet. By the time we arrive at the end-of-summer bash, all three of us are tipsy. The party is packed, and the air is thick with cigarette smoke. Kip is nowhere in sight. After about 10 minutes, my friends and I have to rush outside to the fresh air. Luckily, the nausea dissipates, so we don't vomit in anyone's hedge on the walk back to Jillie's.

TEN

October 1965

THE WEEK BEFORE HOMECOMING, JUST ABOUT every club in school is fashioning a float for the parade. Garages around town, stocked with wire, paper, flowers, fabric, lumber and tools, are blazing with energy. Everyone's welcome to walk in and help stuff tissue into chicken wire or pound a few nails. Shelby and I set off from her house, two cans of malt liquor apiece already downed. We'd gotten them from Jeff, one of her boyfriends. I don't know how she does it, but she's always dating two or three guys at once. I never know who she really cares about.

We sip Cold Duck from a paper cup a classmate hands us near the first float we visit, and accept the vodka bottle being passed around the side yard next to the second. We are on our way to a third garage when Daniel, Shelby's other current boyfriend, pulls up.

"Shelby, what the fuck? You and Jeff? You're killin' me."

She runs up to his window. "Me and Jeff? What about you and Sarah, huh?"

"Sarah? That's over."

"That's not what I heard."

"I got an earful about you and Jeff, honey, and it wasn't sweet."

Being used to these kinds of encounters, I plop down in the grass and watch. Soon Shelby will either ask if I'd be okay if she goes off with Daniel to work things out, or he'll drive off in a huff. I yawn and stretch out my legs.

"Hey, Laura, how's my scarf coming along?" Thomas eases himself onto the grass next to me and hands me a bottle of Michelob.

"I haven't started it yet. Sorry." I take a long chug of the beer and hand it back to him.

"I've been wanting to talk to you," he says.

"You have?"

"Yeah, I really like you. I get a good vibe from when we're together, you know? And when I said I wanted to ask you out, that was the truth. I think you're neat."

"I like you, too," I say.

"No, I mean I really like you."

"Oh." He looks so serious I worry about what's coming next.

"The thing is I have this girlfriend, Tess. She goes to LT, so you probably don't know her."

"I know about her. All the guys go gaga over her because she's so beautiful, right?"

"Well, yeah. But she's not sweet like you. I'd like to go with you. But she started talking about going to homecoming the first week of school. So I couldn't break up with her." He leans his head back and guzzles the rest of the beer.

"I see."

"But I didn't want to disappoint you, you know, just leave you hanging."

"Oh, well, right now I'm so strung out on Kip I probably wouldn't even have gone out with you if you'd called. I have it really bad, and I don't know what's going on with him."

"Kip? You're strung out on him? What could you see in a guy like him?" His body tenses, like a balloon blown up a little too far.

I don't know what he means by "a guy like him." I think maybe his ego is just a little bruised. "I can't explain it." I say.

"The way he two-timed Claire, made promises and then dumped her flat. He's—"

"I have it bad for him."

"You haven't thought about me at all?"

"I wouldn't say that."

He takes a deep breath and relaxes some. "Well, like I said, I have a girlfriend."

"I don't know what to do."

A station wagon full of giggling teens pulls up. Jillie pokes her head out of the window and calls to me, "There's a big party just a few blocks away. Want to go? We've got room."

"Plenty to drink, too," Alice adds.

I stand up and ask Thomas, "Want to go to the party?"

"No, I'm gonna stay here and work on the float and then go see Tess." He gets up and tosses the empty bottle from hand to hand as he walks up the drive toward the garage.

"She's a lucky girl," I call to him. Then I head over to Shelby. "Want to take off with Jillie and them?"

"No, you go on. Daniel and I are gonna get a burger at Topps. Maybe we'll see ya later."

"Yeah, maybe." I cram into the back of the wagon. Alice hands me a Vermouth bottle. I take a swig and pass it on. When we join the party, we dance and make plans to have a sleepover at Alice's, while continuing our drinking with a shared bottle of Mateus Rose wine Jillie stole from her parents' stash.

Then in bounds Kip. I haven't seen him for two weeks, and the last time was the worst ever. We'd been snuggled in his Mustang in Wanda's drive. Making out with him was like being transported to another realm where ancient gods were feeding me ambrosia. He told me he'd missed me and said I was the cutest girl he knew. The longer we kissed, the further and further I went from my day-to-day state of mind. When his hands cupped my breasts, I was enveloped by new sensations. He swirled his tongue in my ear, something I thought would tickle, but the feelings intensified throughout my body. Then he ever so slowly unzipped my jeans, which was more exhilarating than the parachute ride at Riverview. But when he tried to pull my pants down, I pushed him away.

He stiffened, sat up, brushed the hair out of his eyes and put his keys in the ignition. I zipped up and straightened my blouse.

"You really shouldn't eat so much; your clothes are tighter than they used to be," he said, eyes squinting with disdain.

My face burned hot as I opened the passenger door. The last time he'd told me that was on my birthday in September. I weighed 123, two pounds more than the first time he'd told me I was getting fat. Logically, I knew I wasn't at a bad weight for someone who's five foot six. Still, I felt like the Goodyear blimp and vowed then to do better with dieting, to no avail.

"You're way too uptight, too." His hands gripped the steering wheel. "What am I going to do with you?"

I hauled myself out of the car, unable to digest what was going on. I only knew I wanted him to ask me to the movies, walk me to and from classes, call me up just to talk. He gunned the engine. I pushed the door closed and watched him peel out of the driveway.

Since then, he's been out with other girls, but I want more than anything to dance with him now. This is the thing that confounds me most, the thing that I absolutely hate. Every time he returns to charm me, I'm more drawn in than before. I feel like one giant, glowing heart bleeding out love. It's harder and harder to put him out of my mind when he drifts away. I think it should be just the opposite. I don't even date other guys anymore when he's ignoring me. I'm a goner.

Kip works his way toward me through the crowd. We make eye contact. My heart thumps faster, and I can't help but grin. I hope I don't look like Alfred E. Neuman of *Mad* magazine fame. When Kip is close, he pulls me toward him and gives me a hug. Relief ripples through me; it feels so right to be near him.

"Hey, cutie. Want to dance?"

His smile dazzles like no other; I wish I knew why.

"Sure." I hope he's here to be with me, for real, to stay.

"I dig being with you." He gives me a heart-melting kiss, and we sway to the Temptations' *My Girl*. "Are you my girl?" he whispers into my ear.

"I hope so," I whisper back, warmth flushing my skin.

He pulls me closer. "I need you to show me," he says.

I don't know what he means by that. I just keep dancing. And I remain with him in bliss until Alice pulls on my sleeve. "It's time to go. We have to be back home by 11:30 or my mom will kill me."

"Looks like I've got to go," I say to Kip.

"Need a ride?" he asks.

Soon Alice and Jillie are in the back seat of Kip's Mustang, and I'm in the front next to Kip, who opens two cans of Schlitz malt liquor. We pass them around, and I feel dizzy, but happy. When we reach Alice's, he asks me to come with him to his house. I hesitate for a long time, thinking that except for tonight, he's been so mean to me lately I should just get out of the car with Alice and Jillie, but I feel magnetized to the car seat, I gaze up at the moon while my friends get out of he car and walk toward Alice's front door. I finally agree to go with Kip and call out to them, "I'll be along in a little while."

Less than half an hour later, Kip is stretched out naked reaching down through the moonlight for his Winstons and Zippo on the emerald green carpet by his bed. He smirks, lights up, takes a puff. Then he leans back against his pillow and blows a plume of smoke into the chilly air. His 6'3" body is like Andy Warhol's tomato soup cans. Too real. Jarring.

Facing away from him, I slip to the foot of the bed and try to untangle my corduroy Levis, flowered bra and undies, and V-neck sweater. Blood trickles down my inner thighs, which have grown thicker instead of slimmer since I started dieting. I begin each day with a new plan, but they all backfire. I end up stuffing myself in the evening with cold Spaghettios, Twinkies, Lays potato chips, chocolate chip cookies—whatever is available at Jillie's or Alice's or Shelby's.

I'm certain Kip is fully aware I've gained more weight, and I'm sure he's revolted by my wide rear end. I finally shake my undies loose and slide them on. In his dresser mirror I can see he's still reclining. The index finger of his free hand edges the jagged oval of blood on the sheet next to him. Feeling like I've just been smacked in the stomach, I hold the rest of my clothes tight to my skin. My trembling fingers take an eternity to pull the clothes apart and put them on as he watches me with eyes that are anything but loving. I want to run out of the room, but I finish dressing, then grab a comb from his dresser and try to act casual as I run it through the tresses that attracted him to me last summer. He is still on the bed, surveying me, like I'm a horse he might buy. I turn to him and ask, "Should we wash the sheets?"

"Don't worry about it. I'll take care of it." He blows a smoke ring at me.

I stumble out of the room, sit on a kitchen chair, blood oozing into my undies as I wait for him to get dressed and take me back to Alice's. I'm numb, except for the tiny trembles coursing through me head to toe. I'm glad Kip is taking his time getting dressed. I'm not sure I'll be able to get up from the chair and walk out with him.

I am flooded with questions. How much liquor did I chug down tonight? Alcohol relaxes me, makes it easier to talk with people, but it seems once I start drinking, I want to chug everything in sight. Why can't I just be comfortable on my own? Why did I tell Kip I was going to Alice's for a sleepover? Why did I accept his offer of a ride? And why did I stay here when I found out nobody else in his family was home?

I heard he keeps a list of this year's homecoming court in his back pocket. He crosses each one off after he gets a date with her. Whatever made me think I've got anything those far more popular girls don't have? And how could I not have known that when I agreed to come here after we stopped at Alice's, he assumed I was consenting to go all the way? It seems so obvious now, but I didn't have a clue. Even when he wrestled my clothes off and slipped out of his, I hoped he just wanted to cuddle naked like the couple I read about in *Seventeen* magazine. I realized too late how stupid that notion was when he rolled on top of me and ordered, "Put your hands on my back."

I wish to God I'd shoved him off, but I was frozen. All my thoughts spun around and around in my head, and when I tried to turn them into words that might have brought the whole episode to a halt, they jammed in my throat.

"Don't worry. I won't tell anybody" he said as he pushed in.

That thought hadn't crossed my mind. I was overwhelmed with the thought of having sex at all. Now I sit in the kitchen chair, trembling, and going over the scene again and again, feeling worse about it each time.

At last, Kip saunters in. "Let's split," he says.

I stand up, wobble and almost lose my balance. He grabs my arm and walks me out the door to the Mustang. We each get in without saying a word. He whistles *King of the Road* as he starts the engine. All I can think about is how much I want to redo the last hour of my life. The ride back to Alice's stretches on like a long piss. And despite how upended I feel, I'm still hoping he'll ask me to the homecoming dance. I hate myself for this.

At Alice's door, he bends to kiss me; I turn my head so his lips land on my ear. He rubs my rear, which makes me feel slimy. He doesn't say he'll call before he struts back to his car. I feel drenched in shame as I open the door and walk inside. Upstairs Jillie and Alice are laughing. *Help!* by the Beatles is on full blast.

It feels like that song should be my personal anthem, but asking for help, or even telling anyone what just happened isn't something I can do. I am too ashamed. Deep inside, the heartache is breaking loose, working through my blood into my bones. I'm like a warped jigsaw puzzle piece that can almost fit into place, but not quite. And no amount of pushing will make it right.

ELEVEN

November 1965

THE ROOM IS SILENT AS A BOBCAT stalking a squirrel. No one's in the upper bunk, where I used to nod off before Kathy left for college. Mary Ruth, who'd previously claimed the bottom bunk I now occupy, inhabits Kathy's former lair. I stare at the box springs on the bed frame above. No breathing. No creaking. No coughing. No bare feet paddling across linoleum. No hint of Mary Ruth. Just me in mental quicksand. But I'm comfortable. I want to go deeper, deeper, back to wherever I've been in the night. Why fight it? Why get up? Why go anywhere?

"Get up, you lazy good for nothing slob!" Wanda, a jolt from reality, is at the threshold, her palm slapping the doorframe.

I stay put, close my eyes. "I can't. My throat is really sore," I rasp. My throat is always sore on winter mornings and my lips are chapped, too, because my window is open an inch and a half every night. Wanda says the cold is good for me. She won't let me close the window or turn on the heat. I don't mind the hottest days of summer, when even grasshoppers languish, but when icicles dangle from the eaves, I'd sell my soul to escape the cold.

"Sore throat my eye," Wanda snarls, each word a BB pellet hitting my head. "You've been singin' that tune way too much, missy. I'm making an appointment with Dr. Frank. Yes, indeed, I'll show you; you're nothing but a fake. He'll expose you for the liar you are."

"It really is sore." I know it would probably feel better if I got up and gargled with salt water, but my limbs feel too heavy to lift.

"You don't know what pain is. Just you wait. Someday you'll find out, and when you do, don't you come cryin' to me. No siree. When you're eighteen, you're out, out of my hair."

It's been nine years since Wanda has taken me to see Dr. Frank. She says I'm healthy as an ox, so there's no need to waste money on medical visits, especially since Grandpa O'Neill—my dead mother's father, who is a family doctor—gives me a free checkup before school every year. I don't think this threat to take me to Dr. Frank is serious. I succumb again to sleep without answering her. It's the last day of classes before Christmas vacation. I've missed so much school in the last couple of months, what difference does it make if I'm absent for another day?

I drift inward and soon find myself in a familiar reverie, hoping I'll wake up after a long slumber in a new room, new body, new family, new life where everything is sunny and I'm whole again—like when I was a kid racing with abandon in a game of tag.

I don't really want a new family, though. I'd just like my old family back, the one my father held together. I miss him still. It's been five years. Life goes on, the saying goes. But I don't want to move on. I want him back, even though I think he'd be ashamed of me. But then, maybe not. If he were here, I'd be towing the line. He would beat me into submission if he had to, but he wouldn't need to. I'd give away all my freedom just to have him back. I fall deeper into slumber dreaming I'm in fifth grade again, the year before he died, and every scene is etched with a warm golden glow. I am so exquisitely happy. Then footsteps marching down the hall gradually pull me out of the dream. I assume it's Wanda ready to harangue me again. Every muscle tenses, the golden glow is replaced with gray.

"Laura? Are you here?" Shelby calls. "Why weren't you at school this morning? It's already lunch time, you goof." She's in the room now yanking on my blanket. "Come on. Get up."

As soon as I open my eyes, the murk that had possessed me disappears, like a magic trick. I blink and wonder whether it was real.

"What's going on with you, anyway?" She pokes my shoulder.

"I don't know. Nothing. Just tired, I guess."

"Where's Wanda?"

"Beats me. Maybe at one of her card clubs."

"Well, let's get going. Daniel loaned me his car to come get you."

"You don't have your license yet."

"Don't worry, weird one. I know how to drive. I'm taking my test in a couple of weeks."

"I wish I could say the same." My sixteenth birthday has come and gone. I'm too terrified behind the wheel to go more than thirty miles an hour. I don't think I'll ever be ready to pass a driving test.

"Hurry up. I'll be outside." Shelby gives me one more poke before she leaves.

I get ready in double time and settle into the passenger seat a few minutes later. Shelby shakes two Old Gold filters from a crumpled pack, hands them to me, hits the accelerator and drives off in the opposite direction from school. I punch in the cigarette lighter. After it pops out, I hold a cigarette to the orange glow, take a puff and give it back to her. The smell of smoldering tobacco perks me up. I light the second and draw in, feeling the now familiar sensation of smoke filling my lungs. Lately we've been smoking two packs a day apiece.

"Where are we going?" I ask.

"It's a surprise." She turns on the radio.

"I thought we were going to school."

"Nah, why bother now? There's only a couple hours left."

The windows are cracked slightly, so a brisk breeze whips through the car as Shelby speeds down the slush-filled streets and out of town, her red mane and my near-black one flapping up and down as she speeds up and slows down with the flow of traffic. The temperature has risen to 37, so melting snow is making the sidewalks and streets shiny and wet. The radio is up as loud as it will go, tuned to WLS, as usual. We sing along to Dusty Springfield's *I Only Want To Be with You*. I try not to think of Kip as I belt out the lyrics, but it's useless. Then Simon and Garfunkel's *Sounds of Silence* fills the car with loneliness. We listen in quiet, and I am relieved when a Heaven Scent jingle comes on. We sing along to that, too.

The waistband of my skirt is tighter than it was just a few days ago. All my clothes feel uncomfortable these days. When we're not dressed in our below-the-knee skirts for school, the jeans Shelby and I wear are so tight we can only zip them if we are horizontal. Sometimes it takes both of us—fifteen fingers to squeeze the teeth together, and five to pull the slider to the top. Then finally we fasten the button at the waistband. I don't know how we manage to even breathe most of the time, let alone sing. It's not like I want skintight jeans. It's just a mark of pride to be able to fit into the smallest size possible. I'm desperately trying to hold the line at size nine, but I'm up to 131 pounds now, and I've packed all the extra pounds onto my bottom; my breasts are still flat as ever. And every time I diet, my weight goes up instead of down. Shelby still squeezes into a seven.

I don't know where we're going until I see the mausoleum, and behind it rows of headstones surrounded by well-clipped lawns. Shelby drives up to the office; she said they'll have a map, but it's closed. We're on our own. I can't believe Shelby has brought me to Queen of Heaven to visit my father's grave. I told her back on November 5 that it was the fifth anniversary of his death: the day life as I knew it ended; the day I became a sad, lonesome freak nobody really wants to know. But I didn't tell her that part. I said I hadn't been to his grave since the day he was buried, and maybe someday

I should go. I didn't mention that I count every holiday from the day he died, like Thanksgiving this year was the sixth since he died.

"It would have been nice if Wanda had popped for a headstone instead of some little plaque flat on the ground," I say. "It would make his grave easier to find."

"Yeah, that would have been good," Shelby says.

"She used to say she fell in love with Daddy at first sight, and she knew right then he was the one; it didn't matter that he had three kids."

"I guess 'it didn't matter' is better than 'it stopped me cold.'"

"Except if we'd really put her off, then maybe she wouldn't have married him. Maybe he would have married somebody nicer, or nobody at all. She says Kathy, Mary Ruth and I drove our mother to kill herself and we killed him, too, but maybe marrying her is what did him in."

"That's heavy, Laura."

"Yeah, well, that's me." The last time I was here a light rain was falling. I whimpered while nuzzled with my sisters under an umbrella as his coffin was lowered into the ground. Remembering this makes me feel as though a monster from another dimension is poisoning me like an octopus spurting ink to blind predators at sea. I look up at the cloudy sky.

"What are you doing?" Shelby steps beside me; the monster recedes.

"Just looking around." In the distance I spy a stand of evergreens. I'm sure they're the ones I stood by at the burial. "I know where the grave is." I run toward the trees.

Shelby catches up just as I find the marker; it's gold with black lettering. Daddy's first name, Henry, doesn't seem right; everybody called him Hank. I wonder how he feels about that, that is, if he exists in some form somewhere, if there is such a thing as an afterlife. His middle initial E will forever stand in for the name Ethelbert, a name he said we could never divulge to anyone because he hated it so much. He was named after his father, Henry Ethelbert Gross, who was named after his father, Henry Ethelbert Gross, who was named after his father Heinrich Ethelbert von Gross, who lost his land during a political struggle in Germany. Incarcerated for backing the losing side, he was smuggled out of prison in a garbage barge. Then he boarded a ship for America. My gramma says Heinrich soon founded a German-language newspaper in Chicago. Since my father had no sons, I guess all that Henry history rests in his grave now.

Shelby stands by my side. She looks serious. I expect to feel something momentous as my eyes move to the dates that denote my father's life: Feb. 9, 1916 to Nov. 5, 1960. I think of him filled with formaldehyde and covered with pancake makeup and with that awful buzz cut he had when I saw his body at the wake. I wonder if his hair and nails have grown like they say happens after people die, whether his skin is all withered, whether icky things have crawled into his coffin and eaten him up.

"I wish I had some flowers or something." I poke through my jacket pockets looking for something to leave behind. I find a plastic charm Kip gave me one of those nights he came to my door to woo me. It's a little beagle, like Muffin, the dog my family owned for one year. Wanda gave him away right after Daddy died. I place the charm on the horizontal line of the H in Henry. The Lord's Prayer glides through my mind. I see the words move like sing-along lyrics on a movie screen with a happy, bouncing ball, telling me what to sing next. But I don't say the words out loud.

TWELVE

December 1965

SHELBY AND I PUFF ON OLD GOLDS at the Hinsdale Oasis restaurant, a novelty of sorts because it straddles the Illinois Tollway. Cars zoom by beneath, and people from all over stop in for greasy hamburgers on stale buns and French fries growing cold because waitresses have too many tables at their stations and the heat lamps warming their orders aren't strong enough. We grow restless while waiting for our onion rings and cokes.

"Sure is taking a long time." Shelby takes the tops off the salt-shaker and sugar server.

"The old sugar and salt mix up, huh?"

"It's a bummer that you'll miss all the parties tomorrow." She bursts into giggles as she pours salt into the sugar.

"Yeah, I guess." I giggle, too, and begin stirring the sugar and salt mixture with a spoon.

She screws the lids back on and slides them to the side of the table by the napkin holder. "Why are you having your tonsils out on New Year's Eve?" she asks.

"Wanda and Dr. Frank decided, not me. You have a date with Daniel anyway. What does it matter?"

"It's a dumb way to bring in 1966."

"Yeah, but when school starts again, I'll be recovering. I won't have to go, and there's nothing Miss Malice can do about it."

"Our uptight dean of girls will be pissed about that."

Flashing holiday lights line the restaurant booths; Santa and his reindeer sailing through the sky and other holiday motifs are painted across a wall of windows; a tree with tinsel, red and silver balls and fake presents brightens a corner. I feel no joy. I wish I could tell Shelby about Kip. It's been more than two months, and I haven't said a word to anyone about what happened. The whole topic is blocked off with yellow caution tape, and I'm standing guard, facing away from it. I sense that since that night I'm once again living a different life than before, one that's sliding into a place I don't want to go. But unlike the altered life that came with my father's death, this new life is my own doing.

Shelby snaps her fingers in front of my face. "Where are you? Didn't you hear me?"

"Um, what did you say?"

"Daniel's friend Zack's kind of interested in you. What do you think?"

"I kinda don't know. I've never even talked to him."

"We could double date sometime."

The waitress brings our food, and my tummy grumbles at the smell of fried batter and wilted onions. I slather an onion ring in ketchup. Then I see Carleton shuffling toward our table. His skin looks even whiter than it used to. His green, horn-rimmed glasses are as prominent as ever. "Oh, man, it's Carleton, making a beeline right for us."

"Carleton Cramer? Doesn't he go to some big league school back east?"

"Yeah, Yale or Dartmouth, I think."

"He's staring at you. Do you still know him?"

"I haven't seen him since freshman year."

"Hey, Laura." Carleton slides into the booth next to me.

74

"Nice to see you, too, Carleton," Shelby interjects.

"Nice to see you're still a wiseass," he replies.

"Yeah, and you're still a giant twerp."

"Touché." He turns to me. "So Laura, can we talk? I really need to talk to you."

"You mean right now? I'm kinda busy."

"Yeah, she has a life, you know," Shelby says.

"It's been two years." Carlton knits his brows and leans toward me.

"Seriously?" I thought he and Jay must have forgotten all about me by now.

"We're still waiting."

"You and Jay?"

"And Jodie. You can't forget Jodie, our fourth."

"What is going on here?" Shelby asks.

"This is for Laura's ears only, Red," he snaps at Shelby.

"Is this guy nuts or what?" Shelby frowns. She hates being called Red.

"Yeah, but he's harmless." I shrug. The whole group bonding based on *Stranger in a Strange Land* seems too odd to explain.

"What do you want to do?" she asks me.

"He has me blocked in here, so I may as well get this chat over with."

"This is a little too out there for me anyway." She slides out of the booth.

"Catch you tomorrow?" I ask.

"Sure thing. When do you go in?" she replies.

"The morning sometime, don't know exactly when."

"Call me, and let me know," she says. Then before sashaying away, she turns to Carleton. "Just in case, I'm calling her house at five. She'd better be there to answer, or I'm gonna raise hell."

He waves her away. "No worries; I'll get her home long before that."

The waitress stops by, and he orders coffee, pointing to an unused cup and saucer on the table. She pours the steaming liquid from a pot already in her hand. He takes a sip and then tries to make his case. I nibble on onion rings and look out the window at the traffic zooming by below.

"So, Laura, how was your Christmas?"

"Okay, I guess."

"It's a good time to reconnect with family," he says.

"I wouldn't know." Wanda, Kathy, Mary Ruth and I haven't spent the holiday together in years. Most of the time, Wanda visits her relatives, and my sisters and I go to our separate ways, visiting friends' families.

Carleton clears his throat. "We're having a reunion tomorrow night. I think it's time you renew your commitment."

"New Year's Eve? I've got plans."

"We could move it to New Year's Day."

"I've got plans then, too."

"What sort of plans?"

"I'm having my tonsils out if you have to know."

"On New Year's Eve? What doctors schedule surgery for New Year's Eve?"

"Apparently, mine does."

"Bummer. I think you really need our help."

"You, Jay and Jodie?"

"Yeah."

"How's that?"

"Well, for starters, what are you doing still hanging out with a wild girl like Shelby? She'll only bring you down. We can lift you up.

You have to pull it together if you want to get into the Ivy League like Mary Ruth."

"Oh, so you heard Vassar came knocking with a full scholarship?"

"Yeah, my mom told me."

"Word sure gets around. Then you probably know my grades have taken a nosedive this year, too. It'll be a state school for me, I guess."

"You can get over a little slip. It happens to the best of us."

"It never happens to Mary Ruth." The indisputable truth lands like a slap.

Carleton pauses, takes another swig of coffee. "How about if we visit you at the hospital?"

"No. I'm done, done, done. I want to go home." I shove him. "Move over. I need to get out."

"You don't have to be rude." He slides from the booth.

I slip out and stand facing him. "You're right, but you have no business telling me who my friends should be. I'm not the girl you once knew. I've got to go."

"Let me give you a ride. A cold front's moving in; you might slip on the ice."

"No thanks. I'll be careful."

He eases back into the booth, takes a sip of coffee. "You have no idea who you are, do you, how special you are."

"You're nuts, Carleton. Totally nuts." I button my jacket and speed toward the exit.

THIRTEEN

April 1966

THIS APRIL MORNING IS SUNNY, FRESH, and green. It's warm enough to pull out a light jacket and leave the heavy winter coat behind. That's worth a skip, a song, a smile. Instead, I'm at the sink studying a double-edged Gillette. This year, my hopes have crashed like Jan Berry, who drove his Corvette smack into a truck yesterday. And since my tonsillectomy, I'm behind in every class. I missed three weeks of school after the surgery when I was supposed to miss only one.

I know lots of kids who've had their tonsils out. I thought it would be no big deal when Dr. Frank saw white spots on my tonsils and said, "They have to come out, the sooner the better." I was even a little pleased because Wanda had taken me there to expose me as a fraud, a hypochondriac. But when I woke up in the recovery room, the pain was staggering. Then, after I was wheeled to a regular hospital room, the wound wouldn't stop oozing blood. My mouth filled with salty liquid that had a chemical taste, too. A nurse kept handing me paper cups, and I half spit, half drooled out goop that looked like snot, bits of charred chicken skin and blood all mixed up. Dr. Frank had to cauterize my throat again and again to stop the flow of blood. My scorched flesh smelled worse than burning hair. And when I came home from the hospital, my throat oozed even more. So back to Dr. Frank's office I went for more cauterization. So much for thinking I'd turn things around in the new year. It's as stupid as John Lennon thinking the Beatles are more popular than Jesus.

I look at the razor blade and imagine blood will spurt all over my black, red and white plaid empire waist dress when I slash my wrists. A few days ago I stole a kitchen knife, took off my blouse and held the cold tip to the smooth skin of my belly. But I couldn't force the dull blade in. It was then that I remembered the old razor blade in the medicine cabinet.

Self-loathing buzzes throughout my body all day every day. A lifetime of festering fears have been merging, building momentum—only a blip at first, like a cloud covering the sun briefly on an otherwise sunny afternoon, but now dread drones like locusts caught in my gut. I can't control it. I hate my life, hate that I can't get it together. Why can't I put my feelings aside and just function like everybody else? I run my finger along the edge of the blade and wonder how hard I'd have to press to slice the tip right off.

I think of how quietly condescending I was to Jillie last year when she told me she gets up in the middle of the night to eat. She cooks a pot of rice, melts butter into it, and scarfs it down right from the pot. That's the appetizer. Then she gobbles up just about anything edible in her kitchen—salty Spam, buttered toast and jam, cold hot dogs sliced down the middle and stuffed with strips of American cheese and pickle relish, Ritz crackers with Jiff, chocolate ice cream scooped from carton to mouth. Soda after soda after soda.

Freshman year, Jillie's mom told me she hoped my eating habits would rub off on her daughter; Shelby's mom said she wanted my good grades to inspire Shelby to crack the books. Now I'm up to 133 pounds, eating right along with Jillie. That's a gain of ten pounds in seven months. I've introduced Shelby to the all-night pig-out, too. Her upper thighs are starting to bulge. Plus, I've spread Shelby's habit of skipping school to Jillie. I'm like one of those disease carriers; everyone would be better off without me.

I hold my right wrist over the sink, palm up. Gripping the blade in my left hand, I cut into my skin, drawing a few drops of blood. Going in is harder than I thought. I hold my breath, grit my teeth, find a new spot, dig a little deeper. Blood dribbles out.

Mary Ruth knocks on the door. "Laura, hurry up. I need to brush my teeth."

"I'll be right out." I grab a couple of tissues from a box on the counter and press them to my wrist. I thought my sister was done with the bathroom for the morning. I slip the razor into my dress pocket, step out of the bathroom and nearly crash into Mary Ruth in the hall. "It's all yours," I say.

"Groovy." She smiles and slips past me. I turn away.

I turn away and bolt to my room where I fish through the mess on the floor to find my U.S. history and algebra books, binder and the little suede Daveys bag I bought with babysitting money. Lots of girls at school have Daveys bags. When I carry mine, I feel a little less creepy.

I press the tissues over my veins where blood oozes. Mary Ruth knocks on my door. "Do you want to walk to school together?" Since we both sleep more and more often at friends' houses instead of at home, this is a rare opportunity. Her voice is warm; gone is the air of constant exasperation she used to have around me. She likes me now, tells me jokes, goes out of her way to check in with me at school, but I don't deserve it.

I open the door just a crack. "I'm not ready yet. Go ahead. Maybe I'll catch up."

When I step through the front door a few minutes later, my wrist isn't bleeding much. I kick a piece of stray gravel as I inch down the blacktop driveway toward the street, but instead of trudging toward school, I spin around and dash to the backyard. A tiny hill slopes about five feet down from the house to the part of the yard where our garden used to be. I remember weeding with gusto, planting and watering oh so carefully, and then the joy of little sprouts of carrot and lettuce pushing through the black earth. I throw my books down at the foot of a cherry tree Kathy, Mary Ruth and I used to fill with strips of aluminum foil to scare birds away from the ripening fruit. Kathy, the leader on the top rung, stretching her skinny frame precariously to reach the farthest branches. Mary Ruth and me directly behind, egging her on. All that seems eons ago.

I cut across backyards until I'm a few blocks from home. Then I cut through to front sidewalks and amble toward the train station, following a familiar route along Hinsdale's quiet streets, greeting the trees and bushes, street corners and houses I've seen in the pouring rain and blistering heat, scattered with autumn leaves, and hugged by snow drifts up to my waist. I mark my favorites along the way: a rooster weather vane high on a peaked roof; yellow and white gingham curtains framing a kitchen window rimmed at the bottom with African violets; a three-story green house with a stained glass window in its varnished front door, a home I wished countless times were mine.

At the newly sandblasted and spiffed up train station, my heart quickens the closer I get to the front of the ticket line. I'm certain the man behind the counter, who looks authoritative in his black cap, white shirt and thin black tie, will ask why I'm not in school. I don't know what I'll say. But he doesn't even look up when I request a one-way ticket to Chicago. I just missed a train, but another is roaring behind, ready to board commuters and speed them to work. I stand near the track, swinging my bag and humming John Philip Sousa's *Stars and Stripes Forever*, a melody my classmates and I marched to in grammar school.

When the train pulls up, the conductor's wide smile and firm hand help me aboard. I sit in a window seat by myself. As we progress eastward, I gaze at the houses, shops and train stations we pass. The closer we get to the city, the buildings are more dilapidated, the sidewalks more littered, the people more careworn, some lingering outside of bars. I say good-bye to the neon, the streetlights, the auto body shops, the littered backyards, the manicured grounds of small stations along the way. Everything, from stop signs to passing sparrows, to newspapers blowing along the track seems especially vivid. Certain I will never take this ride again, I want to remember the rhythm of the train on the track, the smell of the worn leather seats, the sound of the conductor's voice calling out each stop, the echo of his footsteps down the aisle, the click-click as he punches tickets.

I have a doublewide seat to myself all the way to Brookfield, where a man with Einstein hair peeking out from a tweed cap greets me, sits down beside me and opens his *Tribune*. I am grateful he doesn't want to talk. I would have had to lie about who I am and where I'm going. And right now, the only inkling I have is that I want to head south where the warmth is, where palm trees sway in the breeze and chameleons dart through the sand.

When we roll into Union Station, I get in an Illinois Central ticket line and learn that Springfield is as far south as I can go with the money I have and still keep a few dollars for food until I figure out what to do next. I board a train and luxuriate in the comfort of a cushioned seat as the train chugs away. Soon, all familiar landmarks are gone, and we're speeding through open prairie. The rumble of the wheels lulls me; I want the ride to go on and on and on. But in less than four hours, we stop in the city where Abe Lincoln is buried.

FOURTEEN

April 1966

AT SOME POINT I'LL HAVE TO HITCH a ride into the unknown. I can't walk all the way to Acapulco, or even to Louisville, after all. But I continue to amble southward alone, comforted by sunbeams warming me to the bones. I kick a stone forward along the highway's shoulder, wishing with each step I knew where to go next while traffic whizzes by on my left and prairie stretches to the horizon on my right. When I tire of walking, I turn around to squint at oncoming traffic and stick out my thumb. My first attempt at hitchhiking. Almost immediately, a big rig slows and screeches to halt in the lane beside me. It smells like all of Chicago is baking under the hood as I grab hold of a steel handle and hoist myself up a few wobbly steps to reach the opening cab door.

"Where you headed?" a paunchy, middle-aged man asks as I climb inside. His skin is a lighter shade of the taupe shirt and pants he wears.

"South," I reply.

"I'm goin' down to New Orleans, could take you all the way there." He eases the truck back into gear. His droopy jowls jiggle, and his grin reveals a set of browning teeth.

New Orleans. I've fantasized about escaping to Mardi Gras since I was seven or eight. I like the idea of being in costume, a mask on my face, strings of beads dangling around my neck, a dress full of sequins and lace. I imagine dancing in the streets, meeting fortunetellers and southern belles, mavericks and voodoo priests. Mardi Gras has already come and gone this year, but still, the thought of going to a place where people celebrate like that intrigues me.

The truck picks up speed, but our attempts at conversation sputter and die. The truck roars along. I like being so far above the surrounding traffic. But I don't like the way the driver leers at me. He's old enough to be my father. To my way of thinking, even kissing him would be like kissing a rotten hardboiled egg. I think he ought to know that. He says his name is James Roberts. I don't' believe him. It's like he's trying the name on, letting it linger on his tongue, listening to the sound of it.

He exits the highway and pulls into a truck stop for gas. "A gal can't go cross country in a dress. I'll get you a pair of jeans and some food later if things —" He clears his throat. "If things work out." He winks before climbing out of the cab.

"I don't need a pair of jeans," I call after him, even though I could use a change of clothes.

He fills the gas tank, goes inside to pay and comes back with Juicy Fruit gum. "Want some?" He throws the yellow pack in my lap as he settles in behind the wheel. I'd love to chew a stick right now, but I'm afraid to take anything from him besides the ride. I brush the gum off my dress. It lands on the frayed, brown seat between us.

The journey continues in silence. With each mile the cab grows hotter, stuffier, and overcome with a grotey smell coming from an area behind the seats where a dirty yellow blanket and pillow are rumpled up. Hours later, the sun sets across the prairie to the west. The sky darkens gradually and turns into a midnight blue. He slows the truck down as we roll into Cairo, Illinois.

"I'll need to stop soon," he says. "Most times I pull over and sleep right here, but I know of a little place where we can get a room. Then we can get you those jeans and some food. How 'bout it?"

"Did you know I'm 16 years old and running away from home?"

"No shit."

"You could get in trouble, couldn't you, for being with me?"

"How do I know you're not really 18? Do you have any ID?"

"No, do you have any ID, Mr. Roberts?"

"Yeah, I got plenty. Stupid girl. What? You think you can just ride for free?"

I edge to the right, grab the door handle. "Uh, I just, I can't imagine —"

"You think you're too good for me? Lotsa women would be glad to be with me." He sneers, eyes bulging.

"I'll get out," I say.

"In Cairo? At this hour? You've gotta be nuts."

"I'll get out here. Just slow down, Okay? I'll jump."

"Bullshit you will."

The truck halts at a red light. I open the door and leap out, sliding on the pebbles of the shoulder as I land. The signal turns green. The truck idles. A car inches up behind it. The truck continues to idle. The car's horn toots. My heart pounds. The car honks twice. The truck idles. The horn blares long and loud. The truck sputters and finally chugs away. When the light turns red, I run across the road and down a side street. Not many people are out, but those I see are black. I feel like a slip showing below someone's hem. It's just a matter of time before somebody notices I am way out of place. I turn down another side street and am afraid to keep walking, afraid of what I might run into.

Cars are parked along the curb. I try the handle of a green four-door. It's unlocked. I crawl into the back seat, curl up and try to sleep. I keep on trying until the sun's rays warm my face. Knowing the car's owner could come at any time, I get out and face a dew-covered morning. The neighborhood looks as bad as I feel. Most of the storefronts are dirty and boarded up. Hardly any people are around.

I turn down an alley and poke along slowly, feeling hidden. Safe. But then I reach the end of the alley and step onto a sidewalk lining a street that is abuzz with morning traffic. I look straight ahead, trying to appear as though I have someplace to go. A police car pulls up alongside me. Inside I scream.

"Hello there, miss," an officer on the passenger side calls to me. He tips his black, gold-trimmed hat. I wonder how they could have tracked me down so fast.

"Um, good morning, officer," I reply.

"Where are you going?"

I spy a diner at the corner and say, "I'm going to have breakfast and then go to school."

"Is that right? How old are you anyway?"

"Sixteen."

"And your name?"

"Lizzie." I figure that isn't exactly a lie because Elizabeth is my middle name.

"Lizzie who?"

"O'Neill." Since that was my mother's maiden name, I think it's only half a lie.

"Well, then Lizzie O'Neill, go enjoy your breakfast," the officer says, tipping his hat again.

"I will, sir."

The officers drive off. Now I have to go to the diner. What if they drive around the block to check on me? Once inside, I sit at the counter and order eggs over easy, rye toast and coffee. After I pay my bill, I have only two singles left in my wallet. Craving a place to hide, I exit the diner. Then I see it: a lopsided wood-frame church with peeling green paint. I walk the side lawn to the back of the building and tiptoe up the rickety stairs. The door is unlocked. Inside is a cavernous room painted bright yellow. Directly to the right is a bathroom. I clean myself up using brown paper towels and a bar of Lux soap at the sink. Then I explore. There is a sanctuary, cool and dark; the church office, which I expect will soon be full of people; a kitchen; two big meeting rooms downstairs; and some small rooms upstairs that don't look like they're used much.

It's Tuesday. If I keep quiet, and if I'm lucky, I'll have until Sunday to plan what to do next. I pick one of the small rooms as my hideout for the day. It's empty. No curtains cover the two, dirt-streaked windows, but it is carpeted. I lean my back against a wall, slide down to the floor and look up through the window to the blue, blue sky. Afraid that someone might discover me if I explore the building further, I remain all day, listening and thinking as pigeons coo nearby and crows call off in the distance.

In the late afternoon and evening I hear the unmistakable sound of teenagers ribbing each other, flirting, bragging. Curious, I crawl to the window and poke my head up just enough to see over the sill. Holding court at a drive-in across the street, the group reminds me of my friends in Hinsdale, the way we joke around aimlessly. I have a stab of longing for the chance to be with my tribe again, to be one small breath from normal. I miss going to bed at night, hoping tomorrow I'll wake up and everything will be okay—having the chance. I see no chances here as I plop down alone on the floor. I'm too afraid to even leave the church.

On Wednesday morning I find a box of Saltines on one of the kitchen shelves and take nine, three for each meal of the day. I hope they won't be missed. My mind runs nonstop through everything I think I should have done in my life but didn't. Time creeps by.

Nights are the worst. Terrifying. But I know better than to turn on any lights. I try to sleep on the soft blue carpet of the church office, where rays from a nearby streetlight keep me company, bouncing off the surface of the desk clock. But sleep doesn't come. By Friday, I am so overcome with worry about what I'll do when folks come to pray on Sunday, and I'm so panicked about being discovered if I leave the church, that I give up on running away. I set out to find the Greyhound bus station and see if I have enough money to get to Jacksonville, where Kathy is a freshman at MacMurray College.

At the station, I come up short. So I pick a street and start knocking on doors. All morning I approach houses that are one step above shacks. People who answer usually say something like, "Sorry, we don't even have enough money for food ourselves." But sometimes they dig through their purses or kitchen drawers or old mayonnaise jars and pull out a dime or a nickel for me. I collect $1.25 this way. Then I try a Phillips station. I ask a man wiping grease from his hands with a rag, "Sir, do you have some money you could lend me toward a bus ticket to Jacksonville? I'm trying to get to my sister there."

"How much do you need?" He threads the rag through the loop at the side of his overalls.

"Anything will help, a dime, a nickel."

He pulls a roll of bills from his back pocket, peels off a five and hands it to me. "Get along now. I have a daughter around your age, and I sure wouldn't want to see her beggin' like this."

"Thanks ... I can pay you back."

"Never mind. Just get home and stay there."

FIFTEEN

April 1966

I SLOUCH IN A CHAIR FACING the dean of girls—Miss Malice, Shelby and I like to call her. She sits erect and taps a pencil on her desk blotter. "What do you have to say for yourself about this running away business?" she asks.

"Not much."

"Well, I have quite a bit to say. Not the least of which is that I'm on to you. This may be the first time you've run away, but it's not the first time you've cut school."

"But —"

"Don't even try to deny it. It'll only make things worse for you." Her mighty chest heaves beneath her aquamarine sweater set. I wish I could have moved into Kathy's dorm room and never returned to Hinsdale. I used the money I'd panhandled to buy a bus ticket to see Kathy at MacMurray College. She was so happy to see me—and amazing overall, like a different person, smiling more and with color in her cheeks and a bounce in her walk. She was drawing, drawing everything all around Jacksonville for her art class, and playing guitar and writing some really good songs. She said getting away from Wanda and Hinsdale made all the difference, and she wanted to let me stay with her so I wouldn't have to go back to Wanda, but of course, there was no way to do that, so after a couple of days of bliss with her, she had to put me on a bus to Chicago. Before I boarded the bus she hugged me and said, "You've just got a little over year to go now. Then you'll be free. You'll see."

Vertical frown lines form between Miss Malice's eyebrows as she scowls at me. "The good news is that you won't be expelled. The bad news is that you'll be getting zeros for all the work done in your classes while you were gone."

"You mean I won't be able to make any work up?"

"What did you expect? You know the rules. But I am giving you a break. Usually, truants are suspended for the number of days they cut classes, but we won't do that this time. You've missed enough school already."

"Okay." I look down at the pile of books in my lap.

"Don't look so glum. You won't get any sympathy from me. When a girl's really in trouble, I'll bend over backwards to help. But that's not the case with you. Look at Kathy. She broke her back in her senior year, and she graduated near the top of her class. And Mary Ruth, she's an example of what a girl can do when she applies herself. You are choosing to go down the wrong path. You can change course anytime." She fills out a pink slip and hands it to me. "Now, get going or you'll be late for class."

I sidle out of her office and down the hall, dreading that I'll have to march to the front of each class today, pink slip in hand, the color meaning my absence is unexcused. I pause at my classroom door just as Mr. Conyers, my Western Civilization teacher from freshman year, struts up to me. "You look like death warmed over, Laura. Come this way," he says.

Relieved that I won't have to see my algebra teacher's disappointed face just yet, I follow Mr. Conyers to his office. His long jaw, bald dome and thick, curved eyebrows remind me of Pluto, the cartoon dog. He plops in one of two chairs facing his desk. I settle into the other one. He moves his chair closer to mine. "I've heard things aren't going so well for you." He points to the pink slip.

"Guess not." I think of Officer Wilkins, Hinsdale's chief of police, who hauled me in to the station when I returned home a few days ago. He said I'd better not run away again or I'd get sent to a place that would make my problems at home look like a picnic. He also said that, unlike my friends, I have no one who'll pay to get me out of trouble, so I should be careful who I hang out with.

"What's really going on?" Mr. Conyers asks.

Kip comes to mind, but I bat that thought away. "Nothin' much."

"Chin up, kiddo. You were a little beanpole a couple years ago, but you've filled out. You've got some nice curves. How much did you gain, about fifteen pounds?"

"What?" I sit up straighter in the chair.

"I get it. Girls don't like to talk about their weight, right? ... Listen, I know it must be hard to follow those sisters of yours."

I don't answer. I think he should talk. He's the one who gave me a D one grading period instead of the B I'd earned because I hadn't scored A's in his class the way my sisters had.

He clears his throat. "I'm going to tell you something important." He leans in close and puts a hand on my shoulder. "If I were going to ask one of the three of you out to dinner, you'd be the one." A grin fills the bottom half of his face. Light from a small window in the office door bounces against sweat beading on top of his head.

I shrug his hand off my shoulder. How could he possibly think his remark was helpful, I wonder. What do I care who he wants to take out to dinner? I slide my chair away a few inches. "I'd better get to class now." I stand, clutching my books to my chest and crinkling my absence slip in my hand.

"Don't look so alarmed. I just wanted to give you some perspective. With a face like yours, you've got it made."

I don't feel like I've got it made, but I don't want to argue. "Um, thanks, I guess."

He stands up. "Mrs. Henderson wants to see you, you know."

"The school psychologist?"

"Come on, I'll walk you there."

"Do I have a choice?"

"She'll pin you down eventually. It may as well be now."

I follow him downstairs to Mrs. Henderson's office, but she's not there.

"I know where she is; just wait here." His footsteps echo in the hallway. I sit in a chair and stare at a stack of file folders teetering on the edge of her desk. I resist the urge to tap the pile so the files would flood the floor. Soon, Mrs. Henderson waddles into the room, a five foot eight inch duck with glasses. Her Kelly green dress swishes against her calves.

"Hello, Laura. Mr. Conyers is a fan of yours." She eases herself into her chair.

What a cow, I think. I peer at the dimes I put in my scuffed penny loafers.

"Laura?" she says.

I look up and see a wide face overflowing with kindness. I feel guilty for likening her to a cow.

"I've been investigating your life, honey, and I think it's tragic what's gone on. Not just your father's death when you were, what, twelve?

"Eleven."

"Yes, that. But also your mother's suicide when you were, let me look here ..." She opens a file on her desk.

"Two."

"Yes, a toddler."

"Does everybody on earth know about that?" I feel suddenly hot behind the ears.

"Oh, no, no, no, no, no. And whatever we say is completely confidential."

"But you've got a folder full of stuff about me."

"It's for my use only, and when I'm not here, I lock it away." She points to a green metal file cabinet in the corner. "This folder just has my research notes. I've spoken with your teachers, not just the ones you have this year. I even talked with some of your grammar school teachers."

"No kidding."

"Yes, and I spoke with your neighbors and with the pastor at the church where you used be in the youth group."

"That was just for a few years. I'm Catholic. Well, not exactly. I was born Catholic."

"I see. Does that matter to you, being Catholic?"

Nobody has ever asked me that before. I pause, not knowing what to say. I was so young when Daddy slammed the door on the church, I didn't even know what being Catholic meant. I feel like none of this should matter, but I realize that somewhere deep inside it does. "Well, sort of, yeah. I never had a choice about leaving."

"You could go back to the church any time," she suggests.

"I suppose, but Jillie and Shelby are both Catholic, and they skip mass all the time. They think the church is a bunch of malarkey. "

"I spoke to both of them."

"You did?"

"It appears your stepmother has significant problems." She pursed her lips and shook her head in disapproval.

"You believe them?"

"Why wouldn't I?"

"Nobody else does."

"Most people aren't trained to look at things the way I do. There is no doubt that your stepmother is abusive, but she stays within the law, and she puts on a good show."

I can't believe an adult just spoke those words. "Kathy, Mary Ruth and I have been saying that for years, and all you grownups, you pretty much just tell us to stop complaining."

"It may be because there's not much anyone can really do. She adopted you. It would be very difficult for anyone to take you away from her."

"Well then. I guess that's it."

"No, not at all. I want you to know that you can come see me any time. And I do mean any time. You can leave English class in the middle of a test, you can come here dripping wet from swim class, you can come here five times a day if you need to. When you have to get away, you can come here to me, and you can sit in that chair and not say a word, or you can talk, and I'll listen."

"Really?" I doubt I'll actually return to her office, but the possibility of not getting in trouble for leaving class is like having a get-home-free card in my pocket.

"Yes."

"Can I go now?" I slide to the edge of the chair and put weight on my feet.

"Not yet, dear. I have to bring something up."

I lean back into the chair.

"What's this I hear about you trying to kill yourself?"

I flick my hand in the air, dismissing the notion of offing myself the way a teacher might fend off a wisecrack in class. I'm sure the incident in the bathroom was just a fluke. "I was just experimenting. I wondered how hard it would be to cut through my skin," I lie.

Shelby is the only one who's seen the slivers of pink on my wrist. I figure she must have blabbed.

"It's normal for adolescents to experiment, Laura, but not like this. It concerns me. I'd like to see if we can get you some help, okay?"

"Can't you just help me?"

"Like I said, you can come see me any time. But I want you to see someone outside of school, too."

"Wanda will never pay for anything like that."

"Who's Wanda?"

"That's what I call my stepmom: Wanda the Wicked Witch of the Western Suburbs."

Mrs. Henderson takes a deep breath. I think she's suppressing a smile. "I'll speak with your stepmom about an evaluation."

A bell sounds. "I just missed my whole algebra class." I groan.

"Don't worry. I'll talk to your teacher." She takes my pink slip, rips it up and fills in a blue form, indicating my entire absence was excused. "Just this once," she says.

"Thanks." Clutching the blue slip, I stand and walk out the door. Soon I blend in with the crush of students passing from one class to the next.

SIXTEEN

May 1966

IN THE LITTLE COMPANY OF MARY HOSPITAL parking lot, I steady Wanda at the elbow as she limps beside me. Her left leg is slightly atrophied since a long-ago Chicago bus-stop robbery and beating she mutters about every now and then. When we enter the building, we are slapped by smells of bleach and other cleaners that don't quite mask heavier odors I don't even want to identify. Uncle Thomas, a doctor who is also my dead mother's brother, greets us in the lobby and escorts us to the elevator. He and Wanda strain to make small talk. This always happens when she has to deal with anyone from my mother's family. She says they think they're better than she is. I don't know what they think. I only know the tension in the elevator permeates like the smell of singed hair. After we ascend several floors, we follow him out of the elevator and down the hall to a conference room.

Three of Uncle Thomas' colleagues stride up, two men in gray suits and one woman in a royal blue suit. Her skirt tastefully covers her kneecaps, a cameo pin adorns her lapel. They are all wrinkle free. Wanda and I are all lumps and creases and twisted seams. Uncle Thomas does a round of introductions. One of them is a bigwig shrink, but I don't know which one. They're all Dr. somebody or other. Uncle Thomas asks Wanda to wait outside the room. He points to a row of orange plastic chairs bolted together against the wall.

Uncle Thomas and his friends take seats across from me at a table so large there is barely enough space for the chairs surrounding

96

it. He sits still while the others take out pads and pens. Thoughts of my father surface and dive through my mind, pulling me with them: This is the place where Daddy took his last breaths. I wonder whether he rode up the same elevator I just used, whether he walked down the same hallway, whether he ever thought of me as he lay in his hospital bed. I wonder whether Uncle Thomas feels bad that he couldn't save him. Round and round the thoughts go. I can't shake them.

Then the questions begin. I stare at a crucifix on the wall and wonder if there's some trick to answering them. I don't want these people to lock me up somewhere. It happened to a girl at school. One day she was walking down the hall with her boyfriend; the next day she was at River's Edge being pumped with drugs. Not that I'd get sent there; it's an expensive place for rich kids. God only knows where I'd end up.

I've never sat at a conference table before, let alone one where three adults are jotting notes at my every shift and sigh. I stick with short answers.

"How old are you?"

"Sixteen."

"Where do you go to school?"

"Hinsdale Township High School Central."

"Do you like school? "

"No."

"Do you have any hobbies? "

"No."

"Do you have many friends?"

"No."

"Boyfriends?"

"Not now."

"Did you love your father?"

"Yes."

"Did he love you?"

"I don't know."

"He never said so?"

"No."

"How old were you when he died?"

"Eleven."

"Do you remember him?"

"Yes."

"Do you think about him?"

"Yes."

"Do you remember your mother?"

"Not much."

"How old were you when she died?"

"Two."

"Do you know how she died?"

"Yes."

"What happened?"

"Suicide."

"Do you think she loved you?"

"No."

"Do you think about her?"

"No."

I expect they'll start asking questions that will require more thought from me. But they don't. The evaluation is over in a few minutes. Uncle Thomas walks me back to the hallway and asks me to wait there. He offers his hand to Wanda, inviting her into the room. I plunk down on one of the orange chairs. My thighs sweat through my panty hose into my skirt. Staring at cracks in a framed picture of Jesus, I wonder whether my father wasted away on this very floor. I watch people come and go from the elevator. Some of them nod; some even say hello. Wanda finally comes out, looking timid as she thanks Uncle Thomas and the other doctors. She crosses her arms and scratches her chronically itchy elbows through her jacket as Uncle Thomas walks us to the elevator. He has another meeting to attend down the hall, otherwise he'd walk us to our car, he says. Wanda and I enter the elevator. The door closes.

"Now you've gone and done it. They say you need help, so now I've got to go find some psychiatrist, and where in God's name do you suppose I'm going to get the money to pay for something like that? You nincompoop. There's nothing wrong with you that a good kick in the pants wouldn't fix. But I'm boxed in. The idea. I hope you're happy now."

I say nothing. I know it must have galled her to ask a favor of my mother's family. But that's her problem. Not mine.

A few days later, I enter Dr. Scott's sparse waiting room. No receptionist is there to greet me. I'm ready to bolt; it all seems too weird, me going to a head doctor right in downtown Hinsdale. I don't see blue people darting across lawns or anything. What's the point? I'm not happy, but that's nothing new. I plop down on the sole leather couch and decide against picking up one of the *Time* or *Newsweek* magazines on the end table.

Dr. Scott pokes his head out of his office door and calls me in. Two matching chairs face his desk. I wonder which one I should choose. Does it make a difference? Is one better than the other? What will he think? I pick the chair closest to the door. I'm sure he knows now that I'm a coward. On the desk is a wooden sculpture of what resembles a nude woman. Its smooth curves make me very uncomfortable. The shrink studies me from behind his wide, teak desk. By his desk calendar is another sculpture. It's black, swirly, unrecognizable. Probably very expensive.

"Well?" he says peering at me through black-framed glasses.

I feel badgered by his intense, beady eyes. "Well?" I challenge.

He stares at me. I return the gaze until I can't stand it anymore. I look beyond him to the window that lets in muted light from an overcast day.

"So why are you here?"

"Beats me. Nobody told me." I look around the room, study the nap of the beige carpet, the books in the bookcase; they're all hard-bound volumes, more than two inches thick with gold lettering. They probably detail every known mental disease on earth.

"Why do you think you're here?"

"You know more than I do. Why don't you tell me?" I cross my arms over my chest and glare at him.

The doctor remains silent, occasionally looking down at his desk, then returning his gaze to me. I'd like to tell him it looks like he washed his face with rancid oil instead of soap and water, but I have to be careful around all grownups, especially a shrink. Wanda probably poisoned his thoughts already. The clock ticks on. I cross and re-cross my legs, wiggling my toes inside my loafers. Neither of us speaks until he says. "Time's up. See you next week."

"Okay." I nod, repressing the urge to say, "Fat chance, weirdo."

I race out the office and run most of the way home. When I blast through the front door, I tell Wanda I don't want to see Dr. Scott anymore. She picks up the phone and dials him right away, sugar flowing through her voice as she breaks the news. I knew she'd be pleased. She can save money and blame this failure on my lack of willingness to give therapy a try. I leave it to her to deal with Mrs. Henderson and Uncle Thomas, but I expect telling them about this development isn't high on her list of things to do.

SEVENTEEN

May 1966

PARKED AT A DESK IN THE LAST class of the day, I doodle on a piece of notebook paper. The drill is always the same. A teacher explains a chunk of math or English, history or whatever, assigns homework in a textbook that re-explains the material, goes over the homework the next day, reviews the lesson yet again, and then presents a new segment to learn. It goes on and on like this day in/day out, year after year.

Words about the Battle of the Bulge spew from my history teacher's mouth, but they don't engage me; I'm stuck in the world inside my head. I hope I'll study up on what he's describing later, but I'm not counting on it. I used to be able to concentrate with the TV blaring, radio blasting, phone ringing and Wanda screaming, but not now. Even when all is quiet, my mind often abandons my eyes as I read, so I look at pages of text, but comprehend little.

I am a lost cause who has tumbled overboard into mental whitewater rapids. Battered by rocks, I cling to a tree root to catch my breath. The current yanks me away, and miraculously, I catch up with the bouncing raft that ejected me. I crawl back in and find that nobody aboard missed me. Then I feel something inching up the back of my neck. This jolts my attention back to the classroom. I shift positions at my desk, flick my hair away from my collar bone and shake my head to make sure nothing's really crawling on my skin. The teacher writes the next assignment on the chalkboard in light yellow letters against a deep green background. He finishes, turns to the class and asks, "Any questions?" Before anyone raises a timid hand, the dismissal bell rings.

I find Shelby at her locker and ride home with her. I've been crashing at her house for about a week; it's probably the longest I've stayed there in one stretch. When we walk into Shelby's room, her mom is at the dresser, pulling underwear, sweaters and pants out of the drawers and throwing them around. Sweat darkens her short, mahogany-colored curls.

"What are you doing, Mom?" Shelby asks.

"You're leaving messes all around the house and not cleaning any of them up, and I don't like it." She raises her voice. "I don't like it one bit." She tosses a pink angora sweater into the air; it lands on Shelby's head.

Shelby laughs and throws it back at her mom. "Cool it, Mom, will ya?"

Her mom pulls a drawer completely out of the dresser and dumps the contents onto the floor. "There! When you finish cleaning this up, clean up the living room, too." She turns and scowls at me. "You, too, Laura." Then she marches toward the door.

Shelby grabs a pillow from her bed and whacks her mom on the back of the head. Her mom spins around, wrestles the pillow away from Shelby and bops her in the face. The two of them jostle, lose their balance and fall, laughing, onto Shelby's bed. I see the duo entwined and feel as out of place as a blob of orange acrylic on Mona Lisa's nose. I make a quiet exit while Shelby and her mom continue to tussle.

I stop by Daniel's on the way home. He's one of Shelby's boyfriends, but he's taken me under his wing, says he's my big brother, calls me Sis. I like him a lot, even though all we do when we're together is drink malt liquor and pop whatever kind of pills he has on hand. Daniel lives in a mansion, but his friends aren't all wealthy.

He's pulled together a group of misfits from all sorts of families. Mine is probably the poorest since we're living on Social Security, but the differences sort of melt away in his den. Most nights, at about 9 p.m., his parents retreat to their private wing on the third floor and put earplugs in. Daniel and his friends stay up till all hours playing pool or poker, listening to albums, watching TV or just goofing off. It seems somebody is always there hanging out, so it's a place where I can just show up unannounced. When dread creeps in and taints my days, coming here puts all the negativity at bay, and for a little while, I don't feel quite as alone.

It's around midnight when Daniel drives me home. Light from the streetlamp at the corner of the front yard floods the hallway as I step inside. All of Wanda's pills are lined up by the yellow phone on the yellow-flecked linoleum counter between the kitchen and dining room. Wanda's been seeing doctors for so many years—for her sore back, her limp, her elbow scratching, her anemia, her female troubles and who knows what else—that she has maybe twenty vials of prescription medicine by the phone. Plus, she keeps over the counter painkillers and cold remedies in a kitchen cabinet.

In that familiar scene, I see a solution. I could put an end to all my misery with her pills. It would be so much easier than trying to slit my wrists. I'm ready to say good-bye and face whatever death might hold, even if it's nothing. It has to be better than the life I have. I can succeed at this one thing. All I have to do is swallow pills, go to bed and wrap my covers around me. Then it'll be over. The thought makes me feel better than I have in months.

I decide to do it first thing in the morning, before Wanda is up. I crawl into bed and try to sleep until 5 a.m., when I get up and move in slow motion. Wanda hears even the slightest sound, but I know how to creep toward the kitchen like a ghost. I don't creak one board beneath my feet. Once there, I slowly, very slowly, open the cabinet that holds the glasses. I grab a former jelly jar with a band of oranges painted on its rim. I tiptoe to the sink, turn on the faucet ever so slightly and let the water trickle down the side of the glass. The silence delights me as liquid fills the glass.

I creep to the pills by the phone and try each vial. If it opens easily, I consume about a third of the contents, not wanting to use up all of Wanda's medicine. I down each round of pills with a few gulps of water. If a top doesn't come off quickly, I put it back down, just a little edge of the bottom touching the counter at first, then a little more, until the bottom of the plastic cylinder is solidly on the surface again. I do this, refilling the glass as necessary, until I'm done with the pills by the phone.

Next, I edge to the cabinet with Wanda's over-the-counter remedies. Staring at the grain of the blond wood, I feel calm, strong and completely resolved in my decision to say good-bye to this life once and for all. I pull the door open slightly. It creaks. I pause, praying that Wanda hasn't stirred. I pull again, but at a snail's pace. No noise. I pull again until I can view the shelves. The bottom two are full of medicine. The two shelves above are loaded with cake mixes, some from before Daddy died more than five years ago. That's Wanda—buying things on sale, filling the shelves and storing endlessly for the inevitable catastrophe to come. At least she'll still have plenty of cake to choose from—sponge, devil's food, white, pineapple upside down cake—after I'm out of her hair.

She has loads of aspirin: five little jars. I down one. Two jars of Bufferin; I take about two-thirds. A row of cough syrup; I pass on that. Then there's half a shelf of antibiotics she's gotten from Grandpa O'Neill over the years; I down a whole vial, figuring the more, the better. I spy more vials of prescription medication near the Pepto Bismol and Alka Seltzer and take a few capsules from each.

I swallow my last pill and final gulp of water, rinse the glass, and put it in the dish drainer. I place the empty containers in the garbage bag under the sink. All this time I haven't dropped one thing, haven't made one sound except for that little creak. I am satisfied. I have no regrets as I slip down the hall back to my room. I feel at peace as I crawl back into bed, and am soon carried away.

I don't know how much time passes before I feel buzzing in my head, a cross between a swarm of mosquitoes, cricket songs and a chain saw. I wonder where I am and what is going on. Then I hear a gush, gush, gush, gush going rhythmically through my brain, pounding especially hard at my temples. All the while the swarming buzz is still there like a demented backup band. I become aware of my heart. I don't so much feel it as hear it banging in my chest to the same rhythm that is going through my head. And still, I don't know what is going on or if I should be concerned. Then I hear Wanda's voice.

"Get up, Laura, you lazy good for nothing. Get up. If you think you're going to skip school again, you've got another think coming."

Mary Ruth responds. "Stop it, please, just stop it. Don't you see what she's done?" My sister, my angel, sounds scared, not like her sarcastic, confident school self.

"All I see is someone who's not worth a damn."

"Look at her. You can see what's all over her blanket as well as I can. We have to help her."

"Help her, my eye. She doesn't need help. She needs someone to light a match under her sorry ass."

Right then I realize I'm there in the bed I hate, in the room I hate, with the life I hate, with the stepmother I hate spewing spite at me. And I must have thrown up all over my blanket.

Mary Ruth says to Wanda, "Can't you ever think of anyone besides yourself?"

"You'd just better get ready for school, miss high and mighty know-it-all. I'm the parent around here, not you."

My speeding heart sinks. My plan has failed. I'm right back where I started, but my body is alive in an evil sort of way. I can feel blood sloshing through every part of me. I hear it scraping down to the tiniest capillaries in my toes. I want to open my mouth and scream, but I can't. I can't move. I can't even open my eyes. I feel worse than ever. What if I'm a vegetable after this and have to spend the rest of my existence right in this room with some sort of IV feeding system set up? If my body weren't so busy pushing what feels like some sort of thick putty all through my brain, if I weren't consumed by the buzzing and throbbing and swarming sounds, I just might howl at my incompetence, my failure to even pull off killing myself.

Mary Ruth comes to my side, sits on the bed and pulls my arms forward. "Come on, Laura. I want you to sit up," she says. I understand her, but I can't move. She keeps talking. "You've thrown up half-digested pills all over your blanket, but there's probably more in there ready to come up, and you might choke if you don't sit up." She pulls harder and somehow gets me in a sitting position. I'd forgotten how much Mary Ruth and I have been enjoying each other this year, how many times we've chain smoked in her room, taken long walks in the rain and danced together at the youth center. She has become a good friend, maybe my best friend. I open my mouth to thank her, and up from deep inside comes a ghastly glob of rotten tasting stuff, blasting through my mouth and burning through my nose. My eyes pop open and I watch brown liquid with variegated colored lumps splash out onto the blanket's itchy pink wool.

Mary Ruth grabs some of my rumpled sweaters and jeans from the floor, wads them into a big clump and puts them behind my pillow. Then she leans me back so I'm supported instead of flat. She folds the blanket so all the vomit is caught inside. She lifts it up and steps away. I close my eyes, listening to the cacophony inside my body, wondering if it's going to be permanent.

"She needs to go to the hospital," Mary Ruth says.

"She needs to go to school," Wanda insists.

"Her stomach should be pumped. That's what people do when this sort of thing happens."

"Stomach pump, my eye."

"You don't get it. You really don't get it, do you?"

"I'm warning you, get ready for school or you're out on your ear this morning permanently. Remember, this is my house. You and your derelict sister are only here by my good graces. And when you're 18, you're out. That's it, sister."

"What if she dies?"

"She won't die. She has a cast iron stomach."

I feel like I'm turning to liquid and merging into some sort of soft fuzz. Everything is slowing down, fading out. I vow that if I am spared, and if I'm not a vegetable after this, I will not try to kill myself again. I will get by somehow, knowing things could be a lot worse. I could be stuck in my room, totally dependent upon Wanda for everything for the rest of my life.

Early that evening, I wake up. The noises in my head and sensations in my body are muted. I move my fingers, wiggle my toes, roll my head from side to side, and thank God I am not a vegetable.

EIGHTEEN

June 1966

ON THE BACK LAWN OF A HOME overflowing with tipsy teens, I'm having sex for the second time. While the Troggs' hit *Wild Thing* thrums from a distant radio, Pierre leans over me and professes his love. He's been my boyfriend since he sauntered up at the youth center one Friday night in May. I hadn't even flirted since before I downed all those pills, but his dark eyes and Beatles-with-a-Mediterranean flair looks drew me in.

The rumor about Pierre, a graduating senior, was that two girls who had made love with him became addicted to his touch the way people in anti-drug movies get stuck on heroin. I wondered if he could push Kip out of my head and heart. I've steered clear of Kip for months because he treats me like a Brand X product, but my mind wanders back to him incessantly. I catch myself hoping he, not Pierre, will whisper words of undying love in my ear. I haven't been able to will this sick sort of wishing away. I thought if I went all the way with Pierre, my feelings might shift.

I'm a little woozy from the punch I drank at the party, but I'm not feeling upset like I was the night Kip claimed my virginity. Pierre didn't pressure me into having sex. But there is something he's pressuring me into: he wants me to move in with his family when he leaves for summer school next week. He was conditionally accepted at William Jewell College in Missouri for the fall. He just has to pass a remedial English class first.

I'm uneasy partly because Wanda says if I go, I'm not welcome back at her house and partly because his mom is beautiful like the actress Tippy Hedren, who starred in Alfred Hitchcock's scary movie *The Birds*; his dad looks like Robert Mitchum, who's been in lots of movies; and their house is so flawless it could be featured in *Better Homes and Gardens*.

Pierre and I pull our clothes back on and amble barefoot back toward the party. He takes my hand and pleads his case again. "I told my folks all about Wanda, and they want to look after you. All you need to do is help them with Nanette and Chloe. It'll be a piece of cake." Nanette and Chloe are his three-year-old twin sisters, unplanned children his parents are too old to chase after, Pierre says.

I hesitate. "I don't know. I've only met your parents once and it was just for a couple of minutes."

"They really like you. And besides, they know I love you. In fact, they're the ones who suggested you move in."

"I'm taking algebra in summer school. There's a ton of homework."

"You'll have plenty of time. My cousin did the same thing last year. She had a blast. You've gotta give it a go."

"I do want to get away from Wanda, but I don't know. I have to think about it some more."

I remain undecided until the morning Pierre leaves. I wake up to one of Wanda's habitual harangues, so I gather my summer clothes and put them in an A&P shopping bag. A few minutes later, I pause at Wanda's recliner.

"Remember, you won't be welcome back here once you step through that door, young lady. You think life will be so much better there. Ha! You've got another think coming. They won't want you once they know who you really are. And when that happens, don't come cryin' back to me."

I soon find out Pierre's description of life with his family is about as accurate as a commercial showing how you can transform limp locks with a mere spray of Adorn. His parents want a full-time maid and nanny. They don't even want me to go out to lunch with Shelby. After three weeks of summer school, followed by childcare, cooking, cleaning, and then homework, Daniel comes to my rescue.

He takes me to a friend of his whose parents are gone for the month of July. She's hosting one long party, and there is no quiet place for me to do homework. I keep up with algebra for a few days, but one morning, I start trembling and can't stop. I don't want to go to class until the shaking stops, but it goes on intermittently for two days. I can't sleep; it feels like ice is ripping through my veins. Then this beefy blond guy pulls me onto a couch and takes me into his arms. "It'll be okay, it'll be okay," he says again and again. Finally, I stop trembling and fall asleep. When I wake up the next afternoon, I've missed three days of algebra, which in summer school is like three weeks. I withdraw from class and spend all the money I have on a bus ticket to Liberty, Missouri.

When I arrive, Pierre sneaks me into his dorm and brings me food from the cafeteria, which works well until the end of the term, when the cafeteria closes, and Pierre, his roommates, Carl and Gary, and I are just about the only young people left on campus. Carl and Gary, both heavyset and good natured, don't want to go home to the farms where they were raised and are looking for work in Liberty. Pierre's parents aren't coming to pick him, and me, up for a few days. We're all hungry and out of money. I suggest we pretend to be on a scavenger hunt and put food on the list. The boys are skeptical but decide it would be better than begging. In addition to listing canned beans, bread, bologna, tomatoes and potatoes, we pencil in a red rubber band, pop bead, Band-Aid, toothpick, yellow rose, and Coke bottle cap in the hopes it will make our hunger less obvious.

We walk to a well-kept neighborhood near campus and split up. Two blocks of scavenging later, I jump, bulging bag in hand, from the porch of a tidy, mint-green home. From the front walk, I swivel and wave to the salt-and-pepper-haired woman who beams kindness from the porch after having plucked items from her pantry for me. She's around Wanda's age and size, but seems as different from her personality-wise as an ice cream sundae is from a bowl of sour cream. She opens her mouth, and I think she might burst into song like Julie Andrews in *Sound of Music*, but she just says, "Good luck!"

"Thanks." I feel guilty about putting one over on her, but that fades when I spot Pierre looking suave as a rock star at the corner. He lifts his own paper bag of goodies above his head and does something like an Irish jig. Bouncing up and down, he still manages to look cool.

I run to him, and we race to the park where Gary is opening cans of pork and beans with a Swiss army knife. Flames already dance in the fire pit. At a nearby drinking fountain, I rinse off the potatoes we collected. Then I wrap them, slathered in butter, in foil; and put them on the coals. Carl turns on his transistor radio, and we all sway to Smokey Robinson's *The Tracks of My Tears*. I think it's the ideal song for me. These guys think I'm perfectly happy when inside I'm corroded like an old battery sitting in the sun. We scarf down cold beans and sandwiches and later devour baked potatoes, fresh from the fire.

As the sun begins to paint streaks of purple, orange and gold across the sky, Pierre and I meander along a trail to a patch of grass hidden from view by a tangle of wild roses. We've been here many times in the past three weeks since there's no privacy in the dorm. He strips off his clothes, then pulls mine off, too, throwing each piece high into the air as he goes. Soon we are on the ground, making love. He moans as he comes and says into my ear, "You are so sexy. So sexy. I love you. Love you. Love you forever. You. Drive. Me. Crazy."

I cannot reciprocate. I am wet between the legs, but my heart is untouched. I realize that if I haven't fallen in love with him yet, I probably never will. He rolls onto his side, sits up and tells me to pick the pimples on his back. It's what he likes after lovemaking. I hold my breath and squeeze the smattering of little white buggers that dot the suntanned skin of his upper back. When every last white head is popped, I pick a blade of grass, wipe dirt off the root and stick it in my mouth to chew, something I've done since before I could read.

"So, it's back to Hinsdale with us," I say.

"Hey, let's get married. We can live in student housing right here." He leans toward me. "What about it?"

I spit out the grass. "What?"

"Living here with me, being married. Wouldn't it be cool? All the guys will say I've got the prettiest wife on campus."

"I have another year of high school." I think this is a good enough reason to end this line of thinking.

"You could finish right here."

"That would be weird."

"Why? You hate Hinsdale, right? Here's a chance to get away."

"I don't think it's a good idea," I say.

"There are so many girls who would jump at this chance."

He has a point. He may have pimples on his back, but the smooth olive skin of his face is absolutely clear. To-die-for long, black lashes rim his black-coffee eyes; his thick, sun-streaked brown curls are tucked behind his ears; and he carries his slim, muscular body with the authority of a matinee idol.

"I know how attractive you are."

"Come on. We have to get married. It'll prove to my parents how much we love each other. Plus, it'll help cement my deferment."

"You already have a student deferment. That's enough to keep you out of the Army."

"What if I flunk out?"

"I don't think being married would change anything."

"I bet it would if we had kids," he says. "Let's do it right away." He grabs his cutoff jeans and shakes them out. "Let's go tell the guys at the dorm."

I can't picture me living with Pierre in Missouri with a baby in tow. I gather my scattered garments while he pulls on his jeans.

"Come on. Hurry up," he says.

"Why are you in such a rush?"

"What's with you? You're not even happy."

"I'm as happy as I ever am," I say.

"You don't really want to marry me, do you?"

"I didn't say —"

"No. I get it. I can see you don't care if I get shipped off to some jungle halfway around the world. You don't care if I get picked off by some Viet Cong sniper, or blown to pieces by one of their land mines. I know the score now. Take your sweet time." He throws his shirt over one shoulder and heads back toward the trail.

"Hey, wait up," I call half-heartedly.

He strides on without looking back. I sit down naked on the grass, pull my matches and Old Golds from the back pocket of my cutoffs, and set my clothes aside. The pack is squished, but the cigarettes are still whole. I put one in my mouth and light up, enjoying the sulfur smell as I cup the flame with my hand to shield it from the breeze. I take a puff and exhale slowly while looking up at a squirrel jumping from bough to bough overhead. Between puffs, I hum *California Dreamin'* by the Mamas and the Papas. If I had the money, I'd buy a bus ticket to the West Coast and never look back.

NINETEEN

September 1966

IN A THRONG OF STUDENTS THAT stretches from one end of the long, fluorescent-lit hallway to the other, I throw a couple of books into my locker and pull a few others out. It's senior year; I'm living with Wanda again. I didn't know where else to go when I came back from Missouri. Her front door was locked when I arrived, but I sat on the porch, hoping she'd unlock it eventually like she always had. And just before the streetlight at the corner of our front yard came on, she did. Not one word passed between us as I stepped across the threshold, walked past her twisted scowl and trudged to my room.

I'm hoping to stay focused this year and pull my grades up, but I still can't concentrate like I used to; my mind wanders incessantly. I'm relieved that it's Friday. The click of locks; the jumble of texts, yo-yos, basketballs and what-not hitting metal; the voices of friends greeting one another; the slam of door after door: these all add to the excitement in the air. The weekend is here, and the first autumn frost of 1966 has yet to arrive. Perfect weather.

"Hey, Laura!" I turn to my right and see Shelby loping toward me, red hair in Heidi braids. "I just talked with Caruso."

"Daniel's friend? Didn't he graduate?"

"Yeah, but he started going out with Deb—you know, the stuck up one with that long pony tail she flaunts like a fuckin' mink stole." She leans against the locker next to mine, tossing her braids over her shoulder with a free hand.

"Deb's not stuck up; it's her friends who are."

"I don't know what they see in each other. She's headed for the Ivy League, and he works full time at his dad's auto body shop."

"I wouldn't put the two of them together."

"Yeah, well, here's a bigger surprise." She moves closer to me, whispers in my ear. "He's spreading lies about you."

I pull away. "Me? I hardly know the guy."

"He's not saying he did anything with you."

"That's good. I mean, you know, me and him, I can't picture it."

"He's says you went all the way with Kip."

"What?" I hold tight to my locker door. I think I might pee right there in the hallway.

"He told Daniel he saw proof."

"Proof? What proof?" I gaze into my locker, pretending to be absorbed by its contents.

"Remember last fall when Kip and Dave both asked you out, and you liked Kip but not Dave?"

"Yeah, I remember."

"Caruso said they saw you shopping downtown one day and made a bet on who could fuck you first. The one who scored would win $50."

"What?" My throat suddenly feels lined with sand.

"I told him he was full of shit. I would know if you'd done something like that."

"Well, that should have shut him up, right?" I slam my locker door closed.

"Nope. You know how those guys were always playing poker, right? Caruso said Kip brought a bloody sheet to the game one afternoon, said it was your blood, and Dave forked over two twenties and a ten right there at the table. Kip hung the sheet on the wall."

I picture my dried blood on a sheet tacked up like a trophy while all those guys were playing cards and sipping beer. Every part of me stiffens, except for my face, which is flushing with such force I feel like a fire hydrant unplugged. I press my lock closed until it clicks, turn the dial and lean a hand against the door.

"There's more." Shelby says. "Later on he stuck the sheet out in some field where guys could drive by and look at it. Isn't that fucking wild? I told him it was total BS. It was probably chicken blood or something. Isn't that just fuckin' messed up? I mean I almost beaned Caruso right there."

"I appreciate that." My knees quiver.

"I'm gonna track Kip down." She steps away from the adjacent locker and kicks it several times, each time with more force. "I'll drive to whatever college he's going to now, and I'll clobber him, and Dave, too, wherever he's gone off to, and the rest of their gang."

"Let's just drop it." My voice is raspy, harsh, not at all what I'd intended.

"Drop it? These jerks are spreading lies about you and you fuckin' want to forget it?

"Well ... not exactly ... lies." I long for a fairy godmother to come through the ceiling, wave a magic wand and whisk me away to a place where I never get charmed and taken in by a guy who turns out to have been far meaner than I'd ever imagined possible, a place where I never slouch and am so charismatic that everyone I meet is smitten with me, so situations like the one I'm facing would never arise.

"What the fuck are you saying? Are you, I mean, did you?"

I nod.

"We've got to talk." She tugs on my arm.

I follow Shelby outside, where we sit on the steps, both of us clutching stacks of books to our chests. Neither of us speaks for an unbearable minute as classmates stream past us. Then she asks, "You didn't tell me about this because ... because—why?"

"I don't know. I couldn't talk about it, still can't."

"Jesus, I thought I knew you. I tell you everything, and you don't even clue me in on something as fuckin' big as this? How do you think that makes me feel, huh?

"I probably feel worse."

"You're so messed up. I swear"

I put my books on my lap and lean back, elbows against the stair behind me, and look up at the cloudless sky. I think the Rolling Stones' song *Paint it Black* could be my anthem. I'm suffocating in darkness.

"Earth to Laura. Earth to Laura." Shelby taps my shoulder. "Where are you?"

"Does it matter?"

"Hey, at least Caruso's the only one from that crowd who's still hangin' around school."

I search the sky and wonder if I'll look down from there when I die.

"I'm going to keep fuckin' denying it. You should, too," Shelby says.

"Yeah, I guess." A gust of wind shakes leaves from branches and sends them tumbling across the school lawn. I wish I could tumble away with them. "What now?" I ask.

"Dunno. I'm still pissed at you, you know."

Deb bursts through the door, full of the weekend excitement I felt only moments ago. Statuesque in tan slacks, off-white sleeveless crew-neck sweater, tan leather pumps with matching bag slung over her shoulder, Deb looks like she stepped right out of *Seventeen* magazine. She waves at us. "Hey, Laura, Shelby. Have you seen Gail?

We were supposed to meet at her locker, but she didn't show." Gail has been Deb's best friend since grammar school.

"She hasn't come out this way," I say.

Deb sits next to us, pulls a natural bristle brush from her bag and starts brushing her silky ponytail. "Hey, what are you guys up to tonight?"

"I have a date with Daniel," Shelby says. "We're going downtown to some restaurant at the top of a building that spins around." She stands up. "I'd better get to the corner. Mom's coming to pick me up. We're going to Oakbrook to get a dress."

"Have fun," I say.

"You could come, even though I haven't forgiven you yet." Shelby frowns at me, then breaks into a smile.

"To get the dress, or on your date?" I say.

"Very funny, moron," Shelby laughs. "You comin' with or not?"

"Nah, I'm still kind of sorting things out right now."

"Don't go run away or do anything drastic, okay?"

"I'll try not to."

"It'll be okay, I swear it will. Wait and see." Shelby saunters down the stairs then breaks into a run when she sees her mom's blue Ford LTD pull up. "I'll see ya tomorrow," she calls to me, her braids bouncing against her back.

"What are you bummed about?" Deb asks me.

"Oh, it's nothing." I can't imagine telling her about Kip, and I hope Caruso didn't say anything to her either.

"Let's go for a ride, get some fries at McDonald's or something. It'll cheer you up," she says.

I think about the 18 pounds I've packed on in the last year. "No thanks, greasies are the last thing I need right now." I slap my thighs.

"A ride then. I need to cut loose a little," she says.

"Okay, a ride." Hoping Deb will get my mind off of what I just learned about Kip, at least for a little while, I follow her to the school parking lot, where we both fold into her tiny Renault. She drives off, no destination in mind. We meander, weaving through Hinsdale's quiet streets, and soon we're in an unincorporated area. We turn onto a road paved so recently the smell of tar lingers in the air. Houses on one side are in various stages of completion. Last time I passed through here, the road was gravel and no houses were in sight. Deb turns the car onto a dirt and gravel road and speeds toward a farmhouse in the distance.

"Let's see how fast we can get to the house," she says. Then she shouts à la Speedy Gonzales, "Aye, aye, andele, andele," and I join in for the rest, "arriba, arriba, yee ha!"

I love the sound of the tires whirring on the stones. I open the passenger door, let out a whoop and say, "Let's see if we can fly!"

Deb opens her door, too. Steering with one hand, she presses the gas pedal to the floor.

"Look ahead, a bank of storm clouds," I say.

"Oh, no—turbulence!" She cries out as we bump over a few ruts in the road.

I point to an abandoned tractor in a fallow field. "Hey, look, a UFO!" Laughter rolls out of both of us.

When we reach the farmhouse, we climb out, leaving the doors open. We find a rickety picnic table beneath an old apple tree with some fruit still on the branches. We climb onto the table and into the tree, where we each perch on thick limbs. I pick an apple, rub it on my shorts and start eating. Deb does the same.

Chewing the crisp fruit, I survey the countryside, the fields, the sheds, rusted water pumps, jackrabbits and stands of trees on one side, and the houses in orderly rows on the other.

"Nobody else I know would understand about a flying car," Deb says.

"Aw, you probably say that to everybody."

"Why don't you come to the party tonight. It'll be fun."

"Your friends don't like me, Deb." I feel like the last crumbs in a potato chip bag whenever I'm around the group Deb grew up with. She comes from one of the prominent Hinsdale families that have lived here for generations and are always being written up in the *Hinsdale Doings*.

"My friends like you. They just don't get you," Deb says. "They don't know why you have to spend all that time with Jillie and Alice either. You could do so much better."

"I like them. And I think plenty of other people do, too." I start swinging my legs and think about jumping down to the ground.

"I shouldn't have said that."

"I know you mean well." I throw the rest of my apple as far as I can into the field.

"I think things will be different when we go to college. We'll all be free," Deb says. "Free of cliques, free of gossip."

The mention of gossip sends a chill down my spine. I wonder if Caruso did say something to her about Kip and me and bloody sheets. I hope not as I close my eyes and try to envision a future but can picture only a dense charcoal gray fog.

Deb climbs down the tree and sits on top of the table. "I have to fly home soon or I'll never get things ready for the party. You want to stay for supper?"

"Nah." I jump from the tree and sit next to her on the table. I ate at Deb's house once. It was four of us in a formal dining room, everyone spaced far apart at a long table. A maid came in and out serving the courses. Later, I spent the night, but I was in a separate bedroom with my own bathroom and fresh towels. Lights out at 11 p.m., no conversations long into the night, which totally negated the purpose of an overnight.

"It was fun flying here with you," Deb says.

"Yeah, it was." I slide off the table. "Hey, let's race to the plane."

"You're on!" Deb bolts ahead.

I run to catch up, as the terrible mix of feelings about what Kip did gains on me me like a noxious cloud of exhaust from 1,000 idling buses.

TWENTY

October 1966

IN HER RECLINING CHAIR, WANDA IS a sentinel half watching Shelby and me walk through the door and half watching her new color TV. This one has remote control, so when she settles in with her *TV Guide* and *Good Housekeeping* magazines on a stand to her right and her water and vials of pills on the table to her left, she doesn't have to move for hours. While the Lennon Sisters sing some sappy tune on TV, Shelby and I greet Wanda and then try to convince her to let Shelby spend the night.

"That girl is not staying here tonight," Wanda says.

Emboldened with Shelby by my side, I challenge her. "I've never had a friend overnight. I'm 17."

"I said no overnights, and I mean it," she says.

I stand a little taller, with attitude, like Lesley Gore singing *You Don't Own Me*. "Everybody else has friends stay over. I should be able to, too."

Wanda licks her lips. "Don't go telling me what you should and shouldn't be able to do here. You came crawling back, crawling back, mind you, with no place to go after you followed that boy to godforsaken Missouri."

I cross my arms over my rib cage and lean against the wall by Wanda's chair. "Since you're my parent, I think you pretty much had to take me back."

Shelby smiles at me and sticks both her thumbs up.

123

"Don't get smart with me, young lady," Wanda says.

"What's wrong with asking to have a friend sleep over in my own room?"

Wanda raises her voice. "Listen, missy, this is my house, not yours."

Shelby stifles a laugh.

Wanda crosses her arms and digs her nails into the flesh on her elbows, which are raw from years of scratching.

I sense one of her monologues coming and keep quiet, knowing she'll wind down at some point.

She squints and begins her rant. "I decide who stays and who goes. You never know what sorts of diseases somebody might bring in here, and dumb ideas. Jesus, Mary, Joseph, I never had a friend stay overnight when I was young. I never argued with my mother either. Good girls don't make demands. Good girls do what their parents say. Good girls go to school. Good girls help around the house. Good girls bring money home to help out." Wanda pauses and looks up at the ceiling. "Just who does this one think she is? I thought she was sweeter that her sisters, but no, she doesn't even tell me where she's at for days at a time, and now she wants this wild thing here for the night. Oh yes, I know all about Shelby and her ways. I won't have it. I won't have it in my house. Lord, why have you done this to me? Am I that worthless? Am I some sort of peon? Saddled with three girls that aren't even mine. I was the one who wiped their smelly behinds when they were little. Of course they don't remember that. No. They don't care what I've sacrificed. And now this one, this one—the neighbors see her doing who knows what with those boys in their fancy cars in my driveway, my driveway, mind you. The shame of it. What's coming next? Well, she'd just better not bring any babies home to me. No siree."

Wanda takes a gulp of water and remembers Shelby and I are standing nearby. "What are you two gawking at? Get out, get out before I call the police."

"Maybe it's Laura and me who should call in the police and report child abuse or something," Shelby says. She glances at the canary-colored phone on the counter nearby.

"Wait a minute here now. There's no abuse going on here. Nothing like that," Wanda says.

"I think there's plenty going on here that people would be interested in," I say.

"Drop dead. Both of you." She grabs the remote and turns up the TV's volume. "The idea. Reporting me to the police, Ha! For what, trying to be a mother? Go on, stay in that filthy room, then. See if I care."

"You mean Shelby can stay?"

"Get out of my sight. I don't want to see you until morning."

Shelby and I dart down the hall to my room and slam the door. A Keep Out sign on the doorknob sways as we flop, laughing, onto the bottom bunk.

"Aren't you glad you didn't come out of her?" Shelby asks.

"Yeah, I think about that. If she'd been there from the get-go I'd have no hope, I mean, man, I'd probably believe all the stuff she says."

"She might not say it, though, if you were hers."

"There is that." I grab a folder from the floor and bop Shelby on the top of the head. She grabs a sweater from the foot of the bed and whacks me on the shoulder. Laughing, I push her off the bed. Then she gets hold of my foot and pulls me down to the floor, where we tussle until we're both panting, out of breath and wondering what to do next. I crawl to my closet door, slide it open and see some old oil paints on the floor.

125

"Hey, let's paint the walls," I say. "I'm tired of this yucky beige. Maybe we could do a landscape or some combination of pictures and words, be avant garde."

"I'm not much of an artist."

"Neither am I, but let's give it a whirl. Maybe we'll surprise ourselves."

We dig into the brushes and pungent oils. I paint a tree with branches that wrap around a row of windows. I put a few leaves on each branch. On one leaf I print October 9.

Shelby looks up from a row of ghoulish shrunken heads she's painting above my dresser. "October 9. What's so special about that?" she asks.

"It's the anniversary of that night with Kip."

"Oh, cover that up, then." She blots it out with deep purple paint. So I cover one of her shrunken heads with orange paint. We giggle and paint, and then re-paint long into the night, filling every section of my walls with color. We run out of ideas around 4 a.m. and both agree the walls look ghastly and we'll have to fix them. But we decide it would be grand to catch the sunrise by Lake Michigan first. After that, we can buy some paint somewhere, probably three coats' worth by the looks of things. We wash up in the bathroom and sneak into the dining room, where I scribble a note to Wanda, telling her we'll re-paint the room when we return from watching the sunrise in Chicago. Then we slip out the front door, skip most of the way downtown and board the first train to the city.

We pose for pictures at a booth in Union Station, 25 cents for each row of four in a vertical strip. We buy sweet rolls at a coffee shop and lick sugar from our fingers as we progress toward the lake. We make it to the shore in time for sunrise. Then we walk to the old water tower, the only building in that area that survived the Great Chicago

Fire. Later, we eat French fries in a cafe's window booth on State Street and wave at all the people passing by. We try on clothes at Marshall Field's, leaving piles of Villager skirt and sweater sets in the dressing room. We try on flats at Chandler's. On the way back to Union Station, I tear off one of my photos and throw it into the Chicago River and watch it fall through the air and land on the murky water. I'd like to follow, but I promised myself I'd stop the suicide attempts.

When Shelby and I get off the train late in the afternoon, Officer Wilkins is sitting in a cruiser right by the station. He calls us over.

"Get in," he says.

"Why?" I ask.

"Defacing personal property, vagrancy, underage drinking ... oh, and running away, again, after I warned you, Laura."

"You've got the wrong girls," Shelby says. "We were in the city all day."

"Just get in and don't give me any lip."

I fret silently on the short drive to the station. Pretty soon Shelby and I are sitting across from Officer Wilkins at his desk.

"I thought I wasn't going to see you for a while," he says. He looks me right in the eyes.

"I didn't run away," I say.

"Maybe you did, maybe you didn't, but what about defacing your mother's house?" he asks.

"What?" Shelby and I say in unison.

"Don't look so shocked. I saw what you did in there."

I am so surprised that Wanda called the police over the painting that I don't know what to say. I look down at my hands in my lap.

"It's only Laura's room we painted. My mom wouldn't have me arrested for painting my own room. That's not exactly destroying private property," Shelby says.

"What business is it of yours, Miss I-show-up-at-school-whenever-I-feel-like-it?" Officer Wilkins says to Shelby. "I warned Laura not to hang out with you."

"That's not fair," Shelby says. "You don't know me at all. When have you ever brought me in here before? Never. And you're all set to believe the worst. But Laura's so-called mom? Talk about destroying, what about destroying Laura's whole childhood? Are you going to arrest anyone for that?"

"She didn't destroy my whole childhood. We had some good times," I say.

"I don't fuckin' believe you, Laura. You're defending her? Fuckin' unbelievable." Shelby kicks a leg of the officer's desk.

"Okay, okay, settle down, you two," the officer says, his voice softening. "I heard you have a mouth on you, Shelby. But I'll put your bad manners aside and listen to what you have to say."

"Go ahead, Laura. Defend yourself," Shelby says.

"We didn't mean for the walls to turn out so ugly," I say. "We were just having some fun. And besides I left her a note. I said we'd repaint it."

"I didn't see any note," Officer Wilkins says.

"I left it right on the dining room table. It said we were going to Chicago to watch the sunrise. It's Saturday today. We didn't even have school. What's vagrant about that?" I ask.

Officer Wilkins leans back in his chair and sighs. "Maybe you two just got a little carried away, went a little too far."

"I never thought she'd have a conniption fit about this," I say.

"Laura's so-called mom has a fit about everything. Like grades. If I got good grades, my mom would probably take me out for a steak dinner. But not her. She yells whether Laura gets good grades or bad," Shelby says.

"She can't afford steak dinners," I say.

"Christ, Laura." Shelby says. "So now she's a saint or something?"

"Stop bickering, you two. I get it that you have some grievances, but ..." Officer Wilkins sits up straight in his chair, pulls a quart of Queen Anne scotch from a paper bag on his desk and looks at me. "This was sitting smack in the middle of your dresser."

"Somebody gave that to me for my birthday," I say.

"You know you're not supposed to drink at your age."

"It's not opened. It was decorating my dresser. That's all," I say.

"It's nice that somebody remembered her birthday," Shelby says. "You can't count on Wanda for presents."

"Wanda?" Officer Wilkins cocks his head.

"That's what we call Laura's stepmom. It's short for Wanda the Wicked Witch of the Western Suburbs."

"Well, we are living on Social Security, so it's not like she has money to spare," I say.

Shelby glares at me. "Listen to yourself. She just bought herself a new color TV, and her little Chevy is less than a year old. Some of that money she gets is supposed to go to your care."

"Nobody's perfect," Officer Wilkins says.

"Call up my mom and ask her what she thinks of Wanda. This having us arrested business? It's bunk," Shelby says.

"Don't worry. I'm planning on it. In the meantime, go on home, and don't paint any more walls ... and, Laura ..." He holds up the scotch. "I'm keeping this."

As soon as we're out the door, Shelby socks me on the shoulder and asks, "Why were you fuckin' defending Wanda in there?"

"I don't know. Stuff just popped out."

Shelby fishes through her purse for a cigarette. "Want one?"

"Do you want to get hauled back inside?"

"Oh, I forgot about that." Shelby puts the cigarettes back in her purse. "I told Daniel I'd stop by tonight. Want to come?"

"Nah. I'm tired." I pull two Chocolate Kisses from the bottom of my Daveys bag, and hand Shelby one. "Here, a parting gift," I say.

"Thanks," she says.

"No, thank you. If it weren't for you, I'd still be in there." I point to the station.

Meandering alone toward home, I unwrap my candy and pop it into my mouth. Milk chocolate melts under my tongue, and Kip seeps into my thoughts. I plunk down on a set of disintegrating steps near the train tracks, and I think of that night with him, wishing with every ounce of my being that I could just erase it. I feel like I've been treading water for an eternity. Then it occurs to me that if I'd known about the bet and the sheet last year, I probably would have found a way to succeed in killing myself. So, maybe it's a blessing I only learned about it this year. I get up and trudge toward Wanda's. She will be surprised I'm not stuck in juvenile hall. She just lost a round in a battle that seems to have no purpose and no end.

TWENTY-ONE

November 1966

DANIEL DRIVES A DODGE CHARGER HIS mom bought for his trek to California, where he'll start junior college in January, just a couple of months from now. He's been stocking grocery store shelves all semester because his grades were so bad last year he almost didn't graduate with his class. His parents said he'd have to demonstrate some maturity before he left home. In the death seat next to him, I breathe in the new car smell as I hold a white pill in my palm. In my other hand is a can of Dr Pepper. It's Friday night, and neither of us has plans.

"Go ahead, take it. You'll really like it," Daniel says.

"Why not?" I slurp the pill down with several gulps of soda.

"Atta girl."

Shelby's been spending lots of time with Jeff lately, so Daniel often asks me to ride along while he looks for her. Sometimes he just wants me to hang with him while he mopes, because that's not something he can really do with his guy friends. Be sad. I don't mind; I'm in a funk anyway.

"What did I just swallow?" I ask.

"Could be acid." He has a wild look in his eyes.

"Oh, wow! I've never had acid. What if I have a bad trip?"

"Don't worry. I'll watch out for you." Daniel lifts his hand off the steering wheel and pats my shoulder. Shelby told Daniel all about Kip and me, and ever since then, he has pulled me further under his wing, but we never talk about what happened. I don't know if I'll ever be able to speak of it with anybody, or if I even should.

As we ride along, I grow increasingly aware of my surroundings. The streets that usually look so ordinary seem transformed, more colorful, like a magical kingdom far from the Chicago suburbs. The air blowing across my face smells edible, like a confection I can't wait to eat. Feeling happier than I have in a long time, I glance at Daniel. He grins. "Good stuff, huh," he says.

"I'll say."

"Want to go to a party?" he asks. "It's kind of a long ways away."

"I don't know. How far is it?"

"Chicago. Lake Shore Drive."

"That's not too far."

"Yep, not too far."

"You just happened to meet a girl who lives there, right?"

"Uh ... " He stares straight ahead.

"What about Shelby? You know she loves you. She's just mad because you're always meeting other girls."

"It's one of those chicken or egg things with us," he says. We ride in silence for a few moments. Then he asks, "How about it. Want to go?"

"Sure. Okay."

"I'm gonna see if some of the guys want to come," he says.

I groan.

"Come on, we'll have fun."

By the time we merge onto the expressway, Daniel has gathered one additional car full of friends ready to party in the city, as well as packed three more friends into the Charger. Halfway there, we stop on the shoulder to make sure we're still together and know where we're going. Daniel runs to the other car to bum a cigarette. It feels like my body has merged with the car seat, so I stay where I am. He returns with a pack of Camels. We all light up as *Gloria* comes on the radio. It was recorded by The Shadows of Knight, a local group that played at our youth center before they hit it big, so we puff up with pride as we sing along.

We are giddy with anticipation when we turn onto Lake Shore Drive, but when we find the high-rise where the party's supposed to be, none of the apartment numbers and names match what Daniel has scribbled into his pocket-size address book. We find a phone booth under a street light a few blocks away. To prove to me that I haven't really merged into the seat, Daniel pulls me out of the car and into the phone booth. He gives me a dime and tells me to call the number. I drop in the money, dial, and the phone just rings and rings. It feels like the sound is coming from inside of me, not the receiver. Daniel tries the number and gets the same result. So we decide to return to Daniel's and have a party there. When we pull into the driveway, passengers pile out, one after another, and clomp inside through the back door. I've never entered through Daniel's front door; nobody ever does, as far as I know.

When I walk inside I see a guy I don't know cooking hamburger in an electric frying pan. He isn't paying attention to the meat; he's looking out a window at the row of cars in the driveway. My friends all blast through the kitchen to the den. Some say, "Hi, Michael," as they pass, and I realize this guy must be Daniel's older brother, whom I've heard about but never met. I linger in the kitchen. I've never seen an electric frying pan before. I lean over the counter by Michael's side to peer at the sizzling meat. Michael's hair is dark brown, his eyes a shade lighter, his smile warm as summer sand. I want to touch his tanned hand as he taps the edge of the pan with a spatula.

"Who are you?" he asks.

"Laura." I reply. My face is suddenly glued into a smile. My legs feel wobbly, so I push away from the counter and lean against the stove, which is in an island in the center of the kitchen. Michael is wearing tan corduroy jeans and a forest green V-neck sweater, sleeves rolled up. His body looks slim, solid, perfect.

"One of Daniel's friends, I see," he says.

"Yeah, and you must be Michael."

"That's right."

"You're the one who's traveled all over the world and dropped acid a bunch of times."

"Is that what you've heard?"

"Uhuh. I think I might have had acid tonight, but I'm not sure. Daniel didn't know what it was. It made everything more real than real, if you know what I mean. It kinda still seems that way." I feel like an idiot because I can't stop smiling, but then I see that he's smiling, too. I watch him slide the spatula under the burger, lift the patty from the pan and onto a bun that's already slathered with condiments. Next to it are potato chips and a couple of dill pickle spears that are so glossy they look varnished.

"Do you want one?"

"One what?"

"A hamburger, silly."

"No, thanks. I just ate a little while ago." I don't tell him that I'm always eating these days, have gone all the way from a size five to an 11 in the past couple of years. I can't remember the last time I was actually hungry, except for when I'm starving myself, which doesn't count.

"You sure?" he asks.

"You mean you'd really make me a hamburger?" Butterflies swarm my stomach as I look into his eyes. I wonder how it's possible for brown eyes to twinkle the way his do. Then I think his eyes might not really twinkle; it could be the pill I took.

"Yes, I would," Michael says

"Just because I happened to walk in?"

"Sure. Why not?"

"We don't even know each other."

"I know you're Daniel's friend."

"You're not offering to cook for all the others."

"You're the only one with me now, aren't you?" He strides to the refrigerator, opens the door, bends down and pulls out a coke. "Want one?"

I'm not thirsty. But I want to accept something from him. "Is there a Dr Pepper in there or a crème soda?"

"Picky, picky. Let's see. Yeah, here's a vanilla crème." He pulls the drink out. Then he opens a drawer, rummages through it and finds a bottle opener. He opens mine, then his. I feel like I've landed smack in the middle of a James Bond movie. Michael is 007, and I hope I'm not Miss Moneypenny.

"Here." He hands me the cool, wet bottle.

I grab it, touching his fingers briefly before he lets go. "Thanks, Michael." I enjoy the sound of his name coming from my lips. "I guess I'd better see what everybody's up to."

"Nice meeting you," he says.

"You, too." I back out the kitchen door. In the hallway, I lean against the wall, replaying in my mind what just happened. I feel a surge of energy, like I could jump up and tap the ceiling, or maybe bound up the nearby stairs five at a time. I don't know if it's Michael or the pill that's making me feel so alive. I step away from the wall just as Michael comes through the door. We collide. Drinks slosh, but don't spill. Potato chips slide to the edge of his plate. He tips the plate to slide them back. It all appears to be happening in slow motion.

"Why are you standing around in the hallway?" he asks.

"I just stopped to think for a minute," I say.

"Oh, I do that sometimes." He walks up the stairs. When he reaches the landing, he stops, looks over his shoulder and says, "See ya."

"Yeah, hope so," I say. When he's out of sight, I run down the hall to join my friends. As I enter the room, everyone and everything seems to be pulsating. I see the energy as multicolored dots flowing and shifting through the room. "Wow," I say, as I plunk down on a leather couch. I'm already thinking of reasons to come to Daniel's house more often.

TWENTY-TWO

December 1966

LIGHTS OUTSIDE AND IN RADIATE JOY and possibility this Christmas night at Daniel's, but I am on edge. His folks are upstairs, earplugs in, while a party is in full swing below, fueled by booze pilfered from parents' liquor cabinets. The back door opens. I glance over, hoping it's Michael. But it's more of Daniel's buddies, snow dusted, prancing in with armloads of malt liquor purchased using fake IDs. Michael is out doing whatever a twenty-four-year-old guy who has traveled the world does when he's back home for an extended visit. Reveling with a gang of high schoolers can't be high on his list of things to do.

I edge toward the dining room, where the table is full of treats: plates of Christmas cookies decorated with green, red and white frosting; potato chips and onion dip; mini ham sandwiches, dill pickles on the side; a box of fudge. I steer clear, knowing that once I start eating, I won't stop until I feel like a giant balloon filled with mud. I head into the living room. It takes a few moments for my eyes to adjust; it's so dark. Not one light is on. Dean Martin's rendition of *White Christmas* wafts from a built-in stereo, while a couple makes out on the couch. I feel I don't belong here or anywhere else. I long for simple things that can never be: my father alive again, carrying presents from hiding places and arranging them under the tree on Christmas Eve; Unc and Gramma coming over on Christmas Day and staying long past dark, playing board games, telling jokes, eating so much turkey and stuffing we have no room for pumpkin pie;

watching Christmas specials on TV until the screen is nothing but fuzz. I was part of an odd little family, but it didn't matter much to me. They were mine, and I was theirs, and we belonged. No words, no invitations, no explanations needed. It all began to unravel when my father died. Now, we go our separate ways on Christmas, joining friends who invite us to share in their family celebrations. I don't belong with Shelby's family. They took me under their wing for the holidays this year. I don't belong with Wanda either. At the heart of it, I am unclaimed.

I move on to the family room, where it's wall-to-wall people. Shelby is holding her own in a game of pool with Daniel's sister, Kaye. I watch for a while, but grow bored and a little too hot. I circle back toward the kitchen to see if there's some soda in the fridge. I stop in the doorway, surprised to see Michael walking toward me. I wish I could look cool, alluring, like supermodel Jean Shrimpton, but Bugs Bunny hijacks my face.

"Hi, Michael." I lean on the jamb.

"Hi, Laura. You're standing under mistletoe, you know." He stops a few inches from me.

"No, really?" I look up at the white berries and green leaves above. "Oh, you're right." A giggle breaks free.

Michael comes closer, smiling. Our eyes lock like they have several times since we first met. This has usually happened after I've sought him out while trying to appear like I was doing something other than looking for him. A few days ago, though, I was watching TV with Daniel in the den, and Michael came in with a plate of steak and salad. There were plenty of spots open, but he sat right next to me. He asked if I wanted some of his food. I said sure, why not. And he sliced a piece of steak and fed me with his own fork. I looked into his eyes as I chewed.

Michael stops just inches from me. His brown eyes look brighter to me than the string of lights on his parents' tree. I think he's fond of me, but I'm not sure. I thought Kip liked me, and I was wrong as a wool coat in July.

"I guess that means I have to kiss you, then." He leans down, touches his mouth to mine and pulls me close. I shut my eyes and swoon to the taste and feel of his lips, the smell of his breath, the warmth of his body. We wrap our arms around each other and stop kissing but stay close. "Merry Christmas," he says, and kisses the top of my head before meeting my lips again. We open our mouths slightly, touching our tongues, playfully exploring, getting to know each other in this new way. We press our bodies even closer together. I feel lit up but also relaxed. Swept away, but not anxious like I felt with Kip. We break apart and gaze at each other, grinning. Still embracing, we step from the doorway to the kitchen, where he leans his back against the center island, and I lean into him. Our necking continues unnoticed until Daniel taps me on the shoulder from behind. Michael and I stop kissing but continue to hold each other. Daniel gets a Coke from the refrigerator, opens it and leans against a counter.

"So you two are ... into each other?" He raises an eyebrow.

There's a long pause. Daniel glances from Michael to me and back to Michael.

Michael's kisses are better than any Christmas gift I could have imagined, but I think it would be foolish to say something like that. "Could be," I mutter.

Michael nods his head with a laugh.

The wall phone rings. Daniel picks up the receiver, says hello. He listens for a little bit and says, "Okay, Yeah, Shelby's here. I'll let her know. She'll be right there." He hangs up. "I've got to find

Shelby," he says to me. "You guys have to go. Her grandparents are at her house, and they're all waiting for you to get there for hot chocolate and pie or something." He leaves the room.

Michael and I resume kissing. We don't break apart until Shelby blasts into the room, followed by Daniel.

"Knock it off, you two. I don't see any mistletoe above you, do you?" Shelby grabs her coat from the back of a chair and puts it on while also slipping her feet into her knee length, fur lined boots, which are near the door.

I reluctantly pull myself away from Michael, then find my coat and boots by the door and put them on. Shelby and I are wearing mini dresses and mini coats, so our legs are bare from the top of our boots to midway up our thighs.

"I can't believe you're going out like that," Daniel says. "It's 15 degrees outside."

"We'll be okay. We're used to it." I put on a hat and mittens and then wrap a scarf around my neck. Shelby grabs her hat, mittens and scarf, but doesn't put them on.

"Merry Christmas," Michael calls.

"Merry Christmas to you, too." I wave to him before dashing with Shelby into the burning cold night.

While we speed through the twinkling night toward her home, she says, "What on earth were you doing with Michael?"

I tell her, "Michael isn't like anyone I've ever known. Whenever I talk with him I sense an unfamiliar calmness that's reassuring. He's like Daniel and the other guys, but not exactly. I have a huge crush on him."

"Are you nuts?" She shakes her head for dramatic effect. "He's just here waiting for his 25th birthday in March, when he gets a payout from his trust fund. Then he's leaving. He's not interested in some teenybopper train wreck like you. That's all you'll ever be to him, you know."

Shelby may be right, but there is a little flicker of hope in me, and I'm not sure I could squelch it even if I tried. Michael sets me abuzz in a delightful sort of way, but I doubt the same is true for him. I'm only seventeen and probably can't compare to some of the women he knows. But I'm drawn to him anyway.

A few nights later, Michael and I slip away from a gathering in Daniel's den. Holding hands, we tiptoe upstairs to his bedroom. I feel no tension or pressure as we make our way in the dark. This is what I want to do. As we progress slowly from making out to petting to undressing and then embracing, naked, on the bed, a pure, sweet force envelops us. Feeling my hands on his bare skin, and his on mine, makes me think of The Association's song *Cherish*. I find every part of him, even the hair on his arms, gorgeous. He kisses me along the collarbone and moves down to kiss my breasts, something no one else has done. He probes ever so gently. I feel more excited than I ever have. And when he enters me, my sense of connection to him is so complete, I feel like I will be his forever. We snuggle under the sheets afterward. The glow lingers. We hold each other and enjoy the silence as we drift into sleep.

In the morning, I crawl out of Michael's bedroom window and down a tree to the snow-covered ground. He waves from above. I back away, blowing kisses until I round the corner of his house. I skip most of the way to Wanda's. There's a deep stillness in Michael that is intriguing, but he has a wicked laugh, too, and a glint in his eyes that makes him very much a regular guy. I can't think of a better combination of qualities.

TWENTY-THREE

January 1967

I PAUSE AT MISS MALICE'S THRESHOLD. She sneers, primps her kinky curls and says, "Well now, look at what the cat dragged in." I shrivel inside, thinking I deserved that. She sweeps her arm toward a chair in front of her desk. "Don't look so wounded. Have a seat. I want to know what you have to say for yourself."

I clear my throat, uncertain what to say as I settle into the chair. I can't tell her that instead of attending school for the past month I've been making love with Michael most afternoons in the warmth of his room, icicles in the tree outside tapping against the window pane. I can't tell her that instead of reading Shakespeare, Dickens or Shaw from English class reading lists, I've been under the covers, skin to skin, with Michael and reading Aldous Huxley's *The Art of Seeing* and *Island*, him turning the pages for me. I can't tell her it's been the sweetest time, and I wish it would never end, but I know I need to finish high school somehow.

"Well?" Miss Malice says.

"I uh ... think I'm ready to study now, to get it together." I don't tell her that since I broke out of the high school hamster wheel in December, I've been eating less and losing weight, which is a good thing, but I fear that come April, when Michael begins an 18-month trek following his guru across the globe, darkness will poison me from within, and I'll be immobilized like a papoose on a board. The prospect of school is about as appealing as sticking my tongue on a frozen hand rail, but I want to plug back into something constructive before Michael goes.

"You think? What kind of answer is that?"

"I dunno." I shrug. "The final semester of my senior year just started, and it might be a good time to slip back in."

"So you think you're ready to study now, and you think all of us here are just going to jump right up and accommodate you?"

"Not if you don't want to, I guess."

Her eyes narrow, and her ample chest heaves. "Listen, you can come back—it would be no skin off of my nose." She taps the eraser end of a pencil on her desk blotter. "But there's no way you'll graduate with the rest of your class, no matter how hard you work. You've got straight zeroes for last semester, and you won't be able to make that up. It will be on your permanent record." She smiles like the Queen in *Alice in Wonderland*.

"Oh, okay. I'll have to think about that." I stand up.

"Think about it all you want, but if you're not here ready to work first thing tomorrow morning, you won't be coming back at all."

I leave Miss Malice and trudge down the hall to see if Mrs. Henderson is in. She's on the phone, but she grins and waves me in. I plop on a chair and wait. After she signs off and hangs up the phone, she says, "Hello, dear. I haven't seen you in quite a while. What's up?"

"I'm thinking of coming back to school, but I won't be able to make up any of the work from last semester. So maybe I should just take the GED."

"Oh, I don't think that's a good solution for someone as bright as you," she says.

"I just might go nuts if I have to be here an extra year."

"I understand, especially the way things are at home." She pauses, leaning her elbow on the desk, her cheek against her palm.

"Isn't there anyone who can help you?"

I rule out Uncle John, the uncle I feel closest to. Last July, he married a widow with two grown children and several grandchildren, so he belongs to them now. I don't want to burden him. I think of Gramma, but she's 89 years old and riddled with arthritis. She needs care, not a wild child like me to look after. There's Grampa O'Neill, but he's getting on in years, too. Then Uncle Thomas comes to mind. He's Grampa's eldest son and my real mother's brother.

"There's Uncle Thomas. He set up that evaluation you wanted done," I say. "He's my godfather, too."

"You started seeing a doctor, right?" she says.

"I went to Dr. Scott once. He was awful."

"Dr. Scott? I would never have picked him for you. There are several others who relate better to teens."

"We couldn't afford it anyway," I say.

"Well, let's try your uncle. Do you know his phone number?"

"No, but he's a doctor, so I'm sure his office is listed."

She slides a notepad on the desk toward me and hands me a pen. "I have an appointment coming up. Write down his full name, where he lives and where is office is. I'll try to reach him and see what we can come up with."

I print my uncle's name and the few details I know about him. "Thanks," I say. Her phone rings. I step out of the office and am grateful that the halls are silent as a pinball machine unplugged. I exit the school just as a bell rings, indicating the start of a passing period. As I trot along the frozen sidewalk toward Michael's, I don't have much hope that anything will come of Mrs. Henderson's conversation with my uncle.

When I walk through Michael's door, he is about to eat a steak, baked potato and salad again. We settle onto a couch in the den, and he shares his meal with me, feeding me with his fork, like he did once before we'd ever kissed. I ask him what he thinks about my school situation. "Going back probably wouldn't be as bad as you think," he says. "You have to finish high school before you can try college."

He turns on the TV. The spooky music and seashore of the *Dark Shadows* opener comes on. He is about to change the channel, but I convince him to watch the show. He isn't enthralled with the vampire Barnabas Collins and the mix of witches, werewolves and ghosts inhabiting the screen, but he does admit it's not the typical daytime soap opera fare. Snow is falling when the episode ends. Michael says he has to do a few errands and offers me a ride home. I want to prolong my time with him, so instead of getting dropped off first, I opt to wait in the car while he stops at the bank and the post office. It's growing dark outside when I walk through Wanda's door. She's slumped in her recliner.

"Better get packing, missy. Your Uncle Thomas is coming to get you tomorrow afternoon," she says.

"What?"

"You heard me. That school psychologist convinced him this home I've given you—out of my good graces, mind you—is unhealthy, so get packing."

"Uncle Thomas is coming for me?"

"That's right. I could have fought it. I have legal rights, you know. Nobody could take you away if I didn't want them to. He'll find out soon enough what a big pain in the rear you are. And you're in for a rude surprise if you think he's taking you in. You're going off to boarding school—a nice, strict, Catholic boarding school at that."

I think of Father Doherty and how he screamed at Wanda after Daddy died. He said she was going to Hell for sending us to a Protestant congregation instead of the local Catholic parish where he reigned supreme. I don't want to face someone like him every day, and I wonder just what I have brought upon myself. I walk to my room and begin sorting through the mess of clothes and papers on the floor, while Wanda talks herself into a tirade in the other room. I turn on my transistor radio. As Simon and Garfunkel's *I Am a Rock* fills the room, I sing along and I try to decide what to bring along, knowing Wanda is likely to dispose of whatever I leave behind.

TWENTY-FOUR

January 1967

NINETY MILES OUTSIDE OF CHICAGO AND seven miles from the Indiana border, Uncle Thomas parks his Chrysler in front of Holy Family Academy. The campus, where I'll be living until June, is on the edge of a one-block business district we just drove by. There's a bar, a combination post office and general store, gas station and a few houses. That's about all there is to Beaverville, Illinois.

"Here we are," Uncle Thomas says. He sighs, removes the key from the ignition and slips it into his pocket. He grips the door handle, but doesn't open it. I do the same on my side. He looks at me and says, "It's only because of your mother that the sisters are accepting you halfway through your senior year. A few of them remember the summers Mary Agnes spent here as a child. Especially Sister Agatha."

"Who's that?"

"She's your grandfather's cousin. You'll meet her soon. She doesn't teach anymore, but she still lives here."

I take my fingers from the handle and clasp both hands in my lap. I've never thought of my mother as a girl. I've seen pictures of her as a young woman in a portrait on Grampa O'Neill's bedroom dresser, and as a frazzled mom holding her trio of girls in a few snapshots. Those are tucked into an old photo album in Wanda's basement. I wonder if being here will spark something in me, some feeling other than the profound void that claims my insides at the

147

sound of her name, Mary Agnes. What will it be like to walk the halls where she walked, eat where she ate, maybe even sleep in the same room?

At the public schools I've always attended until now, Catholics and Protestants get along. But Catholic jokes like—What's black and white and red all over? An embarrassed nun rolling down a hill—get huge laughs from everyone, Catholics included. Catholicism seems weird and backward to people I know at school, even after Vatican II. I am a little freaked out, but I remind myself that if I knuckle down here, I'll graduate in June.

"Ready?" Uncle Thomas asks.

"Sure," I say.

He opens his door and gets out. I smooth my skirt, grab the handle, let go, smooth my skirt again, chew on my top lip, which is always peeling in the winter. I grab the handle again, take a deep breath and slide out to join Uncle Thomas on the sidewalk. He holds my only piece of luggage, a battered canvas-covered case with leather trim that his wife, Aunt Barbara, hauled up from their basement. As we walk toward the front door, I feel embarrassed. How could I possibly belong at this school? Shelby and Jillie groaned when they heard the news, and they're both Catholic. Neither of them can think of a much worse plan than going to a place like this. No boys? No parties? Nothing but cornfields for miles around? And what if someone cunning, beady-eyed and mean is running the place? On the other hand, the grounds look so peaceful—several solid buildings, including a church with striking stained glass windows, and acres of snow-covered lawn, and trees. I imagine it'll all be gorgeous come spring.

And I am curious. I've lived most of my life on the edge of Catholicism. When Daddy was alive, we always said prayers before meals and at bedtime; we didn't eat meat on Fridays, but we only went to mass at Christmas and Easter and for family weddings, christenings and funerals. And Kathy, Mary Ruth and I didn't attend Saturday Catechism classes the way Catholic kids enrolled in public schools are supposed to do. Still, the fact that I am Catholic is one of the first things I learned about myself, one of the few things I remember about my first two years, when my mother was alive. Maybe it's my chance to be the person I started out to be, if that's even possible now. I mull this over as I walk through the door and into the foyer. Stairs are to the left. Open double doors straight ahead reveal a jumbo room with a stage at the far end. From a hallway at the right a nun emerges. Her wide smile exposes a row of slightly crooked, yellowing teeth.

"Hello, Thomas. It's good to see you again." She gives his free hand a vigorous shake. She turns to me and says, "You must be Laura. I'm Sister Mary Cecelia, and I'm pleased to meet you. I knew your mother, dear."

"Pleased to meet you, too." I look down at the sturdy, lace-up shoes Aunt Barbara bought for me yesterday. She also purchased a plaid uniform skirt, navy blue blazer, several pairs of white socks, new underwear, a couple of blouses, one casual skirt and sweater set, a pair of wool slacks and a new pair of plaid pajamas that I absolutely love. The suitcase in Uncle Thomas' hand contains the most items anyone has ever bought for me at one time.

Sister Mary Cecelia gives Uncle Thomas and me a tour, even though he's seen it all before. My future classmates are all hard at work, leaning over textbooks at old-fashioned desks with scratched wooden tops and inkwells in the upper right-hand corners. I like the wooden floors, the chalkboards that are black, not green like the ones in Hinsdale schools, the intricate molding, the old-library smell of the place, the corridors that twist and turn, revealing unexpected staircases, doors opening to hallways leading to more doors opening to more hallways, and curtained windows closed tight against the winter winds.

Back at the entrance, I bid farewell to Uncle Thomas.

"Behave yourself." He looks stern.

"Oh, I will." I say, fully intending to do so.

A nun named Sister Theresa Clare approaches to escort me to the senior girls' dorm. She's chewing gum. One of her eyebrows is raised a little bit above the tortoise shell frame of her glasses, giving her a slightly impish appearance as she takes me by the hand and leads me up the stairs.

"We're happy to have you here, Laura," she says. "Sister Augusta thought the world of your mother."

"I don't really remember her."

"That's a shame. I don't know what I'd do without my mother." She twists her rosary beads absentmindedly around her fingers as we walk. All I can see of her is her face and hands. Even her neck is covered. Her slightly oily skin has no wrinkles. I wonder how old she is but figure it's not appropriate to ask nuns such things.

When we reach the dorm, I survey the room. It has one walk-in closet, about a quarter of the size of the dorm itself, to hang coats, skirts, dresses and other stuff that could wrinkle up in a drawer. To the right are two rows of beds, a dresser beside each. One wall has several windows stretching from three feet or so above the floor to just below the top molding. They face the front yard and let in lots of light. Sister Theresa Clare escorts me to the sixth bed from the door against the inside wall. Happy I won't be sleeping by a window during the winter, I put down my suitcase in front of the dresser that will be mine.

"We've got thirteen girls in the senior class now, including you," Sister Theresa Clare says. "Julie lives in town, but everyone else stays right here."

"That's really small. There's more than 650 in the senior class where I come from."

"That's really big." She stifles a giggle.

She lifts up my suitcase, puts it on my bed and opens it. "Your dresser will be inspected regularly, and if your drawers are messy, you won't be able to go into town on Saturdays, or go home for an occasional weekend visit."

"I'm a slob. I'll be stuck here for months," I say.

"Oh, it's not that hard to pass inspection," she says. "I'll show you just how they're supposed to look." She gently lifts my new clothes one by one from the suitcase and shows me how to fold them so my wardrobe will fit into the limited drawer space without getting crumpled. Nobody has ever helped me fold and put away clothes before. I think this can't be right. Nuns are supposed to be mean and cold, but the two I've met here are just the opposite.

"Do you think the other girls will like me?" I ask.

"Of course. Why wouldn't they?" she says.

I can think of lots of reasons. I might say something stupid straight off that will turn everyone against me. They might not like the way I dress, the way I walk, the look in my eyes, or they might take a dislike to me on general principles, like at home, where it seems I have to earn every scrap of acceptance I get.

TWENTY-FIVE

March 1967

MICHAEL, ALREADY DRESSED AND RUNNING A comb through his thick chestnut hair, reminds me of Kookie in *77 Sunset Strip*, only more earthy and not so slick. I pull my green knit dress out of the overnight bag I borrowed from Terry Lynn, my best friend at Holy Family, and slide it over my underwear. I wish I could wind the clock back, even for just an hour. I don't want to accept that only moments from now Michael and I will be heading southeast toward Beaverville in his mom's Cadillac. It's Sunday afternoon, time for me to return to school.

This has been my second trip to Hinsdale since January. I spent an afternoon with Michael last month, but I spent most of my time during that visit with Shelby, because Michael hadn't asked me to come see him, and I didn't want to be a pest. This visit has been different. Michael wrote a few weeks ago that he missed me. I was already scheduled to take the SATs this weekend, so I arranged to stay with him and told Uncle Thomas I was going to stay with Wanda. I've been with him all weekend, except for Saturday morning, when I took the test at my old high school and then hung out with Shelby for a while afterward.

I plop on Michael's bed and put on my knee socks and loafers. He reaches into his pants pocket and pulls out his gold ring with a large, oval stone of jade. "Here," he says. I rise and stand inches from him, drinking in the smell of his clean skin. I've admired this ring when he's worn it on the ring finger of his right hand. Now it's on a golden chain. He slips the chain over my head so the ring dangles just below my breasts. "Jade stands for immortality, just like our love," he says. Then he pulls me close and kisses me for a long time.

When we break apart, I say, "I wish you didn't have to be gone so long."

"I'll be back by your nineteenth birthday."

"That's almost a year and a half away."

"Not so long in the overall scheme of things, don't you think?"

"Not right now I don't."

I pick my jacket off the hook on his door and put it on. Michael lifts my overnight bag and then takes my hand. We walk downstairs and through the kitchen where we first met. By the back door, he dons a beaver coat that used to be his father's. I am elated that he's wearing that coat even though it's far too warm for this March afternoon. He knows I love the way it looks on him. At the car, Michael opens the passenger door for me and tosses my bag in the back. As I get in, I thrum with joy about the ring and what Michael said about our love, but then I remember I have only the next hour-and-a-half to be with him, and I stiffen inside. He just turned twenty-five, received money from a trust fund, and will soon fly across the Atlantic to begin the next phase of his spiritual journey, a quest I comprehend only vaguely.

Michael starts up the engine. I slide as close to him as I can get. He puts his arm around me, and I relax again, thinking maybe I can trust that he loves me. The day is sunny and seems almost as shimmery to me as the time I took what was probably acid with Daniel. We pull out of the drive and get on the road to Beaverville. The Turtles' *Happy Together* comes on the radio several times during our drive. Michael sings along with just as much enthusiasm as

I do. I've never heard him sing before, and I think his passion for this particular tune is a good sign.

Just as we pull up to the curb in front of Holy Family, the Turtles' voices singing, "Imagine me and you, I do. I think about you day and night; it's only right, to think about the girl you love ..." fill the car again. We stay put, belting out the words. When the song ends, we are both out of breath. We kiss. Then I remember that nuns might be watching us. I slide across the seat toward the passenger door, thinking it would be better to get out on that side. We both rest our hands on the handles, like Uncle Jim and I did back in January. It isn't fear of what might be in store for me that's making it hard to open the door now, though. Sister Theresa Clare was right about the girls at Holy Family. They welcomed me into their fold.

The first couple of years after Daddy died, I used to lie in bed and wish that Wanda would move us to a place where more families were like ours, a place where folks weren't so affluent. I've found what I've longed for here: a group of peers. We've all either been orphaned or have been neglected in some way, or were sent here because our parents couldn't control us. Others have parents who want a phalanx of nuns to keep their daughters away from the opposite sex. But in Michael, though I am poor and he is rich, I've also found something I've longed for. He's not my peer the way my friends here are, but there is a deep connection I don't have with anyone else.

I glance at Michael and see in him sadness, as well as joy. I wonder if I see that because I'm feeling bittersweet right now. I slide back toward him, and we kiss again. Then I follow him out on his side, thinking if people are watching, they've already seen us kiss, so it makes no difference how I exit the car. We amble up the drive, my overnight bag in his hand. The snow is gone now, the trees, lawn and shrubs are green and vibrant with new life, just as I imagined they would be when I first saw the campus frozen in winter.

On the porch, Michael puts down the bag and takes both of my hands in his. The sun is setting over the cornfield ocean surrounding the school grounds. I gaze into his long-lashed, brown eyes. It feels like he is exploring every pore of my face. His smile widens the longer we stand toe to toe. My smile widens, too. Tucked into a zippered pocket in my purse is a scrap of notebook paper with the address in Ibiza, an island off of Spain, where he'll be staying while waiting for a group of friends to gather for their trek through India, Nepal and who knows where else. Also in that pocket is a picture of Michael on a beach in Ibiza. In it he is suntanned and smiling, his blue work shirt open, his khaki shorts wrinkled but clean, his sandaled feet in a casual stance.

Michael and I kiss again. "See you in a year and a half," he says.

"I'll be here. I love you," I say.

"I love you, too. Be happy." We kiss one last time. Then he turns, walks down the porch steps and follows the path toward the Cadillac. I grab the bag, open the front door to the academy, run through the foyer and up the stairs two at a time to the dorm. Several of my roommates are in there, milling around before supper.

I run to the window just as Michael reaches the car. "Look, look!" I call out. "You can see Michael. He's right down there." I pound on the window and call to him, watching him take off his Beaver coat, open the back door and toss it on the seat. I wonder if there's any significance to that, whether it means he's already starting to forget me before he's even out of sight. I try to banish that notion as my friends gather at the window. Several girls start pounding windows with me. Michael looks up, spots us, smiles and waves. Half a dozen of us wave back.

"Damn, he sure looks fine," Bonnie says. "To tell ya the truth, I didn't think he was real. I thought you made him up."

"Oh, he's real all right, and he loves me," I say.

"I knew he was real all along," Terry Lynn says. Her bed is right next to mine in the dorm, and we often whisper together late into the night. We talk about Michael and her boyfriend, Mitch, who is also older, but by four years, not seven and a half years like Michael. Terry Lynn and I have dissected and searched for hidden meanings in just about every string of words each of our lovers has said.

Michael gets into the car. He waves again before pulling away.

"Sure is some car he has," Gloria says.

"Oh yeah, that's his mom's," I say. "His family's rich."

"Must be nice to be part of a Cadillac-driving family," Bonnie says.

"Honestly, they don't really seem any happier than a lot of people who have way less money," I say.

I wave one last time as Michael's car pulls out of sight. Pressing my nose to the glass, I wish I could see through the row of dilapidated commercial buildings that now block my view.

"Hey, do you guys want to get a closer look?" I bend to the floor where I threw my purse and Terry Lynn's bag. I pull out Michael's picture. Bonnie reaches her long arm from behind me and has it in hand before anybody else has moved. Most of the girls gather on her bed to examine it. Terry Lynn takes a step toward Bonnie's bed too, but I ask her to wait.

"I've got something to show you." I sit on my bed and cross my legs. She settles in across from me on her bed.

"What is it?" She leans into the aisle between us.

I pull the ring up by the golden chain. It slides out from under my coat. I hold it out for her to see.

"Is this what I think it is?" She moves across the aisle, sits next to me and holds the ring gingerly in her hands.

"It's jade. Michael said jade stands for immortality, just like our love."

"Jeez, that's big. I mean that's the real deal," she says. "You're practically engaged." She hands the ring back to me. I stuff it inside my blouse and feel the smooth metal slide down my skin just as we are called to dinner.

"I'm never taking it off." I uncross my legs and stand up. Bonnie hands me Michael's picture. I put it under my pillow.

"Come on. You'll have to take it off when you shower," Terry Lynn says as we rush to join our classmates filing out the door.

"Well, maybe then. But the way I feel, I don't want to shower for a long, long time."

"Eew, what did you say?" Bonnie asks. "Did you guys hear that? Laura says she doesn't want to shower for a long, long time."

"I'm glad I don't sleep near her," Gloria says.

"Me too," Bonnie says.

We all laugh and tromp down the stairs, the ribbing continuing throughout supper into the evening's free time all the way to lights out when Terry Lynn crawls into my bed and whispers, "Okay, tell, tell me all the details."

TWENTY-SIX

May 1967

LOUNGING ON A GREEN BATH TOWEL and relishing the heat, I'm one of a half-dozen girls on the lawn between the main school and the gym. Sunshine penetrates bare skin. We pass around two bottles of baby oil mixed with iodine and tune a trio of transistor radios to a station blasting from Kankakee. The hits serenade us in stereo, accompanied by the scent of flowers blooming in beds of rich black soil tended by Sister Agatha.

"Hey look, there's King Kong, poking in the dirt. She's probably outside to spy on us," Bonnie says. The others laugh at the pet name they have for Sister Agatha, my grandfather's cousin. She's a small, bent, kindly woman in her 80s. She looks nothing like a gorilla, but they've got derogatory names for all the nuns except Sister Theresa Clare.

"Better her than Pickle," Gloria says. Pickle is their name for Sister Mary Cecelia.

"Yeah, Pickle would probably get all bent out of shape about that bikini," Bonnie says, pointing at Gloria, whose boobs look like they're about to pop out of her white top.

"Hey, can I help it if I grew since last summer? And you should talk. You don't even have your top on," Gloria says.

"I don't want to have a stripe on my back," Bonnie replies. She swats at a fly hovering near her shoulder.

"Well, if anyone's going to get demerits for this, it's you," Gloria says.

"Nobody has to worry about demerits with King Kong out here." Terry Lynn points at Sister Agatha. "She probably can't see us from where she is. The old bat probably can't even hear us either."

I ought to defend Sister Agatha. She is family, after all, but the best I can do is not join in on the bashing. My classmates don't know I'm related to her. And she and I haven't said more than an occasional passing hello since I arrived. I had hoped she would take me aside and tell me something about my mother—what she used to do here as a little girl, whether she liked to run, maybe, or whether she helped in the kitchen, whether she hated peanut butter—any little thing. But Sister Agatha has never sought me out, and I can't bring myself to approach her.

I close my eyes and bask in the heat, the loose Saturday schedule, the camaraderie. Each girl in this group—skin tones ranging from pasty white to deepest olive—wants to be radiant by graduation in two weeks. We're hoping this sunbathing will help.

Terry Lynn hands me a pack of Wrigley's spearmint gum. I sit up, unwrap a stick and pop it in my mouth and pass the pack on to Marlene, who's been thumbing through back issues of *Seventeen* magazine. She's searching for any ideas that may be useful in making our class the spiffiest looking group that has ever graduated from Holy Family Academy.

"Hey, look," she calls out holding up a page with an ad for lip gloss. "This gal's lips are shimmery, almost white. We could get some of this and all wear it. What do you think?"

"Cool. Shiny, white lips. I like it," Bonnie says. Usually, if Bonnie endorses something, the rest of us follow. So, in just seconds, the matter is decided. We just have to figure out how to get the gloss.

"They might have some in town," Marlene offers. She takes a stick of gum and throws the pack on to Bonnie.

"What planet do you live on?" Bonnie catches the pack. "I've poked through every single thing in that store, and I guarantee you, there won't be any shimmery, white lip gloss there." She slides the last piece of gum from the pack and holds it up. "Anybody else want this?" There are no takers, so she unwraps it and consumes it in a series of small bites.

I open a paperback, *I Never Promised You a Rose Garden*, which I've found reassuring because, troubled as I am, I am not controlled by imaginary characters like the girl who wrote the book. I've been using Michael's picture as a bookmark. Terry Lynn grabs the photo from me and tucks it inside of her copy of *Faust*, a book we're reading in English class. I am about to grab her book, but then The Fifth Dimension's *Beautiful Balloon* wafts from the radios. Terry Lynn sits up, starts to sing along while sticking her arms out pretending to fly. We all do the same. Then Gloria stands up. The rest of us follow her lead, arms waving, stretched out at our sides, legs in motion. We dance around our towels, each of us spinning away in her own dreams.

"I feel just like that song," I say to Terry Lynn when the music ends and we are returning breathless to our sunbathing. "And after graduation, that's what it'll be like; it'll be like flying away in a beautiful balloon."

"Maybe for you," she says. "I'm going back to Indiana to live with my Aunt Libby. And she doesn't like me much."

"Well, maybe you can run away, and we'll hitchhike to San Francisco or something."

"Yeah, maybe." She hands Michael's picture back to me. I kiss it and tuck it back into my book.

My guitar is nearby in the grass. I brought it to school after my first weekend visit to Hinsdale. I know about six chords. I pick it up and start in on *Blowin' in the Wind*. My friends turn their radios off and start singing along. We move on to *If I Had a Hammer*, then *Freight Train*. My repertoire is about ten folk songs I learned back when hootenannies were popular. But I just wrote a song called *I Want To Be Free*. Some of my classmates like singing along to the chorus:

I want to be free, to think like I want to

To be what I want any time

They're tryin' to change me, and rearrange me

But I'm just not their kind

When Pickle heard the song, she asked me, "Who is 'they'"? It was a good question; it made me realize "they" is too vague. So my attempt at a protest song isn't the world's greatest. "Time" and "kind" don't even rhyme. But it's my first song. Girls even sing snippets of it at random moments during our days here. It must have something going for it.

A bell rings out across the grounds. It's time to go inside for lunch. Later, those of us who haven't gotten too many demerits can go into town. I appreciate being able to walk off campus and poke around the general store. It's not much, compared with what I used to do in Hinsdale, but it's an outing at least.

"Last one there has to give me her dessert," Bonnie calls. She scoops up her towel and dashes for the building.

The rest of us are jockeying for position right at her heels. We're all chattering about how much we can't wait to leave this place, but I wish secretly that I could spend more time here. The weeks have rushed by. I haven't really drawn in enough of the calmness, the smell of lilacs, corn silk and moist, black earth, the lack of social pretension. And I've been a model student for the most part. I've done a year's worth of work this semester and will graduate on time. The only thing Pickle would have a conniption fit about, if she knew, is the weekend when I went back to Hinsdale to take the SATs. If she knew I'd stayed with Michael instead of Wanda, she wouldn't let me off the school grounds again until I had my diploma in hand.

I'm going to miss Holy Family. Sister Theresa Clare says I must go to college in the fall, that I'm too smart to waste away at a typewriter or on an assembly line somewhere. My SAT scores were good, too. There was a space on the test application form to select schools to receive scores. I picked St. Mary of the Woods, a Catholic women's college in Indiana, because my mother's aunt lives there. She's a nun and a retired art teacher who used to send my mother birthday cards when she was a child.

I just received a letter from St. Mary's admissions office with an application enclosed. They are impressed with my SAT scores and want me to apply. I figure they wouldn't want me if they saw the row of zeroes I earned for the first semester this year. I'm nothing compared with Mary Ruth, who graduated first in her class last year and won a full, four-year scholarship to Vassar. I attended an awards assembly for her class. She was the undeniable star, as her name was called time after time, and she walked up, grace emanating from her blue eyes, gleaming brown hair flowing down her back, teachers with tears in their eyes, handing her the plaques. I tucked the application into my math book and probably won't apply. It's sure to be too late by now. Besides, all I really want to do is board a plane, find Michael and follow him wherever he goes, just like Little Peggy March singing that old song, *I Will Follow Him.*

TWENTY–SEVEN

June 1967

SUCKING A CHOCOLATE FRAPPE THROUGH A red and white straw isn't as sublime as kissing Michael, but the icy burst of flavor is the perfect treat for an especially humid Saturday. The drink is just a milk shake, like ones I've downed on many a summer's day before, but the Bostonian word frappe is a nifty reminder that I'm not in Illinois anymore.

I feel like a sweepstakes winner as I cross Massachusetts Avenue and head for Harvard Yard. A month ago, I was one of thirteen Holy Family Academy graduates filing out of St. Michael's Church for the last time. I had no plans. Two days later, I was enrolled in college for the fall and on a plane headed for the East Coast with Kathy and Mary Ruth. Two days before our flight, Mary Ruth took me to see Mr. Case, a counselor at Hinsdale Central, who helped me out as a favor to her, one of his favorite former students. I'm headed for Mount Mercy College in Iowa, instead of St. Mary of the Woods, where I'd sent my SAT scores, because Mr. Case knows the admissions director at Mt. Mercy and he said it was a better place than St. Mary's. He got me in with one phone call. My record is spotty, but my SAT scores show I have potential, he said. Then Kathy invited me to spend the summer with her in Cambridge.

Kathy and Don, one of her friends from MacMurray College, rented a flat for the summer for only $25 a month. Don comes from Liverpool and sounds like a Beatle, which is really fun, and the flat is bigger than Wanda's entire house. The first thing Kathy and I did after we settled in was circle job prospects in the want ads in *The Boston Globe*. The next day we landed jobs as replacements for vacationing workers at Necco Candy Factory in Boston. The work is numbing, but about twenty other students on summer break are on the replacement crew, too, so we don't feel isolated. It seems everything is falling into place for me.

I enter Harvard Yard and suck in more of the thick, chocolate frappe as I take in the majestic brick buildings, some of which are older than the United States, and the grassy expanse they face. I hope some of the school's tradition of excellence will rub off on me. A young woman approaches. She has waist-long blonde hair, granny glasses, a dress of purple paisley that touches her ankles, and leather sandals. She smiles. I smile back.

"Excuse me," she says. "I can't help but ask where you got that incredible outfit."

"Oh, my friend Violet made it." I'm wearing a navy blue mini dress with thin lime-green stripes. It has a simple A-line design with straps about an inch and a half wide. The hat is big and floppy and reversible—solid lime on one side and striped on the other.

"The color combination is to die for," she says.

"Yeah, I know. If you have a paper and pencil, I'll give you Violet's number. A couple of boutiques carry her clothes, but she lives close to here and sells them from home, too. She'll give you a good deal."

The woman fishes through her shoulder bag, pulls out a pencil and paper and hands it to me. I write down Violet's contact information and give it back to her. She thanks me and sashays away.

Violet and I met while slapping price stickers on giant posters of assorted chocolates at Necco. She sold me the dress and hat for only

$5. It's part of her business plan for friends to serve as advertisements by wearing her clothes. It appears to be working. Two other young women also stopped me on the street today and asked where I got my ensemble. And when I visited Violet less than an hour ago, one of them was already at her apartment, shopping. Violet was leaning over her sewing machine and punctuating every row of stitches with whoops of joy. She has reason to be so happy; she just quit her job at the factory because her business is doing so well.

I wish I could sew like Violet, but I can't even baste a straight hem, so come Monday it's back to the factory for me. I have to save money for Mt. Mercy because the school can't give me financial aid until January since I applied after the deadline. I have to get by on whatever I'll get from Social Security and what I can earn. I feel uneasy about that school. I don't like the name, Mount Mercy. It sounds sappy, like a big lump of sniveling sinners on their knees, begging for a helping hand. St. Mary of the Woods, now that's a five-word story. But Mr. Case pulled strings to get me into what he said is a much better college. It's his job to know all about which schools are best, after all. And I barely graduated from high school. What do I know?

I leave Harvard Yard and amble along Cambridge Street. Finished with my frappe, I discard the cup in a trash container and walk on. Lighting an Old Gold, I think about how the summer's been unfolding. All along the East Coast, it seems, young people are everywhere, talking politics and the Vietnam war; demanding change; drinking wine; smoking pot; singing along to Bob Dylan, the Beatles, The Rolling Stones; dreaming of grand trips around the world; and pursuing true love and passing infatuations. Kathy and I are swept up in it, too, during breaks at work, with friends at the flat, and on weekend adventures we've taken to Provincetown and Cape Cod. Excitement about what we can do to change the world is everywhere.

The factory work is the only hard part. Sometimes I'm stationed at the fudge machine, where I have a few seconds to wrap each box of fudge as it rolls off the assembly line. The worst days are when I stand at a conveyor belt and face crunchy, cream-colored discs on their way to be covered with chocolate. They're poured from a large barrel at frequent intervals. About three inches above the belt are several iron rods running its length. They rattle back and forth horizontally, forcing the centers into rows. It's my job to pull out the broken centers as they glide by. Occasionally, I'm on the floor where Necco wafers are made. Every several seconds a deafening boom fills the entire floor as the hard candy discs are cut from flat sheets. Kathy and I leave the plant each day with headaches from all the repetitive motions and sounds and the overpoweringly sweet chocolate smell that fills our nostrils and lingers long into the evening.

As I approach our flat on Roberts Road, a dark haired guy with big round eyes calls out to me. He's leaning against a red VW bus, beer in hand, like he often is when I pass by. "Come to California with me," he says.

"No thanks," I reply.

"I'm leaving tomorrow."

"So long then."

"Come on. It's the summer of love, baby."

I keep walking. It's more like the summer of longing for me. Despite all the new sights, possibilities and friends, I'm consumed with desire for Michael.

The young man runs across the street and falls into step beside me. He hands me a piece of paper. "Write to me?" he asks.

"Why? I don't even know your name."

"It's John. I'm John O'Malley, and I just flunked out of BU, and I'm probably gonna get drafted and sent to Vietnam."

I stop at my front door. "Bummer. Will you go up to Canada?" I unfold the note and read his name scrawled in pencil along with an address in San Rafael, California.

"Don't know."

"Where's this?" I point to San Rafael on the paper.

"Just north of San Francisco. My dad lives there. He's cool, you know. He wouldn't mind if you came along with me."

"No thanks, really, but good luck." I open the door to the flat.

"Yeah, you too." He sticks his thumbs in the pockets of his ripped jeans.

I step inside and climb the steep stairway to my summer home. Neither Kathy nor Don is here, so the place is eerily silent. I meander through the rooms, turning on all the lights even though it's well before sunset. In the living room, I put on Don's Eartha Kitt album, walk to the window and look out. John's already across the street talking to another girl. I walk to my room and wonder if he'll convince her to go with him. On the end table by my bed is a stack of prepaid airmail forms—sheets of sheer blue paper waiting to convey my dreams. Every few days, I fill up one of these, fold it, seal it and mail it to Michael. I've been doing this since he left in April. He hasn't written back.

I grab two forms, in case I mess up the first one, and a black ballpoint pen. At the kitchen table, I sit down and attempt to collect my thoughts. I grasp the golden chain around my neck and pull up Michael's ring, which I've worn every day since he gave it to me. I rub the jade stone, then close my eyes and recall my last moments with him. My body fills with a soft, warm glow. Then I picture the beach in Ibiza where he waited for his fellow travelers to arrive, or might still be waiting; I don't know. I imagine I'm in a café by his side as he talks about enlightenment with other seekers. Then I picture us in a village somewhere in India, our bodies wrapped together; I'm listening to his heartbeat as a sitar plays in the distance. I make a cocoon of these imagined moments, this desire, complete and blissful.

But soon comes the thought that Michael hasn't written in the three months he's been gone. It dominates like a teacher hovering over my desk, asking questions I can't answer, and everyone's eyes in the classroom are on me, appearing to savor my discomfort. Michael hasn't written. But then, he didn't promise to write. He only promised to return by the time I turn 19. I brush creases from my dress, enjoying the feel of the thick cotton against my palm. I click the top of the pen to open and retract the tip several times while I stare at the white hearts that signify it's a Papermate.

"Dear Michael," I begin. Then I stop, thinking perhaps it's time for a few of the Spanish peanuts in a dish on the table. I savor them one at time, sucking off all the salt before I bite down. What could I, a seventeen-year-old girl, say that could possibly matter to Michael, a twenty-five-year-old world traveler? What if I'm making a fool of myself, like Shelby has insisted many times? What if he laughs at my letters, that is, if he even gets them? I put several nuts in my mouth and shuffle them around with my tongue. I close my eyes and relive my last ride with Michael. I recall how fervently we both sang along to the radio and think he really does love me.

I open my eyes and begin writing about my day. There has to be something I did that will spark his interest, impress him, make me seem worth remembering. I write on until past dark, finishing off the peanuts as I go.

TWENTY-EIGHT
July 1967

WIND BANGS BRANCHES OF AN ELM against the side of the building, and roaring thunder roils my stomach like a ride on the Bobs at Chicago's Riverview Park. Seated at the kitchen table, Don and I puff Gauloise and slurp Harvey Wallbangers, which are heavy on Smirnoff and Galliano and light on orange juice. The rain began when Kathy, Don, their college mate Tripp and I were hitchhiking back to Cambridge from a weekend at a Western Massachusetts farmhouse. The three of them had been invited by one of their professors from MacMurray College who, like us, came to New England for the summer. They let me tag along.

The four of us split into two groups at an onramp to Hwy. 90. We thought we'd make better time that way. Don and I stepped to the edge of the shoulder first, thumbs out, and caught a ride in a pale blue Oldsmobile with gray seats driven by a blue-eyed man in a gray suit. As I waved goodbye to Kathy and Tripp and greeted our benefactor, I was sure Kathy and Tripp would be right behind us on the road. After a gruff hello, the man who gave us a lift warned us repeatedly about the dangers of hitchhiking. He included stories of robbers, rapists and murders that had victimized people right along our route. I worried that he might be a criminal himself, but he turned out to be a lonesome divorcé who'd looked at some real estate in Pittsfield and was driving home to an apartment in Boston. He even went out of his way to drop us off at our front door in Cambridge. Don and

I were in a celebratory mood as we walked up the steep stairs to our flat. One ride that took us all the way across the state was a stroke of very good luck. But our spirits have been sinking with each hour that has passed without word from Kathy and Tripp.

A chain smoker, I finish one cigarette and immediately light another. I shift my weight in my chair, blow smoke rings toward the ceiling and study Don's blue work shirt. It reminds me of the one Michael sports in the only picture I have of him. "Is there any way you would part with that shirt?" I've been eyeing it since the day I moved in because Don has worn it to a soft perfection.

"I'm very attached to this bloody shirt," Don says. "I'd be daft to give it to ya."

"How 'bout if I just try it on?"

"No, no. They say possession is nine-tenths of the law." He takes a final drag on his cigarette and puts it out in a Playboy ashtray on the table.

"I'll give it back. I just want to wear it while we wait. It'll help keep me from worrying."

"That makes no sense, duck," Don says.

"Oh, but it does." I blow smoke rings at him.

He waves the smoke away.

"Please, please."

"Oh, all right. If you fancy it that much, here." He stands up, peels off the shirt and puts it over my shoulders. We sip our drinks and listen to the Beatles song *She's Leaving Home* drift in from the record player in the living room. The arm is set to swing back and repeat the album each time it finishes, so we don't have to get up, walk down the hall and change it.

"This feels so good. I just might have to keep it." I rub the shirt's worn sleeves.

"So, you want something to remember me by while you're at that Midwestern nunnery, Mercy Me or whatever."

"You're making fun of me, 'cause I can't keep up with any of you," I say. "Like at the barbecue this weekend. Everyone had an opinion on whether Charlemagne had killed his brother. He lived thousands of years ago, right? Who cares? And Kathy and the other art history buffs were going on about the Cubists and the Dadaists and the Surrealists. What did I have to talk about? Nothing."

"You just haven't applied yourself to anything yet."

"Maybe I can't." I take in a deep breath, surprised at the frustration that had just erupted.

"Wait until this time next year; you'll have a whole new perspective."

The front door creaks open. Footsteps echo in the stairway and in the hall, and then Kathy, shoes sloshing and raindrops dripping from her hair, her shirt, and her shorts, appears in the kitchen doorway. "I see you two are having a good time." Her scowl could wither a plastic rose.

"Looks like you got soaked, love." Don nods to Kathy. "What took you so long?"

She doesn't answer.

"You'll feel better after you dry off, I'm sure." He stands and grabs the phone. It's red and has a matching cord so long it stretches into our bedrooms, which are all off of the kitchen. "I've got to ring my brother."

He holds his free hand out to me, palm up. I take off his shirt and hand it to him. He flips it over one shoulder, and retreats to his room.

"What were you doing wearing Don's shirt? Are you after him now? " Kathy asks, exuding disdain.

"It's not like that," I say. "I just like his shirt."

"He's my friend, you know, not yours." She withdraws into her room, leaving wet footprints as she goes.

I wobble up from the table and slouch into the living room, where I settle in at a cluttered table against a wall. I find some notebook paper and a pen beneath a pile of newspapers and books, and start writing to Shelby. I pen every nasty thing I can think of about Kathy. I write that I don't like the way she talks, the way she plays guitar, the way she sings—none of which is true, but I write on anyway, swept up in venting my anger until I've filled two long paragraphs. Feeling confused by the venom I'd just translated to words on paper and a little sick to my stomach from too much liquor, I go to my room and flop down on the bed. I close my eyes, thinking Kathy had a right to be upset about what she'd just been through. So what if she accused me of having designs on Don? I probably wouldn't have been smiling either if I'd gotten soaked in the rain like she did.

A little while later I hear Kathy and Don talking in the kitchen.

"Wow, you devoured that sandwich," Don says.

"You have no idea how hungry I was. My stomach was growling and my head was pounding hard."

"We were getting worried about you, love," Don says.

"It was a nightmare. We waited a long time for our first ride and it only took us to the turnoff for Chester. And then it started raining and we were waiting and waiting and nobody picked us up for hours. The next ride went as far as Russell, and we waiting a long time again, getting soaked to the bone. And then finally we got a ride to Boston, where Tripp and I went our separate ways."

"I don't suppose you still want to go to Violet's party tonight."

"I don't want to go back out in the storm. Violet wanted me to bring my guitar so she could hear Laura and me harmonize. That would have been fun. I like singing with her a lot. Where's Laura anyway?"

"Maybe napping? She had too much to drink while we were waiting. She was getting really worried."

"I'll see if she wants a sandwich. Knowing her she probably drank on an empty stomach."

I hear a gentle knock at my door, then Kathy's voice. "Laur? Hey, do you want a tuna sandwich? We could toast cheese on it the way you like. How about it?"

I remain still, eyes closed. I hear Kathy retreating from my doorway. "Guess she's out for the duration," she says to Don.

I mull Kathy's invitation over and feel like a big ignoramus for everything I just wrote about her. I think I should get up, throw the letter away and accept her offer to fix me a sandwich, but I'm feeling too dizzy and stupid to move.

Several days later, Kathy confronts me in the kitchen, her dark blue eyes glaring. She holds a rumpled piece of notebook paper in her hand. I stop at the table, recognize my handwriting and realize it's the awful rant I wrote about her and forgot to throw away.

"I can't believe you wrote all this about me," she says.

"It's not—

"Listen, I don't know where you're working tomorrow, but it's not going to be with me," she declares. Her upturned chin and quivering mouth broadcasting that I have shattered her heart. I feel low as a maggot.

This is the worst possible development I can imagine because we've just switched jobs to a chain of tiny lunch counters. We're supposed to man the counters alone, but I've been working with Kathy because I haven't gotten the job down yet to where I can do it by myself. I can't think of one thing to say in my defense except that maybe she shouldn't have read the letter, but then I left it out on the table, so I guess I didn't have a right to privacy. I keep mum, mortified.

"I don't ever want to see your face again." She turns her back to me and marches to her room, slamming the door behind her.

Knowing I am guilty, guilty, guilty of scribbling out a rash of hurtful nonsense about Kathy, I believe this could be the end for her and me. How I wish I had gotten out of bed and thrown the note away the night I wrote it. I wish I could take it all back. We are three-fourths, Irish after all. Life-long feuds are second nature to our extended clan. Stories abound about aggrieved parties, including our grandmother, refusing to attend the funerals of sisters, brothers or other relatives and friends who wronged them. Our father was big on grudges, too. He left the Catholic church because of something a priest said to him after our mother's suicide. He didn't return to the fold until he was on his deathbed. But after two operations and six weeks of wasting away in a Catholic hospital, it is possible he wasn't in his right mind in the end.

I retreat to my room and feel like I imagine Alice did when she fell down the rabbit hole. The stuff I wrote has everything to do with how Kathy, as the oldest child in our family, used to lord it over me when we were growing up in Wanda's cruel clutches. It has nothing to do with how kind Kathy's been to me in the last few years. It has nothing to do with the beautiful, generous person she is. I don't know how to make sense of the way creepy feelings burble up unbidden, let alone how to try to explain them to her. I can only hope that if I lie low tonight, Kathy will have a miraculous change of heart by morning.

TWENTY-NINE

July 1967

"OH, SHIT!" SHELBY GRIPS THE EMPTY mason jar in her suntanned hands. "The loot's gone, every fuckin' penny." Panic sweeps through me. I'm sure this sort of thing would never have happened if Kathy and Peter were still here. Not only did Kathy not have a change of heart about my screed, she moved in with a friend on the Necco summer crew without saying another word to me. Peter left a couple days later.

When Peter was all packed and set to fly home to England, I complained that I'd never lived alone, and I was scared.

"You'll be fine. Isn't one of your friends coming to visit soon?"

"Yeah, Shelby."

"So you won't be by yourself for long. Everything will be all right. You'll see." He picked up his bags and strode down the stairs and out the door. I followed and stood on the front porch as he tossed his luggage into the back seat of cab, slid in himself and waved goodbye before the cab sailed down the block and around the corner. I trudged back upstairs, where I found his old work shirt folded on my pillow with a note saying I should wear it well.

The tattered shirt gives me no pleasure now. I'm out of a sister and out of a job because I'm afraid to try doing the job alone, so I stopped reporting in. And now Shelby and I are broke. When she arrived last week, we stuffed a jar with enough cash to pay for our airfare back to Chicago, along with money I'd put aside for college from my Necco paychecks, and hid it behind hat boxes on a shelf in a spare room. We were afraid we'd spend it if we didn't tuck it away. I thought at the time that we would find work together, like Kathy and I had, and add more cash to the jar, but Shelby and I haven't even glanced at the want ads since she arrived. We did several days of sightseeing first. Then, while on our way to buy a newspaper on Massachusetts Avenue yesterday morning, we were sidetracked by a couple of guys packing a cooler, towels and a Frisbee into their VW van. Curious, we introduced ourselves and found out they were Chip and Denny, two philosophy graduate students at Harvard. We asked if we could go along to wherever they were headed. We figured job hunting could wait a day.

They conferred briefly; then Chip pushed his wire-rimmed glasses up his nose and said, "It's highly irregular, and we do feel it is not felicitous, in general, for maidens to be importuning favors such as this, but we assent to your entreaty."

"Does that fuckin' mean yes?" Shelby asked.

Denny lit a meerschaum pipe, took a puff and said, "Affirmative."

We went to Cape Cod with them and found they could talk circles around us, but when the hits came on the radio, they couldn't sing on key. That, and the joints they passed around the car, led to laughter and an easy rapport that lasted throughout the day. When they dropped us off at our flat afterward, they offered to take us to Salem, the scene of the infamous witch trials, the next day. "We aver it is our utmost duty, as gentlemen, to escort you benighted Midwestern adolescents and upgrade your scholarship, which, most regrettably, is acutely lacking. With the right tutelage, you can assimilate much about human nature, history, philosophy and literature in one excursion to Salem," Chip said.

We begged off, saying we would have to go job hunting instead. Later, we went out in search of chips and Dr Pepper, and two scruffy, long-haired guys approached us. One was tall, skinny and dark. The other was average height with sandy colored hair. They had deep bags under their eyes and were a little jumpy, but otherwise seemed normal.

"Hey girls, want to try some dynamite pot? We just scored," the tall one said.

"Sure," Shelby said.

"Yeah, I guess," I added

We brought them back to the flat, where I put on the Beatles' *Sgt. Pepper's Lonely Hearts Club Band* album Don left behind, and we shared a joint. The dark-haired guy tried several times to put the moves on me, while the other tried to do the same with Shelby, but we brushed them off. Finally, they said they were going home to Pennsylvania the next day and asked if they could crash with us for the night. We said sure, and set one of them up in Don's old room and the other on a couch in the living room.

Now we're feeling stupid as Gomer Pyle, because they're long gone with the money we'd hidden in the jar.

"How are we fuckin' gonna get home?" Shelby asks.

"Wow, this is how they say thanks for crashing here?"

"They were probably fuckin' pissed that neither of us put out," she says.

"How could they have found it behind those boxes? The place doesn't look ransacked."

"They were probably just careful. I didn't hear a thing."

"Me neither," I say.

"Man, we're fucked. I'll have to call my mom to wire us some fuckin' money."

"I don't know how I'm going to make it to Mt. Mercy now. I've got $30 to my name, or at least I think I do. I'll have to check my wallet."

"Don't you have a savings account?"

"Yeah, I'll get around five hundred dollars from that when I turn 18, but Mt. Mercy is more than $1,500 a year, and I have no financial aid lined up. I'll get some money from Social Security, too, but Wanda says that won't amount to much."

"It's better than me. I'll be back in fuckin' high school. Too much ditching classes."

"Bummer," I say.

"Let's just call my mom and see how fast she can wire money," Shelby says.

"Maybe we can even leave today. This place is giving me the creeps now."

"I'm starting to miss Jake an awful lot, too."

"What about Daniel?"

"Oh, we split up."

"Say what?"

"We were at a party over at Franks, and I fuckin' walked into one of the bedrooms and found him goin' at it with Allison Tenley."

"Didn't he find you making out in a car with Jake not too long ago?"

"That was different. Whose fuckin' side are you on, anyway?"

"I guess I'd like you to stick with Daniel. Then we can have a double wedding—Daniel and Michael and you and me, that is, when we're all through with college."

"Michael? That fuckin' flake? Are you still stuck on him?"

"Well, duh."

"He doesn't know what side is up. He came home a day after you left in June, and then he took right off again a couple days later. Can you imagine spending all that fuckin' money on airfare to and from Europe for less than a week?

"You're only telling me now that Michael came home in June?"

"Yeah, so?"

"Shit. Why didn't you tell me when I called you after I got here, while he was still there? I could have called him."

"What fuckin' difference does it make? He didn't ask about you, and you shouldn't be fuckin' stuck on him."

"How do you know?"

"He's twenty-five; you're seventeen. Case fuckin' closed."

"Are you sure he didn't ask about me?"

"Okay, he asked where you were, and Daniel fuckin' told him."

"Why didn't you give him my address?"

"He didn't ask me for it, okay?"

"You could have offered, you know." I'm barely able to breathe, knowing Michael came to town right after I left, that is, if Shelby's even telling the truth about that. Is she just messing with me because she's angry that we were robbed? Is it possible he came back to see me? Not knowing Holy Family's school year ended almost two weeks before Hinsdale's did, he might have assumed I hadn't graduated yet.

"I just didn't think it was such a big fuckin' deal."

"Yeah, well, I'm gonna go pack my stuff now." I glare at her.

"Good. Me too," Shelby tosses her long hair over her shoulders and scowls right back at me.

I rush out of the room, still stunned at the news that I missed Michael by a day. I sit on the bed, reach inside the neck of my blouse, pull out his ring and remember the day he gave it to me. I thought then that I'd gotten a new start at Holy Family, that life was on an upswing, that I'd take good care of myself until Michael returned. But now, here I am: Kathy can't stand me anymore, I have no job, I've been robbed and I'm probably going to fly home, defeated, with a friend who wants to keep me from the guy I love.

THIRTY

August 1967

I DOWN THE LAST DROP OF Boone's Farm in my glass and wobble up the stairs like a newborn colt. Brian follows, taking swigs from a bottle of Andre Cold Duck and tapping my rear every step or two. He thinks we're going to fuck. I just want to find a quiet room with a phone. At the top of the stairs, he pulls me close and tries to kiss me on the lips. I turn my face to the side. His wet lips smear all over my cheek.

Brian's a nice enough guy—attractive, too, with sandy blond hair tumbling into his green eyes. And the scent of Canoe on his tanned skin is a turn on. But he's not Michael. I shouldn't have kissed him on the porch swing downstairs.

I was sipping my third glass of wine when he sat next to me, put his arm around me and smiled. I'd been worrying about how to pay for Mount Mercy when I won't know how much money I'll have for school until my birthday, which isn't coming up until after classes have already begun. I was also fretting about the paperwork I opened up at Wanda's after Shelby and I returned from Boston, thanks to the money her mom wired us. I was supposed to have filled out forms and questionnaires and mailed them back to the admissions office weeks ago. I'm not even sure the school still has a place for me, and I haven't mustered up the courage to call. Even worse, old feelings of dread have been surfacing ever since Shelby and I were robbed. It feels like a vampire is creeping around the edges of my mind, watching me make one mistake after another, waiting to suck every bit of happiness out of me, savoring the thought of the kill. Some days I don't get up until Shelby, Jillie or Daniel bursts into my room at Wanda's and drags me off to nowhere in particular. Daniel fetched me today and brought me to this party. Then he took off to find more booze. I was sinking deeper and deeper into my whirlpool of worry. Brian's smile was like a momentary life raft. It felt good, the warmth of his body next to mine, the touch of his soft lips. But I should have broken away from him sooner.

Brian takes my hand and pulls me down the hall. "This way," he says. I follow him to a large room with a door toward the back opening to a private bath. A King James Bible is on top of a jumble of books on the headboard. The golden brocade bedspread and butter yellow sheets are rolled and twisted into a totem pole shape, a pair of undies dotted with little red hearts is on one of the pillows. I wonder whose they are and when she'll miss them. The house is packed with teenagers. Half-empty bottles of booze and cigarette butts are everywhere. Word got around that Brian's parents and younger brother are gone for a week. I don't know how he'll ever get the house clean before his family comes home.

Brian sits on the bed and pats the spot next to him. I put my empty glass on the bedside table and grab a beige touch-tone phone that had been resting on a recent issue of *Good Housekeeping*. I plunk down next to Brian, phone in my lap. He tries to take it away.

"Come on. You don't need this," he says.

"Yes, I do. I have to make a call."

"Right now? A phone call?"

"Yes, right now." I clutch the phone to my chest. My heart pounds. I feel like I will stop breathing if I don't hear Michael's voice immediately. I've been thinking maybe my letters of love have never reached him. Maybe that's why he hasn't written me back. I have to find out.

"I still haven't gotten used to these weird button thingies," I say, looking down at the face of the phone.

"What are you, nuts? It's dial phones that are weird now." He tries again to wrench the phone from my grasp. I hold on tight. He leans close to nibble on my ear. I scrunch away, lift the receiver and hit zero.

"Yes, operator, I want to place a call to Spain," I say.

"Spain? What the fuck, Spain? Who's in Spain? You can't call Spain." Brian tries to press his finger down on the toggles where the receiver goes.

I slap his hand away. "Stop that. I'm getting transferred to an international operator."

"Oh no you're not." This time he succeeds in cutting the call off.

"Why did you go and do that?" I grab the phone and dart into the bathroom, which is just a few steps away. I try to slam the door, but Brian's bare foot is in the way.

He screams, "Jesus! What are you trying to do? Kill me?" He forces the door open and yanks the phone from my hands. He stomps out and slaps it back down on the nightstand. I shut the bathroom door, lock it and slide down, plopping on the cold, tile floor.

Brian pounds on the other side. "Come on, open up!"

"One phone call. I just want to make one phone call."

"You can't call Spain. My folks would have a cow. Come on out."

"Go away. Just leave me alone."

"Fine. You're not really girlfriend material anyway."

"What's that supposed to mean?" I pull myself up by the sink basin and wobble as I reach for the doorknob.

"Fuck. I don't know. What kind of girlfriend tries to call Spain in the middle of a date?"

I open the door and step out. "We're not on a date."

"We could be."

"I can't go on a date with you," I say.

"Just forget it, then." He storms out of the room.

I grab the bottle of Cold Duck he left behind and down what's left in three fizzy gulps. I plop on the bed and brood about Michael somewhere on the other side of the world when in walks Daniel, a brown capuchin monkey on his shoulder. "How much have you had to drink, Sis?" he asks.

"I like that you call me Sis, you know. Maybe someday I really will be your sister."

"You never know," he says.

"I was trying to call Spain, you know, Ibiza, to see if anyone there could find Michael."

"What? You were going to just call somewhere in Ibiza and ask for him?"

"It's not that big. I looked on a map."

"He's probably long gone from there by now."

"But he said to write to that Wagon Lits Cook place in Ibiza."

"They're just holding mail for him. Come on." He takes my hands and pulls me up. The monkey screeches. "This is Domino. He doesn't like girls, but I think he'll get used to you."

"Hi there, Domino." I look into the simian's golden eyes. He hisses at me, revealing his sharp little fangs.

"What are you doing the rest of this weekend?"

"Not much," I say.

"A bunch of us are going to Saugatuck. You can come, too. All you have to do is babysit Domino some of the time. What do you think?"

"Do you really think Domino will get used to me?"

"Sure." Daniel puts his arm around me and helps me wobble toward the door. Domino crawls on top of my head and scratches around.

"What's he doing, making a nest?" I ask.

"Just getting to know you," Daniel says.

We make our way through the crowded party and out the door. Just outside, five guys are already packed into an old Impala. The engine idles as I get in the back and sit on Dag's lap. He's one of Daniel's best friends, and I'm safe with him. Daniel squeezes into the front. Domino wrenches away and crawls onto Daniel's shoulder.

"How long will we be gone?" I ask.

"Two or three days," Dag says. He offers me a sip from his Budweiser. I wave it away.

Carl, the driver, turns on the radio, and Donovan's *There Is a Mountain* blasts out. We all start bouncing to the tune as the car pulls away from the curb. I was supposed to get together with Jillie and Alice tomorrow and then somehow pull the whole Mount Mercy thing together. Jillie's folks are driving her to University of Kansas next week. Alice is flying to join the rest of her family in Virginia. They moved in the spring; Alice stayed behind so she could graduate with her friends. I tap Dag's shoulder. "Will you remind me to call Jillie at a pay phone when we stop for gas?" I ask.

"Sure," he says. "How come?"

"I was supposed to do something with her and Alice."

"Oh, so you're finking out on them to be our mascot," he says.

"Yeah. It's sort of a bad habit I should break one of these days," I say. "They're gonna be pissed."

I lean against Dag's chest. He pats my shoulder in time to the music, and I drift off to sleep. We speed through the night to Saugatuck, where we settle in at a funky little bed and breakfast.

Six single mattresses line the floor of our attic room. Daniel directs me to a mattress against one of the walls. He claims the one next to me, and says, "Sleep easy, Sis. Nobody here will lay a hand on you."

One week later, the Impala pulls into Wanda's drive. I open the door and put a leg out, but then Domino leaps onto my shoulder and wraps his fist around a chunk of my long hair. Daniel has to pry him away.

"Guess he got used to you," Daniel says.

"He didn't have a choice with you driving off to make deals so much of the time." I step out of the car. Domino screeches as my travel companions drive off. I'm wearing jeans and a T-shirt given to me by a friend of Daniel's who lives in Saugatuck. Slung over my shoulder is a bag containing the clothes I wore the night we left and two kilos of pot, which were the reason for the Saugatuck trip. It took Daniel longer than he'd expected to hook up with his dealer. Daniel asked me to hold onto his stash for a while, "Nobody would ever suspect someone with a sweet face like yours of having pot in her closet," he said.

I open the front door and see Wanda in her recliner. "What are you doing here? I thought you'd be in Iowa by now," she says.

"Uh, no I went to Saugatuck." I go to the dining room table and grab the top letter from the stack of papers from Mt. Mercy. "Shit. I'm fucked," I say. "Freshman orientation was two days ago. They'll never let me in now."

"Watch your mouth, Laura."

"Yeah, yeah," I say.

"I knew you'd never pull it together for college. You're not as smart as your sisters. Never have been, never will be." She gloats like a child who's won a spelling bee. "But it's not the end of the world. I could use your help here when I go in for surgery, and you could go to that new College of DuPage that's just starting up."

"You're having surgery?"

"At St. Luke's. I'll be there for a few weeks. Then I'll be at Florence's, probably through November. You could stay here and keep an eye on the place, make yourself useful for a change."

"I don't know."

"Suit yourself. I don't really care what you do."

I plod to my old room. A double bed has replaced the bunk beds that were a mainstay of my childhood. I flop down on the mattress, close my eyes and think maybe I should enroll at the new junior college. But I don't know how I could get to classes. They're going to be spread all over the nearby suburbs until the campus is built. I have no license and no car.

THIRTY-ONE

October 1967

My skirt and sweater sets, blouses, dresses, jumpers, jeans and T-shirts are spread around Wanda's dining room, entry way and living room. Jewelry box, silver dollar collection, underwear, a few scarves and belts are on the kitchen counter. Boots and shoes are lined up near the front door. Warm wool coat is in the closet. I'm trying to decide what to take with me tomorrow, knowing that when Wanda returns from Florence's, she will throw away whatever I leave behind. She's threatened to toss my belongings in the trash when I've left before, but she hasn't followed through. This time, though, since I'm eighteen, she says if I go, no trace of me will be left here.

My latest plan is to move to the YWCA in Chicago and work until I figure out where to go to college in January. Since I didn't pull it together to call Mt. Mercy about my late paperwork and missed orientation, I enrolled at College of DuPage, the new regional community college, and planned to watch Wanda's house while she had surgery and then recuperated at Florence's. I bought a rusted, dented Corvair to drive to classes, but I got into a fender bender on the first day of school and was busted for driving without a license. A week later, I trembled in front of a merciful judge, who reduced the charge to driving with an expired permit. He also ignored the fact that no licensed driver was in the car, gave me a $10 fine, and that was it, for him anyway. For me, it confirmed that I am a major fuck up, and the whole thing eats at me day in, day out, one more thing added to the list of what I've done wrong, wrong, wrong.

A truck pulls into the driveway, headlights beaming through the dining room window. It's Shelby and her new friend Jed. They're going to help me settle a score before I move. I run out, glad to put off deciding what to bring to Chicago. I join my friends in the cab of Jed's '57 Chevy pickup, and we speed off, heading west. Finally, Jed parks the truck on a street lined with look-alike brick houses, all pale beige. He kills the engine, pulls the keys from the ignition and tosses them, jangling, one hand to the other.

"Stop that," Shelby barks. She grabs for the keys with one hand while passing a half-smoked Old Gold cigarette to me with the other. Jed clamps his fingers around the keys and stuffs them down the front pocket of his black jeans. "Oh no, girl. You're not getting these," he says.

Shelby tousles his long sun-streaked bangs. Jed is one of Shelby's new friends from a continuation high school she attends. She invited him along at the last minute since she couldn't get her mom's car tonight. I think Shelby and I could have done just fine on foot.

I take a drag on the Old Gold, blow a couple of smoke rings and put my fingers on the door handle. My heart pounds. "Ready?" I ask.

"You bet." Shelby grins, then blows smoke rings back at me.

"I can't wait to get this motherfucker," Jed says. He opens his door and eases himself out. Shelby follows. I throw the cigarette through the open window, open the door and step down. As I stomp the cigarette into the sparkling gravel, I wish the moon weren't so close to full. What if someone sees us well enough to identify us?

I walk to the back of the truck, which is loaded with tarps, brushes, a ladder, half-used cans of turpentine and other painting supplies. Jed stands in the bed. He hands Shelby a crowbar. Next, he picks up an axe.

"You want this?" he asks me.

"Sure." I grasp it with both hands and hold it at arm's length from my body, my eyes fixated on the blade, like a preschooler about to run with scissors.

""Hey, Jed, you got any extra paint? We could have some fun with that," Shelby says.

"Yeah, I got some bright yellow, leftover from a kitchen job."

"How are we going to get a can of opened paint over the fences without spilling it all over the place and making a racket?" I ask.

"Don't worry," Jed says. "I'll handle it." He stuffs a paint brush in each of his back pockets, takes a can of paint in one hand and a sledgehammer in the other and jumps out of the truck. Shelby closes the tailgate.

Then we creep up the driveway of the nearest house, along its side to the rear. Jed puts down the sledgehammer and paint. He jumps over the picket fence separating the backyard from the alley. I hand him his supplies and my axe, and leap over next. Holding the crowbar over her head with both hands, Shelby takes a running leap and clears the fence with at least a foot to spare. She bumps into Jed upon landing, who then bumps into me, causing the axe blade to scrape against my bare calf, shaving off a little skin.

"Damn." I look at the shallow scrape.

"Didn't I tell you to wear jeans instead of cutoffs?" Shelby says. She bends over to inspect my leg.

"Are you two planning to stand here all night or what?" Jed asks.

"Hey, you knocked into me, remember?" I say.

"Because she knocked into me." Jed points to Shelby, who is now crossing the alley. On the other side, down only about 30 feet, is the back of Hal's used car lot, where I purchased the piece-of-shit Corvair. It was $250 down the drain right off the bat, not to mention the cost of replacing tires that blew out every few days because the car was severely out of alignment. I tried to return the junker and get my money back, but Hal refused to take it, said I'd purchased it as is. And now, I have to pay the cost of repairing a dent in the brand new Buick Le Sabre that I plowed into when the Corvair's brakes failed. At least I think they failed. It's possible I was so flustered I stepped on the gas instead of the brakes when the car sped around a corner just as I was pulling out of a Standard station. Shelby says it doesn't matter if I hit the brakes or the gas. Old Hal should never have sold me, an unlicensed driver, a car in the first place, and he should never have sold anybody that wreck.

Hal's lot has a chain link fence topped with barbed wire. Behind that is an evergreen hedge with new growth sprouting from its formerly crew-cut top.

"Crap, I didn't know it would have barbed wire," I say.

"Don't worry." Jed throws the sledgehammer over the fence. It thwacks the hedge, snapping branches as it sinks in several inches. Jed quickly scales the fence while holding the paint in one hand and drops gracefully to the other side. Shelby and I stare up at the barbed wire. I tap one of my sneakers in the fence. It wobbles. I back away. Shelby throws her crowbar over. Then she begins her climb. She slows as she nears the top.

"Don't stop now. The faster you go, the better," Jed says.

Shelby briefly stands to her full height, leaps, clears the barbed wire and lands softly in the dirt just the other side of the evergreens.

"Come on, slowpoke," she says. I dread the barbed wire, certain I'll rip my skin trying to lift myself over it. Then I see an apple tree growing against the fence at the corner of the lot. I run to the tree, throw the axe over the fence, and begin my climb. When a sturdy branch is within reach, I grab hold and walk my feet the rest of the way up the fence. I crouch at the top, reach for a higher branch and climb into the tree. Then I leap down to the other side. Shelby and Jed are at the bottom waiting.

"Chicken shit," Jed says.

"Hey, knock it off," Shelby says. "She made it didn't she?" She socks him in his well-muscled arm.

"Where should we start?" I survey the hodgepodge of cars. Many makes and models are spread over a couple acres of gravel.

"Look at those Mustangs over there." Shelby points to the other side of the lot.

"No, they're too near the road. See those streetlights? And the traffic? We have to stay near the fence," Jed says.

"All the good stuff is in front," I say.

"No, look, look here. There's a Lincoln Continental just achin' to get smashed. It's mine," Shelby says. She runs to the sparkling vehicle and slams the front windshield with the crowbar. It barely makes a scratch. She hits again, harder. Still, she doesn't have much success.

"Let me help," Jed says. He puts the paint down, lifts the sledgehammer with both hands and smashes it against the windshield, which cracks upon impact like thin ice on a river. He moves on to a white Pontiac GTO and walks around the car, smashing each of the windows. I lift the axe and slam it into the plastic rear window of a red Chevy Biscayne convertible. It gives but doesn't tear. I pull out a pocketknife, open it and stab the window. This time it rips but not as easily as I'd imagined it would. I walk to the front and scratch stick figures in the hood with the knife. Shelby knocks into the can of paint. It falls over and spills onto the gravel. She lifts it up and begins pouring it all over the Lincoln.

I slink over to her. "Want to pour some of that into the Chevy?" I ask.

Just then a gruff man's voice calls through the darkness, "What's going on here?"

Lights turn on in a little shack Hal uses for an office. The door creeks open; a figure steps out onto the porch.

"Run," Jed cries out. He throws the sledgehammer clear over the fence from twenty feet away and follows it. I rush to the axe, lift it and run. Shelby is already halfway over, crowbar in one hand. Floodlights come on as I grab the fence and climb.

"Stop!" the man's voice commands. But I am moving so fast there's no way I could stop even if I wanted to. I feel like I'm about to fly. At the top of the fence, I flip my legs over my hands and somersault down, twisting my ankle as I hit the ground, landing on the seat of my pants. Blood leaks from scratches on my forearms, both of which had brushed the barbed wire. I run across the alley, over the picket fence, through the yard, and past the side of the house where Jed's truck is parked. He's already turned on the engine, and the truck pulls away as I climb in.

"That really sucked. What does old Hal do, sleep there?" Jed says, speeding away and turning the corner as I slam the door closed.

"Apparently." I take the pack of Old Gold filters from the dashboard and light one with trembling hands. I pass it to Shelby and light another for myself. "You want one?" I ask Jed.

"A cancer stick? No thanks," he says. He runs a stop sign, going about forty miles per hour. Shelby and I don't say a word. We know we have to get away fast. I clutch the dashboard, my knuckles white.

"That was harder than I thought it would be," Shelby says.

"Well, we did a little damage," I say.

"Let's go to my house and celebrate," Shelby says. "My mom won't be home until midnight, and I have a bottle of Drambuie in my closet."

"No thanks," I say. "I'm moving to the city tomorrow, remember?"

"There's still time to change your mind about all that," Shelby says.

"Look, no offense or anything, but all I'm doing now is hanging out with you and Jed and your other new friends."

"So?"

"You're all still in high school. I should have gone to Mount Mercy, after all."

Jed merges the truck onto the highway where his speed blends with the rest of the traffic.

"Nobody forced you to stay here," she says.

"I didn't think I could pay for it."

"But you got money when you turned eighteen, right?"

"Yep, a check for $1,200, and with my savings account, I would have had enough for the whole year. Wanda must have known all along I'd have enough and just didn't want to tell me."

"Why didn't you go when you got the money then?" Jed asks. He pulls a beer can from the back of the cab, opens it and takes a chug.

"Because classes were already underway before my birthday, and I hadn't filled out any of the forms they sent me over the summer. How could I have just shown up?

"Well, what's done is done, right?" He passes his beer to Shelby.

I look down at blood drops splattered on my shoes. Jed exits the highway and makes his way through peaceful, tree-lined side streets. When he pulls to a stop at Wanda's, I leap out of the truck.

"Next time you want to do some damage, I'm in," Jed says.

"I think I've had enough of that," I say.

"Call me." Shelby throws me a kiss.

"Hey, Shelby, you've got paint in your hair," I say.

She grabs a clump of her red tresses and inspects the ends. "Damn. How am I going to get that out?"

"Your mom will know how to do it," I say.

"Yeah, that's right." She waves goodbye. The truck putts off down the street and around the corner.

Inside the house, everything is dark. My right ankle throbs. I limp to the kitchen sink, turn on the faucet and stick my bloody arms under the cold water. I remember the axe shining in the moonlit alley. No way am I ever going back for it.

THIRTY-TWO

November 1967

Trixie and i drop dimes on the counter by our half-empty coffee cups, say good-bye to silver-haired Betty and exit Pixley's. Splashed by golden rays from street lamps and passing headlights, I inhale Chicago's potpourri of industrial scents, open my jacket to the biting wind and race along the sidewalk. Trixie follows. Her red waves bouncing behind her, she titters and wheezes as she closes the gap between us. Betty just asked if Trixie and I would like to work at the diner where she's been dispensing coffee, pie and advice to patrons at her counter for 30 years. We both declined. I sleep late in my sliver of a room at the YWCA and spend afternoons typing for a company that loans parents money for college tuition. A dull, low-paying job. Nevertheless, I'm sure I have better prospects than Pixley's in store. Trixie thinks she does, too. So does Patty, another friend I've made since moving to the Y.

The three of us are especially convinced about Patty's prospects for glory. She's got a Twiggy body; long, honey-colored hair that shines like it's perpetually in a sunbeam; and some of the biggest brown eyes you've every seen. She moved from Milwaukee to attend some modeling school, and a fancy agency has already signed her. Patty's boyfriend is a blond version of Warren Beatty. She has it all.

Trixie's hair fans out like a broom at the ends from too many changes of color. She also slaps on multiple layers of makeup as though she were a Broadway actress preparing to take the stage, a habit I'm trying to break her of. I have at least convinced her to pamper her hair, so we're off to Walgreen's right now to pick up some Clairol Condition.

"You won't believe how silky your hair will feel when you're done," I say, as we walk into the store and veer toward the hair care products.

"Maybe I should switch up the color, too," Trixie says. She picks up a box of Casual dye in a dark shade of auburn.

"Put that back!" I try to snatch it from her hands.

She darts to another aisle. I briefly consider picking Flex conditioner instead of Clairol because I've heard good things about it, but decide on the product I know. Package in hand, I round the corner just in time to see Trixie crash into a man with wavy black hair, smiling dark eyes and a winning grin. The Casual pops out of her hands, flies down the aisle, lands on the floor. The man's thick woolen coat swirls around his body as he grasps her elbow with a black-gloved hand, helping her regain her balance. She looks him in the eyes, and falls forward into his arms—on purpose, I'm sure. I trot over, pick up the box, slap it in the middle of a nearby Kleenex display, and approach Trixie and the man. They are gazing into each other's eyes and talking as though they've known each other for years.

"Yes, yes we'd love to," Trixie says.

"Love to what?" I ask.

"Oh, Laura, this is Manuel. Manuel, Laura." She gestures at each of us in turn. Manuel and I nod at each other. "Manuel and his friend Hubert are going to take us out to dinner tonight," Trixie adds.

The name Hubert makes me think of a skinny middle-aged bachelor living in an efficiency apartment above a pizza parlor. I envision someone who spends all of his time playing solitaire when he's not at work refurbishing old adding machines and toasters in a warehouse somewhere.

"I don't think so," I say. "I'm not dating, Trixie. You know that."

"A pretty young girl like you not dating? Why is that?" Manuel asks.

"She's stuck on some guy who's traveling around the world and doesn't even write," Trixie says.

"Thanks a lot. Make me sound nice and pathetic," I say.

Manuel smiles. "Don't think of it as a date, then. It'll be four friends going out for some fine Italian food. Though I must say I'm smitten with your friend."

Trixie silently mouths "please" while Manuel's attention is on me.

"I don't know. It's the middle of the week."

"What do you care? You don't have to start typing envelopes until 12:30," Trixie goads.

I think of the month of mornings I just spent in secretarial school in an attempt to increase my typing speed and brighten my job prospects. Our classroom was crammed with young women sitting in long rows, each of us behind a Remington electric typewriter, trying to hit the right keys as our perfectly coiffed middle-aged instructor blabbed on. She told us how to do everything properly— not just letters and memos positioned perfectly on the page, but also how to dress, how to apply lipstick, how to sit at a desk, how to speak with proper respect to our superiors, how to make coffee, how to look busy when we have nothing to do. I'd look up from the keyboard occasionally during these lectures, thinking I'd share my exasperation and disbelief with some of the other students, but no eyes met mine. I was the only nonbeliever in a sea of aspirants. They reminded me of the victims in the old movie *Invasion of the Body*

Snatchers. I feared if I stuck around too long, I would be snatched, too. So now my mornings are free until I figure out what college I can enroll in.

Trixie, Manuel and I walk toward the checkout. "I care because we have a curfew. I don't want to get thrown out of the Y. Patty and I aren't moving to our apartment for another two days," I say.

"I still don't think you should go," Trixie says. "Can you believe the two of them are moving in together and leaving me behind?" she asks Manuel.

"How could you?" Manuel reproaches me.

I shrug. "We asked her, and she said she didn't want to come." I offer Trixie the conditioner package as we get in line.

Manuel snatches it. "Allow me," he says to Trixie.

"Oh my, I, I couldn't." She gazes up at him in her best imitation of Julie Christie.

"It's nothing." He pulls out his wallet and puts the conditioner on the counter along with some Ambush cologne. "You want to look beautiful for me tonight, don't you?" He brushes strands of hair from her eyes.

"Who's the Ambush for?" I ask.

"Ah ... my sister." He averts his eyes and hands the cashier a twenty. After we leave Walgreen's, he insists on walking us to the Y. He kisses Trixie on the cheek at the front door.

"See you at seven, my dear," he says.

"Seven it is." She is breathless, as though she's just run up a flight of stairs. When we step inside, she says, "This is it. Manuel's the one. I've just met the man of my dreams."

"Aren't you engaged to that guy, what's his name, David, you know, the one you met at the USO last month?" I ask.

"David? Oh, he's like the ace up my sleeve."

"No wonder they have rules about not dating those guys. You're not supposed to play games with soldiers headed for Vietnam. It's seriously messed up," I say.

"I just wanted him to have a good time before going off to war. A lot of those guys are never coming back, you know."

"Please don't remind me. I get so upset thinking about it."

"Listen. Before David left I thought I could wait for him, really, but then I realized I can't waste my life pining over someone who's not here, especially when better opportunities come along," she says.

"You'll have plenty of opportunity tonight, I suppose. You might suddenly realize Hubert is really the one, not Manuel."

The elevator stops at my floor. I step out. Trixie follows like an orphaned puppy. "Come on out with us. It wouldn't kill you to go to a nice restaurant for a change," she says.

I look at her eyes, which are festooned with thick black liner and at least five coats of mascara, and I think of all the laughs we've had late at night, sitting cross-legged on my narrow little bed, eating candy from vending machines, when we're both supposed to be dieting so we can be as beautiful as Patty. I wonder if Trixie is trying to hide something under all that makeup, but I don't know what it could be. "I'm not going to go, but come knock on my door when you get back. I want to hear all about it."

"Yeah, sure," she says. But she doesn't visit that night, nor is she in the cafeteria for breakfast the next morning. I knock on her door again when Patty and I are packed and set to move out, but there is no answer.

THIRTY-THREE

December 1967

DECEMBER'S ANEMIC LIGHT SLIPS THROUGH SOOTY windows, illuminating cracks in the ceiling and spots of dried puke on the itchy blanket that covers my goose-bumped knees, thighs, breasts. Breathing into my ear in his sleep is Little Joe, a not so little thug who hijacked my life the day Patty and I moved into this shabby Old Town apartment.

Little Joe's hairy arm pins my waist. Groggy, I vaguely recall being far, far away, traveling to mental realms I've never encountered before. Relieved that his jeans are on and zipped up, I roll out from under his grasp and cling to the opposite side of a bed so soft I feel it could drown me if I don't get up. The last thing I remember was being at the toilet, too dizzy to stand or even kneel. I barfed all over a shaggy green rug. Beautiful, brittle Patty lifted my head and called for help.

I sit up and pause, sensing I was pulled apart and slapped back together with essential parts missing. I dig around in the bed and find the top sheet balled up at my feet. I pull it up and wrap it around my torso, tossing the blanket aside. Little Joe opens his eyes and smiles, revealing a row of crooked teeth that seem too small for his mouth. "Hey, girrrrrrl, you woke up. I was gettin' worried."

"What time is it?" I survey the room, looking for something to throw on.

"What day is it? That's what ya ought to be askin'" He sits up. "Okay, what day is it, then?"

"Dunno. Les see. Yestadeh was Tuesdeh, so it's Wedsdeh."

"You mean I've been out since Friday night? And you just left me here?"

"I was purdy high too, but I was here, don worry. Les have us a kiss." He leans his pockmarked face toward me. I push him away, cringing at the proximity of his desire. "C'mon, you wan me. Yous men ta be mine now that I watched out for yous."

"I'm not yours, I never was yours, I never will be yours." I stand up, wrap the sheet tighter around myself and tuck in the edges to make a sloppy sarong. I stumble out the door and wobble toward the bathroom. The apartment is eerily silent, no footsteps in the kitchen, no chairs squeaking with shifting weight, no conversations in the air, no sound of someone toking on a pipe.

"Hol on," Little Joe calls after me. "I love you. An' you love me too, chicken. Heck, we din even do it. You was too zonked. I wan you awake wen we do it."

I lurch into the bathroom, close the door and lock it. In the medicine cabinet mirror, I see a silly girl with a pimple forming in the middle of her chin—looks like it's going to be a bad one. I splash my face with water, take a swig of Listerine, swish it around in my mouth, spit into the sink. I don't know how I am going to get rid of Little Joe. Everything I've tried so far hasn't worked.

I perch on the edge of the bathtub, turn on the tap, run my fingers through the cascading water. When the water runs hot, I put the stopper in the drain and squeeze in some golden, gooey Breck concentrate, the closest thing to bubble bath available. I think if only I'd gone to Mount Mercy, I wouldn't be in this mess right now, but then I realize, no, I'd have gotten into some mess or other no matter where I'd gone.

I unwrap the sheet. It drops to a floor dusted with hairs from people I've never met, grime from the Chicago streets, the odd toenail. I study my naked body in the full-length mirror tacked to the door and slap my bulging thighs in disgust. Except for the beginning of this year when I was with Michael and then at boarding school, I haven't stopped overeating since that awful night with Kip. No matter how strong my resolve to diet is when I get up in the morning and have grapefruit or something like it, by late afternoon I'm grabbing fistfuls of Lay's potato chips or downing M&Ms and SweeTarts like a starving grizzly bear raiding someone's garbage.

I lift Michael's ring over my head, ease it onto the corner of the tub near a bar of soap and coil the chain to envelop the treasure like a snail's shell. I step into the water and lower myself, welcoming the painful heat. I submerge my head, trying to clear my mind, wishing I could turn back the clock, do the last couple of years over, so I'd never fall for Kip, skip school with Shelby, take drugs with Daniel, gain weight, get drunk, lose my ability to concentrate, or slip into emotional quicksand.

I turn off the tap and recall the day Patty and I arrived at our furnished flat, with all of the belongings we could stuff into two cabs. Our suitcases and bags were spread on the sidewalk after the cabs took off. Little Joe was standing at our door. Hands in the pockets of his silver-studded black leather jacket, he loomed over both of us, asked us to let him in, said he grew up in this very building and a friend still lived here.

We let him in; his black eyes looked so sad. He darted up to the first floor landing while Patty and I loaded our arms with coats and bags. He ran back down, said his friend wasn't answering. So he put one of our boxes in front of the building's door to keep it open, picked up two suitcases, and said, "Les go. Les get your stuff up."

"You don't have to help us," I said. Patty and I began climbing the stairs.

"Yous chicks thing yous too good fer help from little ole me? Come on." Hoisting one suitcase to each shoulder, he leaped up the stairs two at a time, almost knocking Patty and me over as he passed us. He was standing at the second floor door when I arrived and pulled out my keys.

"How did you know it was this one?" I asked.

"Benny downstairs, he my buddy. He said this the empty."

As soon as I unlocked the door, he barged in. And as Patty and I stepped inside, another burly guy came racing up the stairs in search of Little Joe.

"Hey, Little Joe, did you see that cop car come around the corner?" he asked.

"Hey, Twister. Yeah, thas why I came in. They's afta me. I was hopin' to lay low with Benny, but he ain der. "

"Them pigs parked right down the block. They's just sittin' there."

"Guess I gots ta say here for a while."

He said he'd stay just until Benny came home, but he hasn't left our flat since, unless one of his many junkie friends is in the apartment to let him back in when he returns. It turns out the day Little Joe claimed our apartment, he had just escaped from police custody and returned to Old Town, where he'd grown up. A 17-year-old who looks a decade older, he said he's been in trouble with the law ever since he stole a car when he was 12. On the street, he walks head down, his leather collar up high around his neck and a black knit cap pulled past his eyebrows. Word got out among neighborhood junkies that what was supposed to be Patty's and my apartment is a great place to crash. Little Joe says if Patty or I go to the pigs, he'll fix it so no man will ever want to look at either of us again. He grins then, like it's just a big joke, but it has stopped us from doing more than asking him to leave in as many polite ways we can think of.

Last Friday a guy had some greenish-yellow powder and was mixing it in water at the kitchen table. I asked what it was. He said it was an asthma medicine called Asmador, and he was taking it to get high.

"Does it work?" I asked.

"Sure does." he replied. His smile was dreamy.

Eager, as always, to escape the putrid thoughts that leak into my mind like sewage from a broken pipe, I dumped five heaping tablespoonsful in a glass of water and gulped the bitter mixture down. Shortly thereafter, I began seeing friends right next to me talking into my ear, friends who are nowhere near Chicago. And I saw walls where there are none, and open space where there really were walls. I crashed into plaster every few minutes trying to get around the apartment. Worst of all, I saw terrible, tiny all-white creatures, standing upright and dressed in purple hooded robes. They stood about two feet tall, had long, slightly slanted slits for eyes and sharp little flippers instead of hands and legs. They didn't speak; they had no mouths. They communicated telepathically, conveying that they will always know where I am, I will never escape them, and I am doomed. Recalling this, I tremble in the hot bath water. I never want to see those creatures or anything like them again.

The doorknob jiggles. Someone knocks. I stiffen and pull my knees to my chest.

"Laura, it's me. Can you let me in?" Patty says. "My dad's outside. We were almost at the freeway when I remembered I forgot some things."

"Your dad? What's going on?" I stand, step out of the tub, grab a plush black towel from a nearby rack and wrap my dripping body as I step over to unlock and open the door. In the hall is Patty, bundled up head to toe—hat scarf, gloves, boots.

"Uh, that's my towel." She rushes into the room, snatches her toothpaste, toothbrush and assorted cosmetics from around the sink and the top of the toilet and puts them into a paper bag.

I take the towel off and hold it out to her. "Sorry it's wet," I say.

"No, no, put it back on," she says. "I'll tell my mom I lost it when I get home."

"You're going home?" I wrap the towel around myself again.

"Well, you know, we never got a phone, and I didn't call for a while. So Dad and Mom got worried. He took off work today and drove down here. You should have seen how mad he got when he saw all those slobs crashed in the living room. I swear his face turned bright red. He didn't have to say a word. They all got up and skittered out the back door like roaches when you turn the light on."

"Wow ... "

"He says it'll be a cold day in hell before I leave Milwaukee again, too." She backs out the door.

"Well, I guess this is goodbye then, for a while anyway," I say.

"He said I can't ever see you again either because you dragged me into this." She looks at me like I'm a rattler about to strike.

I feel wounded, realizing it's not just her father who's blaming me for the troubles we've had. I follow her out the bathroom door and walk with her down the hall. We halt, facing each other at the door.

"So, you weren't even going to say goodbye or check to see if I'd woken up or anything?" I ask.

"My dad is so mad. ... He said you should go home, too."

"Home, right. " I open the door, wondering where my home is now.

She clutches the bag of toiletries to her chest and steps into the outer hallway. I close the door and return to the bathroom where I slip Michael's ring back on and tiptoe into the bedroom. Little Joe is snoring. Quietly I don the warm woolen Navy pants I bought at an Army surplus store and two rumpled sweaters I pull from a pile of clothes on the floor. From the closet I grab the suitcases I brought from the Y and quietly stuff in as many of my things as I can. I regret that I'm leaving behind a toaster oven and antique Underwood typewriter Uncle John gave me. But I have to get away fast, while Little Joe is still asleep.

Once I'm safely out of the building and around the first corner, the only place I can think of to go is back to the Y. So I set off, crunching through the snow to the rhythm of Christmas lights tapping in the bitter wind against brick buildings I pass along the way.

THIRTY-FOUR

January 1968

I STRETCH OUT ON A TWIGGY-WIDTH bed at the Y in a room just like the one I occupied before the apartment fiasco. I survey the scratched up dresser; small closet with door ajar, clothes and papers spilling out; the bare window above the dresser offering a view of soot-covered brick. Everything's the same as it was yesterday, but it all looks different—more alive, even promising. I've been awake all night reading, my back on the mattress, legs up, toes tapping against the streaked wallpaper's faded fleur-de-lis design. It's my third time through a slender book Darius gave me.

Darius is a pain. He does collections for Tuition Solutions, where my boss, Trish, welcomed me back after I went AWOL from work during the Little Joe debacle. She even says if I improve my attendance, I'll progress to typing letters and be given the title of new business secretary, and since the company's expanding, someday I could even have her job. Trish, who is gorgeous with olive complexion and thick, black hair, could probably be a model. She spent four years typing her afternoons away here after attending classes at Loyola in the mornings. She wants me to do the same. She's even called the university's admissions office to see if she can speed an application through for me.

I flip through Darius' book again, and think that Trish seems genuinely happy and full of good will for me, which I don't think I deserve because I don't want to follow in her footsteps. But I haven't a clue what

I really want to do. So I'm back to typing envelopes, and Darius fawns over me incessantly. He thinks I'm going to be his girlfriend one of these days. He completely overestimates his appeal to the opposite sex. But the ideas in the little book in my hands have captured me. I think I've found everything I've been looking for in fewer than 150 pages—from whiny, gawky Darius, of all people. I can't believe it. For weeks he's been talking about how I should sign up for this communications class he took, and I've told him I don't need a class in how to communicate. I know how to carry on a conversation, after all.

But he finally talked me into going to an introductory lecture last night. It was in a shabby apartment in Uptown, and the middle-aged guy in charge wore a wrinkled chartreuse shirt and had stains on the front of his baggy, knit pants. He would be as conspicuous in a place like Hinsdale, Illinois, as a fly trapped indoors, bumping against a windowpane. But there was a sparkle in his eyes, and lots of laughter in the crowd of about thirty people, most of whom were young and curious, just like me. I've decided to give the class a try. What harm could it do? It might help me concentrate again, be more stable, happier.

I am taken with the main point of this philosophy with a funny name, Dianetics, and a sort of advancement on that with an even funnier name, Scientology. The idea behind it is that much of what plagues people today is based on past hurts we keep stored in our unconscious somewhere, and instead of suffering, we can do something about them so the past no longer haunts us and makes us feel bad and do weird things. That stupid psychiatrist I visited barely spoke to me and didn't offer me one useful idea. Even Mrs. Henderson, the school psychologist who genuinely cared for me, never said anything about how I could part ways with my ever-present sorrow without killing myself in the process.

I feel on fire in a really good way. At long last, I think I've found the key to personal empowerment. I'm about to put an end to the horrible fog that catches me off guard, seeps into my bones and immobilizes me, sometimes for days at a time. Maybe now I'll be able to make a decision, like where I'm really going to go to college, and then follow through on it—no more twisted complications.

I hear two knocks at the door. I open it, and there is Trixie in her pajamas and robe. Pink foam rollers are stuck every which way in her thick hair. She's grinning like she's just had some dynamite pot. I haven't gotten together with her since I returned from Old Town, so I'm eager to catch up.

"Want to have breakfast with me?" she asks.

"Breakfast? Yeah, sure, I can do that."

"I've got big news for you," she says.

"I've got some big news for you too."

"Fifteen minutes?"

"Yeah, yeah." I close the door and throw the book up in the air and catch it a few times. Right now I feel higher than I ever did on the best of the pills Daniel handed me when we spent long afternoons skipping school and riding all over Hinsdale. And I'm not on drugs. I haven't taken any since I downed all that asthma medicine. Darius said last night staying off drugs is part of the key to living a good life. When I take the introductory class, I'll still have to maneuver around all of Darius' feelings for me, but I'm sure the class will help with that. Plus, I'll have something useful to share with Michael when he returns. He won't be the only one who has grown wiser during our time apart. He might actually learn a thing or two from me.

I leap out of bed and start dancing around the room. Then I grab a roll of tape designed with red footprints on a beige background. It's the same size as regular tape and in the same kind of dispenser.

I break off segments of varying lengths and stick them willy-nilly on a piece of 11" x 17" newsprint I rip from a pad I bought for no particular reason other than I think it's good to have stuff like that around. When I'm done, I tape my creation to the wall above the bed, convinced I've done something extraordinarily artistic. I do another, and another. Soon, footprint-covered newsprint pages cover the walls, doors, window and dresser. I survey the room, satisfied. Yes, I think, yes, I am breaking free already. All that from attending one lecture and reading an introductory book! I imagine once I finish the class I'll be like a genius, free at last to be comfortable in the world no matter where I am and who I'm with.

Seeing that it's been twenty minutes since Trixie stopped by, I pull a sweater from under the bed and throw it over my shoulders. I tuck the book into my purse, pull a small hairbrush out and head for the elevator down to the cafeteria, brushing my hair as I walk. I haven't slept even one minute, but I feel as energized as a child released from a classroom for recess. I can't wait to tell Trixie about my discovery.

I drink in the smell of breakfast fare and wonder why more people haven't made the same discovery I have. Moving through the cafeteria line, I order oatmeal, bacon and orange juice. After I pay the cashier, I see Trixie waving to me from a table across the room. She's wearing a tweed suit. Her hair is brushed into smooth waves, and her makeup is applied.

"You sure got fixed up fast, Trix. You look nice."

"Oh, well, yes. I have the best-ever news."

"You got some high-paying job downtown?" I ask.

"Nah, something better."

"It couldn't be better than what I've found." I sit down across from her.

"What's that?"

"I've just found the answer not just to my own problems, but to everyone's problems," I say. I pull the book from my purse and toss it on the table. "It's all in there."

"Go on, Laura. That's downright silly."

"Think about it: no more sadness weighing you down, no more riots in the ghettoes, no more war in Vietnam or anywhere else, no more poverty, no more kids bullying each other on the playground, no more conflict that can't be resolved by effective communication."

"Well, I can tell you're excited about it; that's for sure."

"And no more overeating." I stir my oatmeal. "No more addiction period, for anybody."

"Nothing works like that," Trixie says.

I push the book toward her plate. "Read this, and you'll change your mind."

"Oh, I don't have time to read that. I've got a stack of Harlequins I haven't read yet." She sips her coffee.

"It'll only take an hour. You can borrow it. I practically have it memorized now anyway."

"No, I really can't. I'm heading downtown this morning, and I'd like you to come along."

"Why?"

"I'm getting married. I want you to be a witness."

"Manuel popped the question?"

"Manuel, are you kidding? That creep is married, and somehow just forgot to tell me."

"Oh, sorry to hear that. Who, then? That boy you dumped for Manuel? Is he back from Vietnam already?

"No, no. My intended's name is Donny. I met him two weeks ago at the USO, and he's just amazing. We've spent every day and evening together since we met—no nights, though, not until after we get married. Then I'm going with him wherever he goes."

"Well, you can't exactly go to Vietnam, can you?"

"He's already been there and he got wounded. They aren't sending him back. He's going to make a career in the military, though. And, you know, by the time we're in our forties he'll have earned a good pension. Then there's all that great education stuff. Donny's smart."

"Wow! I don't know what to say. Another military guy, huh?"

"Not just another military guy. The love of my life," Trixie says. "Plus he said he'd adopt Cole." She pulls a picture of a smiling young boy on a swing. She's behind him pushing. "He's four years old, now," she says.

"You have a son?"

"Yes, yes I do."

"You had a baby when you were 16?"

Trixie looks down and fiddles with the buttons of her suit jacket. "No, ah … no, I was twenty."

"But you told me you're twenty now."

"I lied."

"Why?"

"Why not?"

"You've been pretending to be someone you're not."

"I thought you and Patty wouldn't hang out with me if you knew I was older and had a kid."

"Where's his dad?" I tap the picture of the boy with my fingertips.

"I don't want to talk about his dad." She looks toward the cafeteria line, which is crowded with young women, many of whom will soon be populating the typing pools of Chicago's downtown high rises.

"That bad, huh?"

"Yeah, you know, I thought he loved me, but as soon as Cole came along, he left me all alone, high and dry. I couldn't raise Cole on my own. I just fell apart."

"Who's taking care of him?"

"My mom, in North Carolina, but it's getting to be too much for her."

"I don't suppose you and what's his name will be able to go to a lecture with me tonight, then."

"No, Mr. and Mrs. Donny Tremaine will be on a plane headed to Kansas so I can meet his parents before he reports back for duty," she says.

"You can keep the book, then, Mrs. Donny Tremaine. I can get another one tonight."

"So, will you be my witness?"

"Sure."

"Donny's coming for us in an hour."

"Just as long as I can get to my stupid job by 12:30."

"Sure. We'll take a cab back and drop you off right at the curb."

"Well, congratulations, then." I take a few bites of oatmeal.

"Thanks," she replies.

Feeling too full of energy to be hungry, I stand and pick up my tray. "I'd better go get dressed," I say. "Why don't you read that book while I'm getting ready. It'll change your life. I just know it will."

"Sure, sure." She picks it up and thumbs through the pages, then puts it down and stares at her hands.

As I walk to the elevator, I think that one of the dresses scattered about my room is probably in good enough shape to wear to City Hall. I'll just hang it up in the bathroom so the wrinkles can steam out while I'm in the shower. That'll do for a so-called liar of a friend I probably won't see again after today.

213

THIRTY-FIVE

February 1968

GRAMMA EASES INTO A CHAIR LIKE a patient forced into a bath too hot. Her gnarled fingers hold fast to the carved wooden arm rests until her weight is fully supported by the green brocade seat. Then she lets go, heaving a sign of relief. I bend over and kiss her on the forehead before I settle in on the couch, where she used to hold me in her lap and play *This Little Piggy* with my toes long ago. Back then, love radiated from her stout, warm body. Even now, her smile reaches across the living room like a rainbow.

It's been more than month since I've seen her. When I first moved to the Y, I thought I'd visit every weekend, but that never happened. All the years when Wanda wouldn't allow me to call Gramma—because it was a toll call—seem to have clipped whatever drive I might have had to reach out to loved ones I don't see day to day. I believe this is a serious character defect. I cross and re-cross my legs at the ankles and think about how I disappoint everyone who cares about me, not that there are that many people who care. But that's just as well, fewer people to let down.

I twist the leather strap of my shoulder bag. "I'm leaving tomorrow for Washington, D.C."

"Washington, D.C. My, oh, my. Why so far away?"

I brace for a lecture, but no hint of judgment infects her voice, no sigh of exasperation leaks into the room. "Well, there's this course I took on communication, and I got a lot out of it, and they've got a whole lot of other courses I can take in D.C." I don't mention that it will also get me far away from Little Joe, who's been outside of the Y every day lately, lurking in doorways, waiting for me to come out. He walks behind me, muttering that I am his and he's going to get me in the end no matter what he has to do.

A few days ago, he even came into the lobby of the Y, made a scene. He wouldn't stop calling for me. The security guard had difficulty throwing him out because he's so strong. Later, he waited outside of the building where I work at the end of the day. Darius and I were heading out to talk about my next step after the communications class. Little Joe thought we were on a date. He grabbed Darius by the lapels of his suit, pulled him close and growled, "Stay 'way fum 'er." Then he let go, and Darius stumbled backward.

"Hey, man," Darius said. He threw his arms up in the air. "It's not what you think. Laura won't give me the time of day."

"Little Joe, stop it!" I reached out to touch the sleeve of his leather jacket. He brushed my arm away and glared at Darius. "I wadn't born yestadeh, bub. Stay way. Nes time, I'll come wid a gun." Then he turned around and disappeared into the rush hour crowd.

"Where did you find him?" Darius asked. "He's just like something out of *West Side Story*, or maybe Marlon Brando in *On The Waterfront*, only with a little Frankenstein mixed in. Is he serious about the gun?"

"I don't think so," I said.

Since then, Darius hasn't been bugging me to go out with him as much, which is a relief, but Little Joe is another matter. I never know when he'll be standing in a doorway across the street from the Y or near my job waiting for me to come out.

The sound of Gramma's voice brings my thoughts back to the safety of her flat. "I thought you were going to keep working at that nice little office in the afternoons and enroll at Loyola," Gramma says.

"That's what Trish wants me to do, you know, because that's what she did."

"It sounds like a good plan to me, except I think you should study to be a dietician and work in a hospital."

"I'm really not interested in Trish's plan. I'll die if I have to keep typing envelopes much longer. I don't know how she managed to work there all this time. The bare white walls; the minute hand creeping around the wall clock, the rows of women at metal desks typing all day long; the managers and executives in offices around the perimeter—it's all so boring. Trish thinks it's a big deal that she looks out at the Water Tower."

"It did survive the great Chicago Fire. It's a famous landmark."

"You know she's never been anywhere? At least I've been to Boston."

"Her life doesn't sound so bad, dear. She has a good job."

"I suppose."

"Why not stay in Chicago and study communications at Loyola?" Gramma asks.

"I'm pretty sure they don't teach this in college. It's something entirely new, where you actually learn how to communicate effectively in real life, not in some classroom. Plus there's a lot more. Communication is just the beginning. There are classes that can help me get my life together."

"This is awfully sudden, dear." She fidgets with the buttons on the flowered robe I bought her a couple years ago for her birthday.

I was embarrassed at how much Gramma liked the robe when she pulled it out of the bag the day I gave it to her. She touched it like it was fine china, just because it came from me. It was a cheap discount store robe. I hadn't even wrapped it. I should have saved up my money and bought her something better. But I never save my money. I feel there is so little of it, why even try?

"I know. It is sudden, but I think it's the right thing," I say.

"But where will you stay?"

"There's this girl I went to high school with. Alice. Her family moved to Virginia, and she says I can stay there as long as I want. She has the whole basement fixed up. That's where her room is, and she has an extra bed there, and the walls are painted black, but when you turn on a special light, there's all this bright day-glo paint everywhere that lights up. She even has a drum set. I've always wanted to learn how to play the drums. And she's kind of between things right now, like I am."

"You could always stay here with me. I have plenty of room."

"I'm all set to go now; I've got my ticket and everything. Maybe after I finish all the communications courses. Then I might be able to come back and stay with you and go to school."

"That would be grand," she says. Her face tilts toward the window. I know she's looking at her memories, not outside.

"Yes, it would be grand," I say. But I'm thinking just the opposite. If I came to Gramma's to live, I'd end up doing something stupid, like I always do. I'd promise to cook dinner, and I'd go out with friends instead, get drunk, sleep on some stranger's couch, and come back to Gramma's a day or two later. Or Little Joe would find me and start ringing Gramma's bell, yelling up from the sidewalk, demanding to know where I am. Gramma would end up hating me.

She pulls a $10 bill from her pocket. "How about if you get us some fish chips for lunch?"

I haven't thought of those fresh, deep-fried chunks of goodness in years. We used to pick them up on Sundays when Daddy drove our family to visit Gramma every week. I can't stomach most kinds of fish, but my mouth used to water at the thought of biting into one of those hot, greasy, perfectly seasoned, only-in-Chicago fish chips. "Is that place still open?"

"Yes, indeed, dear."

"I'll be happy to do that." I rise from the couch and take the bill from her hands.

"Get some potato salad, too, and maybe some soda," she says.

"Will do." I walk out the door and down the stairs to the ground floor. When I step onto the front walk, someone steps backward into the shadows of a doorway across the street. I wonder if Little Joe followed me here. I pull the collar of my coat up around my neck and quicken my steps.

THIRTY-SIX

March 1968

ALICE IS LIKE A CHURNING POT of pasta with starchy bubbles boiling over and down her sides. I can't figure out what set her off. She seemed interested enough when Bill started class by explaining how the exercise sequence would help all of us interact better. But right after he asked us to arrange our chairs in two rows facing each other and begin the first exercise, Alice pulled her chair to the opposite side of the room and sat, arms crossed over her heaving chest, face flushed.

Bill looms over her now, all six foot three inches of him, looking like an aging version of James Taylor strung out on speed. "Come on, Alice. You need to do this, okay? To improve the quality of your life, okay?"

"My life is just fine as it is." Her hands fiddle with the knot in her bandana. She often wears something in her hair, which has grown several inches below her shoulders. Yesterday it was a long golden ribbon leftover from Christmas. Today she's wearing a strip of purple velvet wrapped across her forehead and tied at the back of her head.

"Okay. Your life seems fine. I get that. Okay. But it can get much better than fine," Bill says.

"My life is totally groovy now," she says. "This can't possibly make it any better."

I wonder why Alice signed up for this introductory communications class if she isn't willing to participate. I already did these exercises in Chicago. I'm only repeating the class because she didn't want to do it alone. Alice has a point about her life being groovy, though. She's not the same Vidal Sassoon-bobbed girl who moved from Hinsdale to join her family in Arlington last June. She's become a full-fledged hippie, patching and embroidering her bell bottom jeans, donning paisley shirts and long granny dresses she finds in thrift stores. She always wears bright beaded necklaces, dangling hoop earrings and bangles jingling around her wrists.

Her boyfriend, Larry, a university student whose thick, dark waves reach to his shoulders, comes over every afternoon, and they smoke marijuana together in the basement. Sometimes he brings friends along; they all seem to have a crush on Alice. She went from being an outsider in Hinsdale to the girl every guy wants to be with in Arlington. Alice plans to join Larry at school in the fall, after she's an official Virginia resident and can pay in-state tuition. Before she enrolls, they're going to take a cross-country road trip that might include a stop at the Democratic convention in Chicago.

"Laura? Laura, where are you?" Bill's medallion swings in front of my face.

"Um, I guess my mind wandered."

"Okay. Your mind wandered. What are you going to do about that?"

"Pay attention."

"Okay. That's good. And work on acknowledging communications when you receive them."

The woman sitting across from me bumps her knees against mine. Her round eyes and wavy hair tucked behind double-sized ears remind me of an African bush baby. She says whatever comes to mind in an effort to get me to laugh or flinch. I face her calmly, no trace of emotion in my face, even when Alice gets up and heads for the door.

"I'll be waiting in the hall," Alice says when she passes behind my chair.

I wish I'd brought Alice here to visit before she signed up for the class. Byron, the registrar, and Flo, the receptionist, bend over backward to make potential students at the Scientology headquarters in D.C. feel welcome. They have so much love in their eyes. They hug everybody and notice everybody's good qualities. I often hang out with them just to bask in their warmth. They've taken me under their wing, answering all my questions, and explaining the difference between Dianetics and Scientology, and why Scientology, weird as it sounds, is so much more advanced. They would have welcomed Alice, too, and she'd have felt some of the group's power before starting the class.

When the class ends I join Alice in the hallway, and we walk out of the building in silence.

"Well, that sure was uncomfortable," I say when we reach the bus stop nearby. We both look straight ahead at the houses across the street.

"It's way too weird, Laura. All that peering at strangers, practically nose to nose and saying those stupid things. It gives me the creeps."

"But it's for a purpose. You haven't read the book yet. Read the book, and you'll get it."

"There's nothing to get, Laura. They're putting one over on you to get their hands on your money—what little of it you have—and maybe your soul." She turns toward me and puts a hand on my arm. I brush it off.

"They're going to help me clear my head so I can do better in school when I go back. I'm going to clean out the cluttered part of my mind. They call it the reactive mind."

"But what about that weirdo, Bill, who was teaching the class? I never saw him blink his eyes. That's so strange. And his assistant with the pointy teeth? He looks like part of the Adams family. Oh, god, and that woman sitting across from you? She spewed spit every time she opened her mouth."

"You just don't get it." I pull out an Old Gold from my coat pocket and fish through my purse for a light.

"It's like they're living through another depression or something. I mean, did you see the stains all over the shirt of that guy who wanted me to be his partner? And he practically has more dandruff than hair. I wasn't going to get anywhere near him."

"Well, you're wearing the same bellbottoms you wore yesterday and your dad's old shirt from the Navy." I find a book of matches, strike one, light up and inhale.

"That's different. I'm a hippie. Your new friends look like skid row bums."

"After all we went through in high school with everybody judging us based on who knows what, I'd think you'd be more open or something." I blow smoke rings and watch them sail into the night. I offer the cigarette to Alice. She takes it, inhales, hands it back.

"That was different," she says. "These people are real grown ups, and they're sitting around in folding chairs knee to knee, staring each other in the face, trying to be the last one to blink, or whatever. It's like the goal is to stop being human. I'm not interested in becoming some sort of machine."

"I don't want to become a machine either."

"Why don't you just apply to University of Virginia for the fall like I'm doing? You can stay with us. My mom really likes having you around."

"Having someone around for a couple months is a lot different than having someone move in permanently."

"You know my mom loves you like a daughter."

"Let's just drop it. I'm nothing like a daughter to your mom, and I'm not going to University of Virginia." I throw the cigarette on the sidewalk and step on it.

"You're impossible."

"Think what you want." I cross my arms in front of my chest. Alice shifts her weight from one pointed boot to the other. And we wait, glaring at the curb and every so often looking up the block, hoping to see our bus rounding the corner. When it arrives, I board first and take a window seat near the back. Alice sits beside me.

I look out the window at the sturdy buildings as the bus picks up speed. "You're right, Alice. I am impossible. I can't even stand myself half the time."

"Oh, you're not that bad. You're loads of fun, actually. I'm just worried about you."

"Let's talk about something else."

"What about this summer? You have to come with us. We're leaving in June and we're camping all around the country and getting more people to come along to the great yippie gathering."

"Sounds cool," I say. But I'm thinking I'd better move out of Alice's. Byron and Flo have warned me about friends who'll try to pull me away from the group. They say people who do that don't have my best interests at heart. I hope that's not true of Alice. I don't understand why she doesn't understand how much hope this philosophy has given me. Byron says I have to cut old friends who don't understand out of my life, which I don't think I could actually do. But if I move to a room in D.C., I'll be able to at least get some distance.

THIRTY-SEVEN

June 1968

HANDS TIP-TAPPING AND SLAPPING AGAINST HIS body, Leonard alternates palms up, palms down, going chest to knees and back again. He is bliss in motion head to toe. All syncopation eludes me as I struggle to imitate him. I feel like a malfunctioning robot.

"You ain't got no rhythm, girl." Leonard sputters, trying to suppress his laughter, then breaks into a belly laugh that fills the room.

"I'll say." I shake out my hands and laugh along.

I've been trying to learn the hand jive for a couple weeks now, taking breaks in the evening in the accounting office for the Church of Scientology, in Washington, D.C., where Leonard works under Rosalie's so-called supervision. When she's at work, she leaves her desk every hour to visit a bust of the group's founder, L. Ron Hubbard, in the hallway outside her door. There she bends her head, as though in prayer, her tumbleweed hair scraping her pinched face, midriff fat poking against a chartreuse cardigan she wears every day. She mumbles unintelligibly, tears rolling down her sallow cheeks, each time she pays her respects. Often, she'll lose track of time, and another staff member will take her by the arm and escort her back to her post. I was floored when I learned she'd been involved in this organization since the 1950s, back when it was just Dianetics. I still don't exactly know what Scientology is. It's supposed to be a new religion, but it's not like any church I've ever known. There's a lot I don't know about worship, though.

Leonard turns on the radio. Linda Ronstadt's voice on *Different Drum* draws me in, filling me with longing. I feel for both the person being left behind in the song and for the one running away. Moonlight shines through the windows. Leonard grabs my hands, and we dance around the desks. He pauses, his smile bright and wide. I smile back easily, knowing he doesn't expect more than friendship from me: he's attracted to men.

I met Leonard when I joined the staff here. I hadn't planned to become a staff member. When I left Alice's and moved to the city, I found a job as a file clerk in an insurance agency. I earned more than enough to pay $5 per week rent for a furnished room in a building close to my job and to the Scientology headquarters. But my employment didn't pay enough for the extensive Scientology counseling, called "auditing," needed to reach a state of "Clear." That's when bits of garbage from past hurts no longer gum up your mind—and when you get to learn more what Scientology is all about.

Every day after work I'd stop in to visit the headquarters, called the "org," and Byron and Flo would tell me how much fun they were having being on staff. They also told me staff members get free auditing, as well as training to become auditors, in exchange for their labor. I didn't enjoy my job pulling insurance papers in and out of giant metal drawers all day long. So one morning, I walked to the org instead of to work. Within half an hour, I was the new receptionist, replacing Flo, who became an auditor in training.

All seemed to be going well at first. Lots of people came in from the suburbs to take classes and get auditing, and they were all friendly. But I soon learned that org workers often have to wait a long time to receive auditing and training. I've gotten zero of either so far. Plus, a couple weeks after I joined staff, Dr. Martin Luther King Jr. was murdered.

"Don't worry," Byron said, after we heard the news on the radio. "He wasn't his body anyway. He'll be back. So his death isn't a big deal. Remember, we're all 'thetans,' which means we are eternal beings, not these bodies we're occupying."

"But so many people loved him. He was making the world a better place. He wasn't supposed to die. Something is very wrong," I said to Byron.

"Pull yourself out of the mud of confusion, kid. You'll make the world better by bringing more people through that front door. Reel 'em in. Spread the word. Don't worry about old Dr. King. He brought this on himself, he pulled it in."

As news of the assassination spread, riots erupted only blocks away, and a citywide curfew was implemented. Nobody came to the introductory lecture scheduled for that evening. The next day, I looked out the reception area's windows and saw an armored tank rolling by. It seemed I'd walked right into a surrealist painting and belonged neither inside the org nor outside on the streets.

Since then, only a handful of previously enrolled students and auditing clients have walked through the doors. Nobody new has come near the org. And something I didn't know before I joined staff is that our pay depends first on how much money the group nets in a given week, and second, on how well each of us does our particular job. Our results are measured and graphed, and everyone's graph is supposed to show upward movement week to week. We are also assigned "conditions" based on our performance. The better we do, the better our condition. As receptionist, I am judged by how many people walk through the door and how many books and other paraphernalia I sell. If my "stats" don't go up, I am penalized to varying degrees, depending upon how far my graph dips from the preceding week. With nobody coming through the door, my stats have flatlined.

Leonard hasn't been doing well either lately. Part of his job is to make bank deposits, which have gone down week after week. We've each been assigned a condition called "nonexistence." As part of that, we haven't been allowed to leave the premises or shower or change our clothes. The building we've been stuck in must have been an elegant home at one time. Now the exterior is covered with soot; inside the yellowish paint is grimy, the plaster is cracked, the carpet is worn, the faucets drip, the heater rattles ominously. The basement, ground floor and second floor are used as offices and meeting rooms; the third floor provides living quarters for the higher-ups on staff. Too bad maintenance isn't part of anyone's job description.

Leonard and I have been working in the basement long into the night, folding flyers for mass mailings. In the wee hours, I try to sleep on the floor by my desk. Other staff members have been instructed to shun Leonard and me. Not even Byron and Flo have talked to us, which makes me wonder how sincere all their hugs and encouragement were before I joined staff.

But today things changed for Leonard. Someone who owed the org money sent in a large check. That means Leonard is finally heading home to shower, change and then go out with friends.

"I wish I were going with you," I say.

"Don't worry. You'll be out of this soon. Things have to pick up." He pulls me close and gives me a hug.

"Are you still going to talk to me in the meantime?"

"You'll always be my friend." He steps back, touches his finger-tips to his heart and does one last jive up and down his body. Then he spins like Fred Astaire and walks out the door.

THIRTY-EIGHT

July 1968

JUST OUTSIDE THE ORG'S FRONT DOOR, I savor the sunshine on my face. At long last I can leave the building because I sold an E-meter to Graham, a lawyer with salt and pepper hair and a beard that reaches below his collarbone. He comes in twice a week for auditing. An E-meter consists of two cylinders that look like tin cans without labels. The cylinders are connected to a wooden box housing a meter. An auditor draws conclusions based on how a needle on the display moves when a person holding the cans reacts to questions the auditor asks.

Graham already had an E-meter, but he is smitten with me and wanted to help out, so he paid more than a hundred dollars for something he doesn't need. He's divorced, lives in Maryland and has two kids in grammar school. Every time he comes into the org, he asks me to move in with him. The E-meter purchase isn't going to increase the odds that will happen. I made that clear.

Pam and Liz join me on the porch. They share a flat down the street with their boyfriends and several other staffers, along with a couple of spouses who have regular jobs and begrudgingly pay most of the rent.

"You must be happy to be getting out of here," Liz says to me. Her small brown eyes peer through thick granny glasses.

"Just don't pull a Leonard on us, okay?" Pam adds. Her grin reveals a mini rainbow painted on her bottom front teeth.

"I really miss him. I wonder why he never came back," I say.

"Doesn't matter. Leonard's been declared a suppressive person. We'd never let him back in now," Liz says.

"Just like that?" I shiver at the thought of being declared suppressive, the lowest condition of all. If you're suppressive, you're an enemy of Scientology. "I don't see why he has to be off limits just because he left."

"You can't just skip out like he did after signing a contract." Pam twirls her wavy light-brown hair around her index finger. "Say, my mom's coming over tonight with pizza for all," Pam says. "You want to come over?"

"I'm not sure." I have reservations about socializing with people who have ignored me so easily for the last few weeks, but I don't have other friends to spend time with either.

"If you want to know the truth, Ray asked me to ask you," Pam says.

"Oh, him. He and Charlie are always trying to get it on with me. So is Bill."

"They like you. Is that so bad?" Liz says. "And Ray is really cute. I wanted to get together with him last month, but he wouldn't have me."

"Wait long enough, and he probably will. It's like musical chairs, only with beds, around here," I say.

"We're just not hung up about sex like some people," Pam says.

"Or stuck on guys who don't even bother to answer our letters," Liz adds. She looks at me accusingly as she smooths wrinkles from her floor length denim skirt.

"Besides, getting together with Ray wouldn't mean you're going to marry him or anything," Pam points out.

"Yeah, it's like covering your bases," Liz says. "If your guy never comes back, or comes back with another girl on his arm, won't you feel foolish?"

Liz and Pam are expressing doubts that have been galloping through my mind like stampeding horses. I used to write Michael almost every day, but that stopped after I went on staff. There's no time, paper or postage to spare. Michael never answered my letters anyway. He did send me a Christmas card. It arrived a few weeks ago, months after the holiday, but to see his handwriting was a thrill. I carried the card in my pants pocket for an entire week. I'd peek at it every couple of hours, touching it like a talisman, re-reading his message, looking for hidden meaning: "Merry Christmas, Merry Christmas, Merry Christmas, Merry Christmas, Merry Christmas, Merry Christmas, Merry Christmas, Merry Christmas, and Happy New Year for many years to come. Love, Michael." Repeating Merry Christmas eight times, saying for many years to come, and signing off with love are all good signs—better than, say, a simple Merry Christmas and Happy New Year. But for all I know, he could have sent out a dozen cards with an identical message. A bad sign.

Pam taps my shoulder. "When was the last time you had pizza anyway?"

"Can't remember. Maybe I'll come over later. I have to take a shower. It's going to feel so good—if I still have a room. I'm a little behind on rent."

"You can always stay with us. We've got an extra cot right now, but probably not for long," Pam says.

"That's good to know." I jump down the stairs, wave goodbye and practically sprint home. I unlock the ground floor entrance and walk up the creaking stairs to the second floor, where I see the door to my room is padlocked. I find Mr. Turner, the landlord, working in the back yard. His sleeveless, white T-shirt barely covers a potbelly protruding over baggy gray trousers. Beads of sweat glisten on his scalp, which is visible through thinning dishwater blond hair, streaked white at the temples. A wet curl sticks to his brow, and ashes fall from a cigar dangling from thin lips. His biceps ripple beneath flaccid, tattooed skin as he heaves rocky dirt from a hole he's digging near a basement window.

"Hi, Mr. Turner. Could you let me into my room?"

"Ain't your room no more, kid," he says.

"Could I at least get in and get my stuff?"

"Not until you pay me your back rent."

"I have $7 now, and I can pay you the other $3 in a week."

"There's an easier way to pay," he says.

"You'll get your full $5 a week." I push a five and two ones at his face.

He snatches the money and, chewing the end of his cigar, heads to my room, grunting and breathing deeply as he trudges up the stairs. He unlocks the door, motions for me to step in. He follows me so closely I can feel his breath on my neck.

"Why are you practically on top of me?" I ask.

"What little wifey don't know don't matter." He places a hand on my shoulder.

I slap his hand away and move across the room toward a dresser I've never used. I notice one of my suitcases is missing. "Hey, where's my other bag. I had two. Half of my stuff is gone," I say.

"I don' know nothin' about that."

"Who else but you has a key?"

"Like I said, I don' know nothin' about that, but, you know, I might be persuaded to do some lookin' for ya." He leers.

I grab a Bible from the top of the dresser, part of the furnishings the room came with, and hold it up above my head, ready to throw. "You'd better leave." My voice quivers, but I step forward anyway. "You shouldn't even be in my room."

"No cause for you to get all worked up there, missy. I can see you're not interested in making things easy." He backs away. "Just remember you owe me three bucks, and I can collect it any time—if you get my drift."

He walks out, leaving the door open. I stomp over and slam it closed. Then I sink into a chair by the window, which I promptly open to let out the lingering cigar smoke. In my missing suitcase are some of my favorite clothes. I'll replace them eventually. But it also contained a silver dollar collection I started as a small child. My grand aunt Kitty visited from Texas once a year and gave each of the children in the family a silver dollar. Also tucked inside were a pinkie ring with a tiny diamond from Gramma; an embroidered box from my father; a beaded coin purse from a childhood friend; a small doll dressed like a guard at Kensington Palace, given to me by an English pen pal long ago; pictures of Michael, Mary Ruth, Kathy, Shelby, Jillie, and Muffin, the little beagle my family had for a year or so; a journal I'd kept since the day Michael left; and the Christmas card—all taken like treasure swallowed by the sea.

I pat the jade ring under my blouse. It's the only possession I have left that holds special meaning for me. I sit alone, watching people pass on the sidewalk below as I absorb the truth that it isn't safe to remain in this room and probably never was. I pick up a sweatshirt, jeans and underwear I'd left on a chair by the dresser, a pair of black flats on the closet floor, and the one dress I'd bothered to hang in there. I shove them into an already crowded suitcase, sit on it so that I can latch it, pick it up and leave the room.

Down the hall, a door cracks open. A notebook slips out and falls to the floor, and the door closes. I think it's just like the oddball who lives there to slip something into the hall like that. She favors flowered, floor length mumus and bracelets that clank when she moves. Her black curls frame a wrinkled face that exposes two gold teeth when she smiles. In the hallway between the bathroom we share and my room, she has accosted me repeatedly, demanding to tell my fortune. When I've refused, she's followed me to my door and said, "Big sorrow coming to you. Big sorrow. Better take advice now."

Curious about the notebook, I walk to her door and pick up what I realize is my missing journal. I bang on the door. "Hey, open up. Where's the rest of my stuff?" Footsteps echo inside, but she doesn't respond no matter how hard I knock. With knuckles sore from pounding, I haul my remaining suitcase to Liz and Pam's. Ray answers the door. "Hi there," he says, raising an eyebrow. He takes my suitcase. "We were starting to think you weren't coming. Now it looks like you're moving in."

"Well, maybe for a little while." I step inside.

"The more the merrier." He leads me into the living room, where he puts my suitcase down on one of four cots set up on the perimeter. In the center are a couch and a couple of chairs positioned around a coffee table. "This one's open."

"Great. Thanks," I say.

"I've got an extra sleeping bag you can use tonight, and you'll be all set. Oh, and the bathroom's down the hall to the right," he adds.

Moments later, I close and lock the bathroom door, turn on the shower and strip off my dirty clothes. When the water's good and hot, I step in and stand in the soothing stream for a long time before I grab a bottle of Dr. Bronner's soap and begin to wash. As the water sprays my back, I think maybe losing the card from Michael is a sign that I should just move on, but I've been stuck on him for so long now, I can't imagine really being able to let go.

THIRTY-NINE
September 1968

MY NINETEENTH BIRTHDAY IS FINALLY HERE. September 11, 1968. The day I've dreamed about since Michael kissed me goodbye at Holy Family Academy and drove away. I imagined I'd be thin today, suntanned, wearing a mini skirt to show off my long, shapely legs. My hair would swing, shiny and silky, down to my elbows. Michael, too, would be tan from months under the sun in far-off, tropical climes. His madras shirt would be open, showing a sliver of chest with just the right amount of hair; his khaki shorts would be a little loose.

Sometimes I'd picture myself running toward Michael at O'Hare airport. We'd embrace against the backdrop of airplanes lifting off and landing beyond wide panes of glass taller than most buildings. Other times, Michael and I would be reunited in his parents' driveway; Daniel and Shelby would watch from the kitchen window as the two of us would melt into each other. Or he'd send me a plane ticket and directions for a rendezvous. We'd meet, barefoot on the Mediterranean shore, and our kisses would sparkle more than the blue-green sea beside us. Then he would pull presents from his pockets and put them on me: necklaces, bracelets, earrings, a fisherman's hat—all of these gifts proving how much I'd been on his mind.

But today is no such day. I've been alone all morning, cleaning my new office. I've just been appointed the org's ethics officer, of all things, which means when people's stats go down, I'll have to assign them conditions.

I have no idea where Michael is, and it's just as well. The air is as thick with moisture as a pineapple upside down cake just out of the oven. I'm throbbing and swollen all over like an out-of-control infection. My ankles, which have always remained slim no matter how much I weigh, are plump, and my feet are crammed into scuffed loafers that have grown so tight they're giving me blisters. My hair is limp, stringy—no shampoo here to give it a nice shine. My skin sticks to the blue and red striped knit dress I found in the org's free box, a trove of ripped, faded and wrinkled wares left behind over the years by departed clients and staffers. I haven't had my period since July, but I've skipped more periods than I've had since I began menstruating, so I'm hoping the blood will flow any minute now.

Bill looms in the doorway, casting a long shadow over my work area. He enters the room, carrying a small bag of Cheese-Its and a bottle of Coke, which is a typical meal for us these days. He puts the Cheese-Its on the table, pulls a can opener from his pocket, opens the soda and takes a sip. Bill, who wears that weird medallion all the time. Bill, the org's current executive director. Bill who begins almost every sentence with "Okay," because that's what's taught in the communications classes he teaches.

"Thanks," I say. I don't look up at him.

"Okay. How's it goin'?"

"I'm kinda glum."

"Okay. Cheer up. We can celebrate your birthday when you're done in here."

"How? Go have coffee and an English muffin at Rand's? That's what you usually want to do." I open the bag of Cheese-Its, pop a few into my mouth and take a sip of Coke.

"Okay. We'll talk about it later. I've got to go now. Leonard sneaked back into the building and was rifling through the free box.

He was looking for some shoes he left behind. Pam found him, and we put him down in the boiler room."

"You what?"

"It was just for a little while—to teach him a lesson. We let him go just now. You should have seen him tear out of here."

"You shouldn't have done that," I say.

"Okay. You'd better not say that to anyone else."

"Why?"

"I can't always protect you." He leans over and kisses the top of my head before leaving the room. I thought he and I would be just a passing thing. It seems most sexual relationships among staffers don't last long. I stayed out of the sexual pairings until I moved in with Pam, Liz, Ray and a slew of other people. Ray climbed into my cot one night, and I didn't resist his lovemaking. I felt awful afterward because I thought about Michael the whole time. I told Pam and said I wanted to find another place. She told me that Nancy, an auditor on staff, was looking for a roommate. Her apartment was near the org and the $7 per week rent seemed doable, that is, until I moved in. Nancy pointed to the bed in the living room that doubled as a couch during the day. "That's yours. The bedding's $4 per week extra. If you use any of my towels, that 50 cents per use. Same goes for the pots, pans, dishes and silverware. You pay per use."

"What? I can't afford that. I'll have to find another place."

"You agreed to live here at least six months." She waved a paper at me. "You signed this before moving in, remember?" she said. "You'll owe me rent for the whole time whether or not you remain."

"That's not fair. You didn't tell me about these extra charges. They're not written into the contract either."

"You agreed to live here, little girl. It's time you grow up."

"I can't believe this." I ran out of the apartment and to the org, where Bill and Liz were on the porch, smoking Salems. They'd been a couple for a few weeks but were now broken up.

"You look a wreck, Laura. What happened?" Liz asked.

"I moved in with Nancy and thought I was going to pay $7 per week, but it turns out I have to rent everything I use—bedding, towels, plates, basically anything that's hers."

Bill chuckled. "Okay, Nancy's at it again. She does it to newer recruits all the time. Got you to sign an agreement, right?"

"She's so in debt on her credit cards, she'll try anything," Liz said.

"Okay. Who uses credit to pay for auditing and training and then goes on staff?" Bill asked.

"Yeah, she'll never pay those cards off now," Liz added.

"I don't know what I'm going to do," I said.

"Okay. Don't worry about it. I'll handle Nancy. Come on." Bill jumped down the stairs and motioned for me to follow. On the way to Nancy's he told me, "I've been wanting to fuck you since the first time I saw you. I know you've been with Ray lately. I asked him how he would feel if I had a go with you, and he said that would be fine with him. He doesn't like you anyway. He wants to get together with Liz. So it would be like switching girlfriends in a way."

"You and Ray can't decide who I'm going to be with. I think you're too old for me anyway," I said.

"Okay. I'm a young thirty-two, and I could show you a thing or two."

I picked up the pace, pulling in front of him. He soon caught up, and we walked together in silence. When we arrived at Nancy's, she and Bill went into the bedroom to talk. A few minutes later, Bill sauntered out of the room, a big smile on his face. Nancy followed. Scowling, she brushed past him and stormed out the front door.

"You are free to leave, no more agreement," Bill said to me.

"Really? What did you do?"

"Nothing much, just helped her see reason."

"I'd better find another place to live quick."

"I've got plenty of room on the third floor," he said.

"That's good to know, I guess."

I walked to the kitchen to get a glass of water. Bill came up from behind, grasped my shoulders and turned me around to face him. He pushed me up against a cabinet and kissed me long and hard. I winced at the knobs jutting into my flesh. I doubted he would rape me if I resisted, but I didn't want to find out. I let his hands explore my breasts and then move down my torso. As head of the local org, if he had it in for me, he could make my life difficult. We had sex on the kitchen floor.

"So, now we are lovers," he crowed just after he came. He reminded me of a skinny, short-haired Tiny Tim about to sing *Tiptoe through the Tulips* in falsetto. I almost laughed, but remained silent, meeting his gaze. Then I pushed him off of me, grabbed my underwear and jeans, and slipped them on as I stood.

He got up and pulled on his pants, too. "Go grab your stuff; I need to get going."

"I'll stay with you just for a little while, till I find a place," I said.

"Okay. That's what you say now. You'll change your mind."

It's been four months, and I'm still living with Bill on the third floor of the org in a huge room with African violets blooming on windowsills along one wall. A self-proclaimed gift to women, Bill thinks I'm in love with him, though I've never told him so, and I've never pretended to love him like I did with Pierre, when I hoped pretending would make it true.

I consume the remaining Cheese-Its and Coke while I finish straightening my desk. I want to end my entanglement with Bill, but I don't know how to bring that about without angering him.

And today, my birthday, I've thought of nothing but Michael. But if he really loved me, wouldn't he have tracked me down somehow, called the group's main number here? Even Kathy, who said she never wanted to see me again, came to visit me when she returned from a year spent working and traveling in Europe. She was radiant with shoulder length blonde hair and a royal blue mini dress that showed off shapely legs. I was plump and dirty, wearing a green knit dress I'd fetched from the free box. It was baggy at my chest and stretched too thin around my rear. She and I didn't talk about what had happened in Cambridge. She just said she was worried about me and offered to take me away. I assured her I was fine.

Mary Ruth stopped in, too. She was gorgeous in a spaghetti strap dress with thin multicolored stripes and brown leather sandals with straps crisscrossing up to her ankles. She wanted to sneak me into her dorm room at Vassar, said I could probably even get accepted as a student there. A pipe dream. Shelby came to visit for a few days. She strutted down the street in a neon yellow dress like a runway model, drawing children in the neighborhood to her like the Pied Piper. Shelby's mom came after that, too, and tried to talk me into flying back to Chicago with her. But not a peep from Michael.

Not long ago, everything seemed so clear, so promising. I was going to reclaim my mind, take charge of my life. And when this thing with Bill started, I was sure he'd move on to someone else in a month or so. Instead, I'm still sharing his bed. The all too familiar feelings of dread are burbling up from deep within, and I'm scared. I doubt I could weather a repeat of the darkness that enveloped me in the last couple years of high school. This sure isn't the nineteenth birthday I'd envisioned. And right now I hate myself, and I hate Bill in equal measure.

FORTY

November 1968

BILL SWINGS HIS ANGULAR ARMS IN awkward, wind-up-soldier spurts. "Take another little piece of my heart," he sings along with Janis Joplin, whose voice thunders from the radio across the room. Every time that song comes on, Bill turns the volume up as loud as it will go. We have no TV, so the radio is our link to the world outside.

"I'd like to see Joplin someday," Bill's pudgy friend Johnson says.

Johnson and his wife, Lucy, arrived a couple of weeks ago, and the only thing I like about them is that they've taken us out to eat several times and paid the bill.

"I'd never go to see Janis Joplin. She's too wild." Lucy tightens her aqua chiffon scarf under her chin. "I'm dying to see Loretta Lynn and Tammy Wynett again. They're the real deal. You haven't heard singing until you've heard country singing."

Johnson, Lucy and Johnson's eight-year-old son, Slate, are staying in a motel in town. They leave Slate alone there watching TV when they come to see Bill, which is almost every day. Lucy said she doesn't like "dragging the brat along" and she doesn't see why the boy can't just live permanently with his mom. To that, Johnson said, "Now, honey, you know that ain't gonna happen 'cause of his blond hair and freckles remind her of me, and so she can't stand him." He guffaws as though he's just told a brilliant joke.

Lucy, Johnson and Slate are moving from Detroit, where Johnson is from, to eastern Kentucky, where Lucy is from. Johnson was fired from his job as an auto mechanic for coming in late all the time, and Lucy was tired of being a telephone operator in a big city, so they plan to get a new start living in Lucy's childhood home, which has been unoccupied since her folks moved into a trailer home nearby. They swung by D.C. to visit Bill on a whim.

Gimme Some Lovin', a hit from a couple years ago, comes on the radio. Bill sings along off key.

"Ah, you haven't had lovin' till you've had country lovin'," Johnson says. He pulls Lucy close and pinches her rear.

Lucy squeals with delight.

"You don't know what you're talking about, man." Bill gestures toward me. "I've got the best young piece of ass right here. Can you imagine how fine she'll be when she's twenty one?" He says this to Johnson as though I'm not there.

"Then I'd like to try some." Johnson leers at me.

"How 'bout it?" Bill asks me.

"No thank you." I glare at Bill. I've heard of people swapping partners for sex, but I never thought I'd meet anyone who does it.

"Aw, she's a party pooper," Lucy says. "Why do you bother with some green girl anyway? How old is she, sixteen?"

"Nah, she's legal—eighteen," Bill says.

"I'm nineteen now," I say.

"I'd treat you real good." Johnson walks over to me, puts his hands on my shoulders and leans down. "Come on, give us a kiss."

Johnson leans in, and I punch him as hard as I can in his soft belly.

He winces and backs away. "Hey, she had no call to do that. I'm just bein' friendly."

"Leave the kid alone. You can see she only has eyes for me." Bill puffs his chest out with pride. Then he mentions a couple of women he and Johnson knew in their community college days in Detroit. This leads to their swapping stories about former lovers. They describe the women's physical attributes as though they were cattle being auctioned at a county fair.

"Why go carrying on about all them old girlfriends when you've got me right here, Johnson?" Lucy asks.

"We don't mean nothin' by it, hon. Say, how 'bout we go back to that little café and have a bite to eat." Johnson sweeps his arm toward the door.

"You two go ahead. We can't afford it, and you've paid for enough meals already," Bill says.

"Forget about it, pal. You'd do the same for me and Lucy, wouldn't you? And besides, we're leaving tomorrow."

"I guess another one of those hot turkey sandwiches and fries would be good right about now." Bill turns off the radio, cutting a Doors song off after "Hello I love ..."

"Does she have to come, too?" Lucy nods toward me. "She did assault my husband."

"I think I can forgive that." Johnson smacks his lips and opens his arms wide, feigning magnanimity.

"Never mind. I don't feel well anyway," I say, even though I'd love to sink my teeth into a club sandwich and a bowl of chili.

"You sure?" Bill asks me.

"I'm just gonna go upstairs and rest."

"Okay. Suit yourself." Bill blows me a kiss and struts out the door. Lucy and Johnson follow.

I turn the radio back on and think about all the news I've heard coming from that little box in the months since I joined staff: Martin Luther King's assassination, Robert Kennedy's a couple of months later, protests against the Vietnam War all over the country,

President Johnson's decision not to seek reelection, chaos at the Democratic convention in Chicago. I wonder if Alice ever made it there and whether she was clubbed by the police the way so many people were.

Steppenwolf's *Born to be Wild* comes on. I sit in a swivel chair and pull a telegram from my pocket. I've been carrying it around for a month. I unfold it and read, again, that Grampa O'Neill is dead. I wish now I'd figured out a way to pay for a plane ticket so I could go to his funeral. Bill leaned over my shoulder as I read the telegram and said, "Don't worry. He wasn't his body. No big deal; you'll see him again someday."

I wonder whether people do return to inhabit new bodies after they die and whether Grampa O'Neill might claim the fetus growing inside of me, a new life I've been hoping doesn't really exist, an interloper who has invaded my body and is turning my life upside down in increments day by day.

Someone on staff might know of a back-alley abortionist, but I could end up dead or infertile if I were to go that route. Besides, I've spent all the money I received for college last year, mostly on rent and food because I earn about $15 per week on good weeks for the org; when income is down I earn even less. Bill is broke, too. I'm probably too far along for that solution anyway.

Leaning back in the chair, I spin myself breathless. Then I curl into a ball, close my eyes and see myself clinging to a capsized boat far out at sea.

November 1968

I'VE SHIVERED IN A CROWD FOR more than an hour, temperature hovering just below twenty degrees, while people from nearby Kentucky and West Virginia towns have come and gone from a makeshift stage. Each has either made a speech or accepted a prize of some kind—a set of carving knives, a blender, a chocolate cream pie, that sort of thing. The community is raising funds to help neighbors in need make it through the winter. I asked Bill to get the car keys from Johnson and drive me back to Lucy's home, which it turns out is a dilapidated miner's cabin, but Johnson said we have to stay until the end; we must be present to win a prize. Why didn't Lucy tell me this raffle was outside? I would have stayed at the cabin where it's warm. Who in their right mind holds an event outside on a windy night in December?

I used to walk to and from school in temperatures far colder than this, but I was bundled in a wool coat, hat, mittens, scarf, leggings, thick socks and boots. Tonight, I wear a sleeveless, wool mini dress, T-shirt and green Army slicker. I have no boots, only loafers, no socks or leggings. I have no warmer clothes because I left most of my belongings at the org a month ago, when Bill woke me just before five a.m. and told me he was going with Johnson and Lucy to Kentucky, and I could come, too—if I hurried.

"I almost left without you. Johnson and Lucy wanted me to. I threw my stuff in the trunk, but then I couldn't get in the car," Bill said.

I sat up in bed. "You were going to leave while I was asleep? That's ... I don't know what to say."

"Yeah, okay, it's lame, but I couldn't do it. And you've got to hurry now. I talked Johnson and Lucy into bringing you along but neither of them is keen on the idea."

"How did you talk them into it?" I asked.

"Lucy can't have children. I told her she can adopt the baby."

"You had no right to do that." I throw the covers off and get out of bed.

"Okay. I thought you'd be relieved. You said you're not ready to be a mother. I sure don't want a kid to take care of either. What's not to like about this? Lucy lit up at the idea of having a little rug rat of her own."

"I will not promise anything to that woman."

"It's your ticket out of here. Take it."

"I don't know. ... I don't know."

"If you're coming, you have to step on it."

I looked at the familiar cracks in the plaster, the faded patchwork quilt on the bed, the African violets soaking up the sun, the sweaters and pants scattered across the carpet, plopped right where I'd peeled them off, a stack of staff bulletins that cover everything from the importance of looking up words you don't understand to dealing with people who criticize your beliefs. I knew if I didn't leave with Bill, I'd have to find another place to stay. I would also have to rely on other staff members to help me figure out what to do about the baby.

Now, outside in the cold, watching my breath puff white clouds into the black night air, I wonder if I should have stayed behind in D.C. I wasn't happy working at the org, especially after a few people from an elite, new Scientology group called the Sea Org arrived and said our org was being mismanaged. Lackluster introductory lectures, shoddy documentation of auditing sessions, insufficient income and rampant promiscuity among staff members were some of the deficits they cited. They said if I didn't start coming down hard on people whose stats weren't going up each week, they'd remove me as ethics officer and put me back on reception, something I never wanted to do again. I've probably been declared suppressive by now, and whatever hopes I had for Scientology are pretty much gone. I had only moments to make a huge decision the morning we fled. Bill towered over me in our room, not just physically—six foot three to my five foot six and a half—but also energy-wise. I felt squished into a tiny spot in my stomach.

"Are you coming or aren't you?" he asked.

"I guess so." I shuffled to a dresser, pulled out some clothes and threw them on the bed.

"Okay. You can't pack anything; there's no room. The car is stuffed to the gills."

"Can I at least put some things in a bag to hold on my lap?" I pointed to an empty Safeway bag in a corner.

"Do it fast. We have to make our escape before someone wakes up and catches us."

I pulled off my nightgown, threw on some underwear, a dress and my slicker; stuffed as many clothes as possible into the bag; slipped into my loafers; and tiptoed down the stairs and out the door with Bill. My pulse raced until we were tucked in the back seat with Slate and rolling away.

Soon, we were speeding west toward Appalachia. Lucy peered over her shoulder, slid her sunglasses down to the tip of her nose, pointed her finger at Bill and me, and said, "My people don't take kindly to outsiders, you know." Then she cackled and faced forward again.

"How bad could it be?" I whispered to Bill. I had gone to school in Hinsdale with plenty of aloof people and survived.

I've since found out just how bad it can be. Every time locals see us in town or on the road, they squint at Johnson, Bill and me like we're vermin worthy of massive doses of d-Con. Plus Lucy's cabin doesn't have a bathroom, just an outhouse. We bathe in the kitchen in a big washtub with water that's been heated outside over a fire. We're on a winding road with Hatfields on one end and McCoys on the other. Lucy says they're still enemies. I thought their famous feud was just folklore. Now, when blasts punctuate the long nights and reverberate down the hollow, I wonder whether a Hatfield or McCoy just got shot.

Bill and I are the only people within miles who have never fired a gun. Johnson and Lucy have several weapons apiece and often march the yard's perimeter, pausing periodically to shoot into the woods. Yesterday, Johnson played with his loaded Luger inside. He tried to spin it around his index finger, like Wyatt Earp. The weapon dropped, crashed onto the linoleum and blasted the hamper, which was full of clothes. Johnson whooped and cackled. Eight-year-old Slate, who'd been standing next to the hamper, peed in his pants.

"What's wrong with you, boy?" Johnson lurched forward and slapped him on the head. "You got shit for brains?"

Slate ran out of the cabin with just a T-shirt, jeans and socks on. I stood at the window and watched him race through the snow-covered backyard and into the woods.

Since then I've often thought about Johnson's recklessness with the gun, the terrified look in Slate's eyes when it went off, the hours the boy spent in the woods before he slipped in after dark and took a seat at the kitchen table, where Lucy told him to go to bed without supper. She said he had no business running off the way he did. I realized then I could never give Johnson and Lucy the child I will soon bring into the world.

Tonight, in the cold, I shift my weight from foot to foot, and wonder how I'm going to break the news that I don't think they're fit to raise a baby. My teeth begin to chatter. Lucy, Johnson and Bill are wrapped in winter coats over layers of warm clothes. Bill and Johnson snicker as they assess the women in the crowd, ranking each by how fuck-worthy they think she is. Lucy flits gaily from one chum to another. Two loud speakers toward the front of the crowd blare out her beloved Loretta Lynn.

I tug on Bill's arm. He looks down at me.

"Please, can we go back to Lucy's?" I ask. "I'm frozen through."

"Why didn't you dress better?" Bill asks.

Johnson laughs, "For a smart girl, she's pretty dumb, isn't she."

"I hardly have any clothes. You wouldn't let me pack anything, remember? Besides, I didn't know this raffle would be outside. I figured it would be in a church hall or something."

"Well, you figured wrong on that one." Johnson grins.

"Please?" I jump up and down, hoping it will help warm me. It doesn't

"Say, Johnson, what harm would it do if I drive her home and then come back for you?" Bill asks.

"That won't fly, man. First off, it's Lucy's car and she doesn't want anybody but me and her driving it. And second, Lucy needs that gas in the car to get to work tomorrow."

"Can I go wait in the car?" I ask. "Maybe it'll be warmer there."

"I suppose that would be all right," Johnson says. He pulls the keys from his pocket and hands them over. Bill and I walk in silence to the car, which is parked a few blocks away. I crawl into the back seat, hoping for warmth, but it feels as cold inside as out. Bill closes the door and heads back to the raffle. I curl into a fetal position and wait. Tenderness in my lower back creeps into my awareness. I try to ignore it, but it intensifies. I wish I could sleep to block out the cold and the growing discomfort.

Finally, the three of them return. Johnson and Lucy wiggle into the front seat. The car fills with the smell of liquor as they tell jokes in speech so slurred I can't understand their words. Bill slides in next to me. He's rigid, as usual. I lean into him anyway and put my head in his lap. "I've got a pain in my back. It really hurts."

"When you get inside and warmed up, it'll probably go away." He runs chilled fingers through my hair.

The next morning, the pain is so severe I can barely move. Bill, Johnson and Lucy confer. Lucy wants to wait and see if the pain goes away. Bill pushes to get me to a doctor. Johnson is noncommittal. In the end, Bill wins out. We all pile into the car and wind through the frozen red hills into town. First stop is Lucy's work. Then Johnson pulls up to the local hospital's emergency room. There, my kidney infection is diagnosed and my pregnancy confirmed. I'm allergic to penicillin, so a frowning doctor prescribes sulfa pills. He tells me to return for prenatal care as soon as I'm feeling better.

FORTY-TWO

January 1969

LIKE WIZENED GAMBLERS, LUCY, JOHNSON AND BILL are playing poker, smoking and drinking Kahlúa in the dining area. Lucy glares at me as I slink by her chair on my way from the kitchen to the dining room.

"Land sakes, that girl could at least smile when she goes by, after all we've done for her," Lucy says to Johnson.

"Some folks just aren't very appreciative," he replies.

I ignore them. Three months of dark days have crept by in one suffocating blur. I've spent most of my time perusing five Readers Digest condensed books, the only reading material in the cabin, while my belly has slowly grown. I thank God I only have to stand this for one more day.

Last week, I received a letter from Kathy, along with a check for $100—part of my share of proceeds from Grampa O'Neill's estate. He was always kindly, but also a little sad whenever I saw him, maybe because Kathy, Mary Ruth and I reminded him of our mother. Based on pictures I've seen of her, I think there's something of her in all of our eyes. There could be more, too. Maybe our voices, which Wanda can't tell apart most of the time, sound a lot like her, and maybe that tugged at Grampa's heart. I wish he were still alive, but what a gift this money is. Now I can leave Lucy, Johnson and Kentucky behind. Lucy, the only one of us who found a job, has been feeding us on her waitressing tips, a burden she reminds me of daily. I'm returning to Chicago, where I'll get $1,000 more from

Grampa's estate. I was going to go alone, but Bill wants to come, too. He reminded me that he didn't leave me at the org, so I guess I owe him for that. He also smoothed things over with Lucy and Johnson, who were furious when I told them I am leaving and not giving the child to them. Bill convinced them that with Johnson unemployed, they can't afford another mouth to feed. He even talked Lucy into vouching for me at her bank so they would cash my check.

I stretch out on the living room couch and think about how eager I am to see Kathy in Chicago. She lives on the North Side now, still sports golden blonde hair instead of the light brown of our childhood, drives an MGB sports car and writes for a suburban newspaper chain. I spoke with her and Mary Ruth on Christmas morning. Mary Ruth was visiting on a break from Vassar. They congratulated me because they thought Bill and I had gotten married, a lie Lucy insisted upon.

"You two have to say you're married," Lucy said the first day we pulled up to the cabin.

"No way," I said.

"We'd get run out of town if anyone knew I was letting a couple live in sin in my family's home, do you hear? Everyone has to believe you're married. Everyone."

"I just want to write to my sisters. I can tell them we're pretending to get married. I don't have to lie."

"You can only send a letter if you tell them you and Bill are married, period," Lucy said. "They might forget and address envelopes with the wrong name. This is my home, and I won't take chances."

I regretted going along with this as soon a congratulatory card arrived from one of Wanda's cousins. Word has probably spread since then. Who knows how many people back home think I've gotten hitched now? I have no idea how I'm going to set the record straight when I get home. I never thought I'd be so eager to return, but I yearn to hold Gramma's gnarled hand and listen to her tell tales I've heard again and again, but never grown tired of. I've missed Unc's tender greeting, "Howdy do." I've missed the smell of fish and sand along the Lake Michigan shore. I've missed strolling past the Wrigley Building and over the Chicago River on Michigan Avenue. I've missed the plaintive whistle of the Burlington Northern train approaching the Hinsdale station. I even take pity on Wanda, slouched in her recliner, yellow telephone in her lap and vials of prescription medication on the table by her side.

The only thing I'll miss about this Kentucky home is Spots, a brown and white puppy Slate carried home a few weeks ago after school. He's a whimpering ball of short hair and lolling tongue who follows me from room to room. The little hound even sleeps at my feet. Everyone in the house except me beats him for peeing and pooping inside—and for whimpering or howling. Even Slate tears into him routinely. I'm also the only one who snuggles with him, talks to him and takes him for walks down the rugged dirt roads nearby. We amble along together. He sniffs the gorgeous red earth poking up between white snowdrifts at the side of the road. I cling to the leash and watch deer dart over hedges and creeks to hide in thick woods behind lopsided shacks. I envy hawks that soar through blue-gray skies toward mountain peaks in the distance. Occasionally, I see the gleam of working stills in the pines, and lookouts guarding their liquid lightning with rifles and sapphire eyes.

Lucy can have this place. She can have the early shift, serving biscuits and gravy to truckers and miners. She can have Johnson, who never says a kind word to his own son. She can have all the people here whose hearts are like safety deposit boxes locked and guarded. After tomorrow, all of this will be just a memory to me. I expect when Bill and I reach Chicago we can rent a little apartment and stay together until the baby comes. Then we'll go our separate ways, unless I can find an unwed mother's home to take me in before then. That would mean I could be rid of Bill sooner.

Bill calls to me from the kitchen table, where he, Lucy and Johnson continue to play cards. "Laura, come join us," he says.

"It's your last night here, kid. Come on and have some fun," Johnson adds.

Lucy chimes in, "Yeah, it wouldn't kill you to be sociable for a change."

"No thanks. I'm getting tired."

"Yeah, sure, go rest and take care of that baby you're going to give to some strangers instead of good folks like us," Lucy says.

"Now, Lucy, let up a little bit. What's done is done," Johnson says.

The puppy scratches at my legs. I pick him up, squeeze him to my chest. His brown hound eyes are so sad. What's going to happen to him tomorrow after I board the train? What's going to happen to me?

FORTY-THREE

March 1969

MY SON IS ASLEEP. I WONDER if I should nudge him awake so I can look into his eyes. But the nurse who cradles him is angled to the side, shielding him; her elbow is a weapon ready to deploy, as though I am Richard Speck, the infamous nurse killer. The elevator doors open. Baby-guarding Nurse Righteous and I step inside. Unspoken judgments splatter me, as they have since I arrived at this hospital six days ago, screaming and escorted by police. Mary Ruth, shaking by my side, spoke on my behalf.

I didn't expect to give birth at Chicago's Belmont Hospital. The baby was supposed to be delivered at a suburban facility selected by my lawyer. It's close to his office, near the obstetrician he partners with for adoptions. I thought I'd stay nearby starting two weeks before the due date, but pains descended upon me in the middle of the night three weeks early. I thought they were cramps and took a bath. I didn't know this would speed the contractions.

Bill slept on until my insides were writhing with such force I knew I was in labor. I sat on the edge of the bed and shook his shoulder to awaken him. Then I called Mary Ruth, who was spending her spring break in Hinsdale. She arrived at Bill's and my apartment on the city's north side about forty minutes later. Clad in gray maternity pants and a knit sweater I'd bought at a second hand store, I donned my slicker and grabbed my purse. Bill, who had recently found employment as a draftsman, stood barefoot in his pajamas. Handing me a knotted rag to bite as I stumbled out the door, he said he wasn't coming along because he had to work the next day. I was relieved; his presence was a persistent headache.

Estimating I'd been in labor only about three hours, Mary Ruth and I thought we had plenty of time. But my water broke as I was going down our apartment building's stairs. Contractions devoured me as we made our way to the car. When Mary Ruth started up the engine, I flailed in the passenger seat, moaned, pulled my hair, punched the door. Mary Ruth, gipping the steering wheel tight and leaning forward in her seat, sped toward the expressway, but while she navigated a pair of 90-degree turns, known as the S curve, on Lake Shore Drive, I felt too confined in the front seat. I shimmied into the back, where I thrashed, howled, slammed my feet against the door. Mary Ruth saw a police car, got on its tail and honked until it pulled over. She braked right behind. An officer stepped out of the cruiser and sped to her open window.

"My sister's having a baby." Mary Ruth's voice quavered; her slender hands trembled at the steering wheel.

He looked in back, saw me churning and said, "Follow me."

He sped off, siren blaring, lights flashing. Mary Ruth, now quivering head to toe, drove in lurches and jolts, but she kept up all the way to the hospital parking lot. Soon the officer lifted me out of the car and carried me inside. "Help me! Help me!" I wailed all the way into the emergency room, where attendants covered my face with a mask. I gulped ether as deeply as I could, anything to lessen the pain that sliced like blender blades through my flesh.

Thinking about that morning as I stand beside the oh-so-lady-like, pseudo-benevolent, Nurse Righteous—my personal version of Ken Kesey's Nurse Ratched—I can't believe how out of control I was. The elevator descends; the buttons light 5, 4, 3. Soon we'll be in the lobby. Not a sound out of the baby, a vanilla ice cream cone: white diaper, T-shirt, onesie, sweater, booties, blanket, hat—all except the underwear look hand-made, a sign that the mother he has yet to meet anticipates his arrival with love. My son's days of almost nonstop crying, which began as soon as the doctor lifted him high at birth, appear to be at an end.

At the sight of the scrawny boy being passed from doctor to nurse just after birth, I exclaimed above the bustle in the room, "A baby!" A revelation, as though he were the first human to ever emerge from a womb. A stout, red-haired nurse at my side nodded at the doctor, rubbed my forehead and said, "There, there." She wasn't haughty like Nurse Ratched, but until that moment, she'd only growled instructions into my ear, first not to push until a doctor arrived even though there was no way I could stop the waves that overtook me. Then, when the doctor arrived, the nurse yelled, "Push, push!" repeatedly from just inches away, when I'd already begun pushing with everything I had. To me, she was Nurse Battleaxe, and I was suspicious of her hand on my brow.

"You have a healthy baby boy," the doctor crowed. He didn't know yet that I wasn't keeping the newborn.

When my lawyer arrived later that morning, he said, "It's a shame the kid came so fast. It would have been a whole lot easier if you hadn't seen him at all. You would have been spared some complications."

Complications seemed an odd way to express the intense love I was feeling for the little boy whose life I'd set in motion. But I was too intimidated by my lawyer's confident stance and professional aura to say a word. He soon left, saying he'd be back when the hospital was ready to release the baby and me. Neither of us knew when that would be. Born premature, my son was only 4 pounds,

15 ounces when he emerged. The hospital policy was to not release babies weighing less than 5 pounds; they wouldn't release me either. So I stewed, oozing blood in my maternity ward room, until he gained another ounce.

I spent the days and nights alone and aching in every way, while my son bellowed in a bassinet down the hall. I longed for him, wanted to hold him, keep him. With each passing day, pressure built. I felt like a stick of dynamite, fuse lit, ready to explode with emotion.

I wished I could talk with my sisters, but neither one was in town. Mary Ruth's spring break ended the day I gave birth, so she had to fly back to school immediately. Kathy was on vacation. I thought of calling Gramma, but she is in her nineties now, getting frail. I didn't want to burden her. I thought of aunts and uncles, but felt too ashamed to reach out to any of them.

Then Wanda came to mind. My feelings toward her had softened since I'd left her home and moved to the YWCA in Chicago. She had surgery, and her friend Florence was supposed to pay a few bills for her while she recuperated. Instead, Florence drained her bank account. So Wanda returned home, reliant entirely on her most recent Social Security check. And her health was no better than before the surgery. I'd felt sorry for her when Bill and I visited upon our arrival from Kentucky. And I found it easier to be around her now that I saw her only occasionally and she no longer ruled my life day to day. I stopped referring to her as Wanda the Wicked Witch of the Western Suburbs, and Kathy, Mary Ruth and I came up with her new nickname: Little Ma. It seemed to have just the right mix of distance and affection.

Still, I dreaded calling her from the maternity ward. All she'd ever done when I was in pain was scream at me—starting from my scraped knees as a toddler, to my childhood attacks of bronchitis, on up to my attempts at suicide as a teen. There was never a kind word, nor a gentle touch. But I was so desperate to make contact with someone that I placed the call. She said hello, and at first I couldn't speak.

"Muh, Muh," the tears began to flow. "Muh, Muh, Mommy."

"Yes?"

"Ih, ih, it's Laura."

"Yes, I know."

There was a pause while I struggled to speak. Finally, I squeaked, "I want to keep the baby."

I awaited the braying voice, the venom, the recriminations, the insults, the barbs. But she said softly, "Of course, you do, of course."

Then it was just her listening to me sob until I finally gasped, "But I, I just don't know. I don't think I can."

"It sure would be nice to have a little one around here. Yes, indeed, babies light things up. But it's something only you can decide."

My sobs subsided. "Okay, well, thank you for listening."

"Sure, sure."

When we hung up, I was breathing more easily. I thought about how through most of my pregnancy I had abhorred the new life occupying my body. I held no kind thoughts, made no plans—except for the baby's adoption, hastily arranged with a lawyer Bill found in the last trimester. How could all of my loathing just disappear at the sight of his slimy little body? How could I adore him so much? How could I be sure my hatred wouldn't resurface when I was alone with him and he started to cry?

Shortly after I hung up with Little Ma, Nurse Battleaxe from the emergency room came and sat by my bed. "You've got a strong love for that baby. You ought to keep him. Not every mother is overjoyed to see her child the way you were."

I wanted to scream at her, "That's easy for you to say. Who do you think is going to help me? You?" But I fumed in silence. I knew I couldn't count on the assistance of strangers. Who would want to follow through with a nineteen-year-old and her baby, a nineteen-year-old with no marketable skills, a nineteen-year-old who has proven herself to be unreliable?

"If you don't change your mind about this adoption, you're going to regret it for the rest of your life," Nurse Battleaxe said.

"I'll think about it." I closed my eyes and waited for her to leave, which she did, quietly.

In the following days, I did think it over. And today, I'm about to do something irreversible. A few minutes ago, the lawyer paid the hospital bill and came into the room to tell me I was discharged. He grabbed my arm as I slipped on my slicker. "Why do you still have your wristband on? There's no sense in that."

He marched to the nurse's station and came back with a pair of scissors, snipped off my plastic hospital ID, and threw it in the wastebasket. I wanted him to look away so I could scoop it up, tuck it somewhere, for always. But he didn't. Then Nurse Righteous came to the door, my swaddled son in her arms.

"See you out front," my lawyer said as he walked out the door

"Let's go." Nurse Righteous glared at me. I followed her out the door. We stopped at the nursing station so she could tell her co-workers what she was doing. Two women behind the counter stared, unsmiling. Their eyes seared into me the feeling that I am now marked for life. No matter where I go, what I do from here on, shame will shadow me.

Now, in the elevator, Nurse Righteous' disdain suffocates me. My son remains quiet in her arms. It's such a contrast to the racket he made all week. The nurses were constantly rushing by my door in response to his cries. "It's the little one again," they'd say. I was certain he was filled with hatred for me. He had every reason to be. I'd resented him with body and soul from the moment I could no longer deny that I was pregnant. Why wouldn't he be livid? I wonder whether he senses now that he's going home to parents who love him, that he'll soon be free of me for good.

As the elevator descends, I reaffirm silently that I will go through with this, must go through with this. A loving couple is waiting for him, longing for him. They have means; they have constant love. I have a spark of love, but could it survive the storm of parenthood? I can't even care for myself. How could I care for a baby? I feel there is too great a risk I would hurt him, if not physically, then certainly emotionally. Plus, if I decided to keep my son, I wouldn't even be able to cover the hospital bill. My lawyer waved the receipt in my face when he paid it: more than $500, not including whatever the doctor is going to charge. He reminded me I'd have to pay him back for that, as well as for the two prenatal visits I'd had, plus the time he'd spent on the adoption so far, if I changed my mind.

On the verge of the hand-off, I wish Nurse Battleaxe were with me instead of Nurse Righteous. In a few minutes I'm supposed to go on with my life and pretend this never happened. That's what unwed mothers who relinquish their children do.

In the back of my mind, I knew pregnancy was a possibility when I had unprotected sex. Of course, I knew. Why didn't I insist on condoms every time? Why did I not consult a doctor about alternatives? It's not like I thought I was immune from pregnancy. It's more that I wasn't thinking, wasn't all there. I was reckless, mindless. It's like all the different parts of me aren't in the same book, let alone on the same page. My conscious mind doesn't want to have sex at all. But there's power in the physical touch, the expression of tenderness that goes way deeper than words.

The elevator door opens at the ground floor. Kathy waits just outside, standing near the slush at the curb. She just got back to town this morning. Now she's on duty, tending to the off-key member of our sisterly triad. Thank God she's forgiven me for the upheaval we had in Boston almost two years ago. Otherwise, I'd be riding a bus back to the hole in the wall I share with Bill. Coming to the hospital after the birth wasn't at the top of Bill's list of things to do. He visited only once while I was in limbo, waiting for the baby to gain weight.

Nurse Righteous scowls and hands me the sleeping child. She has to let go. By law in Cook County, I, the birth mother must carry the child out of the hospital, and I have to be a certain distance from the door, before handing the baby off to my lawyer. Kathy's MGB is parked in the white zone. I limp over and wiggle into the passenger seat, balancing the slumbering babe in my arms. I'd thought of naming him Erin for Ireland, but people are starting to name their girls Erin, so I've settled on Liam instead, Liam Michael. That's who he is right now, for just a few moments. My lawyer said I cannot give him a name officially. On the adoption papers he will just be Baby Boy. It's better that way, he said, because it gives the adoptive parents a clean slate.

Kathy starts up the car, drives half a block and halts behind the lawyer's white Cadillac, which idles in front of a stop sign. A man is in the passenger seat. I expect it's the father to be. Liam's little face is so smooth, made to order, with long dark lashes, plump little cheeks. He slumbers on. My lawyer gets out, slops through the slush to my window and raps with his knuckles. Kathy looks straight ahead. I open the door, swivel my legs, ready to get out.

"No, don't," he says. "Stay there. I can get him." He reaches in and takes the sleeping bundle from my arms.

I swivel back to face forward. He closes the door, sprints back to his Cadillac, gets in. He stretches toward the passenger, who leans over to accept the baby. Kathy and I watch in silence. The luxury car pulls forward, turns right and then zooms out of sight.

"Where do you want to go, Laur?" Kathy asks.

I slump low in the seat. Inside my slicker pocket, I rub a gaggle of tiny red pills prescribed to dry up my milk. "I don't know. I don't care."

FORTY-FOUR

April 1969

THIS IS THE SUCKIEST APRIL I'VE ever seen. Gray clouds in gray skies, gray slush melting in gray gutters, cracked gray sidewalks. So many shades of gray to match my deepest gray spirits. Chicagoans ought to have as many words for gray as Eskimos have for snow. Not even one yellow crocus pokes through the patches of unpaved dirt around spiny trees dotting Clark Street. Naked branches, swaying ominously in the polluted breeze, remind me of hands stretching up from a grave in some old horror movie.

"Excuse me." A tottering old woman jerks her squeaking shopping cart past me. I wince and step aside so she doesn't have to navigate a melting snowdrift.

This time last year I would have raced past someone like her without more than a passing glance. Now I study the wild white curls bobbing against the back of her tattered, brown trench coat. Her feet in scuffed, black flats plod forward, going much faster than mine. I'll never again pass a person on a sidewalk without remembering how I am today, still a teenager, unable to keep up with a bent woman four times my age.

I have no plans other than to get well. Somehow. My healing has been delayed by the return of the kidney infection that leveled me in Kentucky. Each step hurts, every word I speak takes maximum effort. The sulfa pills I swallow every few hours make me incessantly thirsty, but penicillin might kill me. One dose of it when I was three years old puffed me up and turned me red; doctors always err on the side of caution and avoid prescribing the antibiotic.

I know there's more in need of healing than my kidneys and the rips and tears from giving birth. I've sunken into a sort of mental mud bath. It lulls me, comforts me, warms me, traps me. I feel as though I am no longer of this world. People's voices sound far away; answering questions seems impossible. This dark place of hiding has taken me over before, but only intermittently. Now, this is who I am. The girl I used to be is buried deep, probably dead.

Two days ago, I could walk only half a block. I stretched that to one full block yesterday before I turned around, exhausted. Today, I will do two. That is what I promised myself when I put on my slicker at the door to the studio apartment I share with Bill. So that is what I'll do, one step at a time.

As the distance between the old woman and me increases, I hear heavy, uneven footsteps approach from behind. That's the thing about city life. There's always someone in front or in back. I'm never alone while always alone. I look over my shoulder and see a middle-aged man wavering, drunk, his coat unbuttoned and open to the wind, his frayed shirt and baggy trousers wrinkled and stained. My eyes met his minutes earlier when I passed a bar, with its door open, shedding a trickle of light on the denizens within. I recognized in the scruffy man a battered, kindred spirit. He waved for me to come in, but I looked away and took a step forward. I've had a baby, but I've never set foot in a bar. I won't be able to do so legally until I'm twenty-one. I don't know if I'll want to go to bars when the time comes. Alcohol and drugs are not my friends. I cannot visit with them politely, talk small talk.

My thoughts drift to Trixie and how harshly I judged her back at the Y for having a baby when she was too young and unsettled to care for him, and then keeping it a secret. I'll never be able to sit in judgment of anyone else again, not after shame and sorrow have so fully filled my shoes. I take my next step, pause, then take another. This, at least, I can do. I go farther every day until I can walk for miles, lost in time and space and thought.

I have no appetite anymore. That has caused the pregnancy weight to peel off. I probably look like a normal nineteen year old, but I feel like an alien. I want only to hide, but my money is running low, so I must go to work as soon as I can.

So I walk on and on, step by step, hour by hour, and after weeks of going a little farther each day, I am able to to amble at a normal pace without pain. I work up the courage to answer a newspaper ad and land a job right away. Now, every weekday I board the Clark Street bus at Wellington, inch toward the back and slide into a window seat. Bill squints at me from the sidewalk, fists in his jacket pockets. When the driver accelerates, Bill sprints toward his bus on Halsted—the ritual of guarding me from door to bus stop complete.

I am a goldfish swimming in a plastic bag—like the orange babies I used to win every year at my grammar school fun fair by landing a ping pong ball in a bowl. Each victory was accompanied by the congratulatory smiles and nods of PTA moms who cared enough to volunteer at those sorts of things. They would hand over my prize, and I would run home, holding tight to the precious life inside, hoping I could keep the fish alive more than two weeks. Now, Bill is holding tight to the top of my bag, his taut fingers keeping me from spilling onto the anemic landscape of my life.

With the massive wheels churning below, my thoughts spin in circles, around and around, wearing deep grooves of worry in my psyche. This goes on every waking hour, most of which are spent typing installment loan documents at The First National Bank of

Chicago. I feel too undeserving to do anything else. I see my job as a form a penance for all my transgressions, failings and faults, the most egregious of which was bringing a baby into the world and giving him away.

I scrunch closer to the window and gaze at nothing in particular. A middle-aged man in the requisite charcoal business suit boards and shuffles toward the back. He slows near my row. Eyeing the available spots, he absentmindedly pulls on his mustache. I hope he picks the window seat across the aisle, but that would require moving past the woman in the spot next to it. She's absorbed in *Zen and the Art of Motorcycle Maintenance*. Bingo. He flops down next to me, his thick overcoat spreading around him as he lets out a long breath. He opens the *Chicago Tribune*. I am thankful he's not going to try to engage me in conversation, an art that eludes me now. I wish I could peruse a newspaper or delve into a novel on these rides. Then I'd escape from my life for a while. But I've never been able to read and ride without becoming nauseated.

The driver jerks us forward, calling out street names stop after stop; it's the same route every day, most of the same people getting on and off. When I lived in Hinsdale, coming to the city was a lark. Sometimes Shelby and I would ride the busses and laugh out loud at who knows what. I can't imagine what could have been so funny. I would look at people sitting glumly in their seats, and I'd swear I'd never be one of them. But here I am, still a teenager, exactly what I thought I'd never be.

The bus approaches the Loop. A weary man sits in a pawn shop doorway and chews a cigar. He's always there, always chewing, never smoking. He's even at his post on the coldest days, when taking in one small breath sears the lungs. Soon, we reach the Picasso sculpture at the Civic Center. This is my stop. My seatmate angles his legs to the side as I stand and say, "Excuse me." I brush his newspaper as I edge past. I imagine he's reading about the Chicago Seven, who are accused of inciting a riot during the Democratic National Convention last year. Most of my co-workers think the defendants are deranged. I think the opposite.

I wish I'd been in Chicago the night of the convention last year. I wish I'd heard Abby Hoffman, Jerry Rubin, David Dellinger, Tom Hayden and the other defendants speak to the crowd—from a safe distance, though, not in billy club range. I feel like those who were near the fray are my pack, and I've gotten separated from them. They've gone hunting without me, and I'm in the woods alone, winded, unable to pursue them. If I could catch up, they probably wouldn't recognize me as one of their own anyway. I am so changed, so empty, so lost. I'd like to pick up the pieces of my scattered self, put them back together in a sensible order, leave Bill and never look back. But it seems too much of who I used to be has simply vanished.

The last rider to step into the aisle, I drift toward the exit, step down the stairs and leap over the gutter to the sidewalk. I look up and follow the smooth lines of the bank building rising toward the clouds. I'd like to gaze skyward until the spirit moves me to go somewhere, any place I might be interested in. But there is no such place. Nothing in life captivates me, and my IBM Selectric typewriter awaits. I shove off and show my employee ID badge at the bank's gleaming glass door. The guard smiles; I wish I could smile back.

FORTY-FIVE

May 1970

THE DOORBELL RINGS. IT MUST BE KATHY. Who else would stop by on Saturday at 8:30 a.m.? Only Mary Ruth when she's on a break from school. How Kathy and I thrill to see her when she comes to town in her granny glasses, waist-length hair and 1930s style fur coat, a thrift store find. But Mary Ruth can't be at the door. She's studying away at school thousands of miles away. Bill gets up to push the buzzer, assuming it's friend down there, not foe. Without an intercom, the only way to check would be to walk down three flights of stairs. He returns and sits by me on the Murphy bed built into the living room wall.

Soon we hear footsteps in the hall. A knock at the door. Bill opens it. Kathy rushes inside, her cheeks rosy, blue eyes aglow, her hair, back to its natural brown, framing her face. She throws down her purse, dashes past the bed to the stereo, pulls an album from a bag and holds it up. It features three guys with long hair, looking serene on the front porch of a yummy old house, probably in California, I think.

"You have to listen to this." Kathy spins around to put the album on the turntable.

The room fills with Crosby, Stills and Nash's *Suite Judy Blue Eyes*. I bounce on the bed to the music.

Bill smiles and bobs a little, too. Then he stands up and asks, "Anybody want coffee?"

Kathy and I both accept the offer. Bill shuffles toward the kitchen. Kathy pulls me up, and dances me to the window, where she puts an arm around my shoulders and sings along softly. We sway together, looking out at the courtyard below. When the first track ends, I sit down, close my eyes and listen to the next, and the next. I'm swept away by the harmonies and lyrics wrapped around adventures in far-away places.

Kathy hands me the album cover. "I want to give this to you."

I stare at the musicians whose magic has brightened the room. I imagine I'm with them, taking their picture, chatting amiably, as though I'd known them all my life, as though I could still talk like a normal person. I try to give the cover back to her. "You shouldn't. It's not my birthday or anything. There's no reason."

"Oh, yes, there is." She pushes the gift back toward me. "This album reminds me of how full of possibility life is. You used to feel that way. You were bursting with life. I want you to have that back."

"Wow," I say, head down. It's been more than a year since I gave birth, and I've been plodding, broken, through my days ever since, barely able to talk to anyone, feeling permanently on the periphery of the human race.

"Yes, possibility, life, love, adventure, for you, my little sister. Mary Ruth would say the same if she were here."

Bill walks in holding two mugs of steaming coffee, hands one to each of us and saunters back to the kitchen to get his own. I sit back on the bed and take a sip. Kathy does, too. We listen in silence for a little longer. Then it's time for her to leave for a meeting with some folks who might hire her to do PR. After I close the door behind her, I dash to the window. Soon she emerges into the sunlight, looks up and waves as she wends her way backward through the courtyard toward the sidewalk. I wave back until she steps out of sight. Bill comes up from behind and reminds me we'd planned to go shopping to buy me a dress, and the magic from Kathy's visit slips away.

Within an hour, we are at Marshall Field's downtown. I smooth the front of a white mini dress and fasten the small, square black buttons that run down the front, collar to hem. "He's not your boyfriend, is he?" The salesgirl whispers to me, as though we were the best of friends. "I mean ... he's so ... old."

Bill sits in a chair outside the dressing room. With only 149 pounds on his towering frame, he looks like a giant greyhound set to race. Since we arrived in Chicago, we've explored various alternatives to Scientology: Georges Ohsawa's macrobiotics, Madam Blavatsky's theosophy, Edgar Cayce's spirituality, various types of astrology. Most recently we read about the life of nutrition guru Arnold Ehret. Popular in the early years of the century, he advocated a diet of fruit, starchless vegetables and herbs, along with periodic fasting. So we've been subsisting on his regimen, except for when our stomachs growl so loudly, we can't bear it. Then we pop a batch of popcorn and cut up a chunk of Swiss cheese and eat until our bodies can hold no more.

I'm so thin Bill's fingertips almost meet when he grabs me around my waist, and every woman I work with at the bank has expressed envy—except for my co-worker La Donna, who thinks I've gone too far ever since she learned I don't weigh enough to participate in the bank's periodic blood drives. That day I weighed in at 108. I wonder what she would say if she knew I'm down to 106 now.

I study the black piping around the sleeves, collar and waist of the dress I might buy. The salesgirl peers over my shoulder. Her sparkling blue eyes and wide smile make her look effervescent—the opposite of how I feel.

"He's not my boyfriend," I say. It's not exactly a lie. He's thirty-three, hardly a boy. Plus, I'm marrying him next week, so technically, he's my fiancé.

I was sure I'd leave Bill right after the adoption papers were signed. But more than a year has come and gone, and I'm still under his thumb. I left him briefly a few months ago and stayed with Judy, the girlfriend of one of Bill's buddies. Judy's apartment was one block from Chicago's western border and spitting distance from the L leading straight to the Loop. It was a smooth commute to the bank, and the first few days went just fine. But then came the weekend. Judy dashed out Friday night to buy Virginia Slims cigarettes and returned with two guys she'd met on the sidewalk. They made a couple of phone calls, and soon the living room was full of strangers. One curly haired guy with big brown eyes took a liking to me, said he knew Hugh Heffner and could get me a job as a Playboy Bunny, a line so unbelievable, given my Twiggy-like figure, I was immediately on guard. He offered me a joint, put his arm around me. I pulled away and ran to the kitchen, where I grabbed an apple and a bag of chips and withdrew to the bedroom, closed the door, and crawled under the covers.

This is the post sexual revolution. All the old morals have been thrown out the window. What that means to a reasonably attractive woman is that there are guys like roaches everywhere crawling out of the woodwork wanting to screw you, and if you're not interested in them, they don't think, "Yeah, maybe my breath stinks" or "I've got bug eyes" or "The big zit festering on my nose really isn't sexy, and besides she doesn't even know me." No, they think, "Man, that chick's uptight! What's wrong with her? She's like ice, some kind of prude."

Except for trips to the bathroom, I remained in the bedroom until Judy called Bill two days after her impromptu party. She said

I was in bed because I missed him and should go back. I knew it wasn't Bill's absence immobilizing me; it was the dread I first met in high school, only multiplied, cocooning me, mummifying my dreams. When Bill arrived, he pulled me out of bed. I didn't object when he said it was time to go home.

The upside is that when I'm with Bill I only have to deal with him. He has to get his penis inside me every three days or else. As each day passes without sex, he gets more uptight, like a rubber band stretching thinner and thinner in some schoolboy's fingers at the back of class. One time he waited outside the bathroom while I brushed my teeth. He had his ear to the door. When I came out he said, "You were masturbating in there, weren't you."

"Are you crazy?" I said. Masturbation isn't my thing. I've had enough clitoral stimulation to last a lifetime. Bill's fingers works on me like he's prospecting for gold. He never finds the mother lode, but he persists because, he says, if he can get the ecstasy of sex to overpower me, I'll be his forever.

Being his forever, or even just for now, isn't what I want, but I don't see a way out. There are hidden dangers in living with some-one, things you can't really know until you do it. For the generation before me, premarital sex is a no-no, and living together before marriage is still unthinkable to most of them. In snippets of small talk, I heard my elders complain about my generation's lack of mor-als. But just saying breaking their rules about sex isn't good doesn't provide illumination. Why is it bad? Reasons? They offered none.

Now I have reasons. I'm full of reasons. It's not that I think living with a lover is wrong; it seems to work fine for some people. But the thing I didn't know beforehand is that this person you've taken up with becomes part of you. You breathe the same air, sleep in the same bed, fill the same trashcan, share the same dishes. Your toothbrushes are next to each other in a holder by the sink; your shoes are on opposite sides of the closet floor. You become family in day-to-day ways that grow on you. For some, maybe these little bonds hold no power. I didn't think they would matter to me. But I've found that each day I remain with Bill, the less ready I am to part with him than the day before. So when Bill asked me to marry him shortly after my attempt to strike out on my own, I figured I'm stuck with him, so I may as well be married.

Now I'm looking for a dress that will work well enough for a wedding but will also be suitable for work afterward. I only make $350 a month at the bank, so I have to stretch every dollar.

"We've been trying to guess who he is," the salesgirl says. "He doesn't look quite old enough to be your father, so we think he must be an uncle or something like that."

"Yeah, something like that." I offer a perfunctory smile. At the occasional social gatherings Bill and I attend, someone will invariably pull me aside and ask what a good-looking girl like me is doing with a man like Bill. I can't explain it to myself, let alone to anyone else.

"An uncle, then?" The salesgirl bats her eyelashes. I think they must be fake.

"I'll take this one." I undo the buttons one by one and wonder what it will be like when I'm a married woman, whether anything will change.

FORTY-SIX

May 1971

ONE YEAR HAS CRAWLED BY SINCE Bill's and my wedding on the Lake Michigan shore—a mail order minister presiding, his barefoot girlfriend the only witness. I feel dragged through the days as though I'm tied to the back of a Clark Street bus at rush hour. People drive or walk by, but they're so preoccupied with getting home or to their next rendezvous that they don't notice anything is amiss. I'm invisible as I go through my routine, typing the hours away at the First National Bank of Chicago, an IBM Selectric welded to my being. And I'm invisible now as I squeeze into a spot on Shelby and Daniel's couch. They were married a couple years ago when Shelby was four months pregnant, and they have a little girl, Marnie, who is three months younger than my son, whose name and whereabouts I'll never know.

The scent of marijuana permeates the packed living room. Bill and I are here only because Shelby kept phoning, pestering me to come. I finally relented even though I just want to be left alone. Shelby either hasn't noticed or refuses to accept that I do not want to try to make small talk with old acquaintances who party at her home. Since I became pregnant a year after graduating from high school, when I was a couple months shy of 19, it's not like everyone in Shelby's circle knows I gave a child up for adoption, although I'm sure Shelby has told quite a few of them. But here's the thing: based on what I'd heard about teenage pregnancy, I thought giving my son up would make for a better life for him and for me. I'm certain he's in good hands with a couple who had wanted to start a family for a long time and had the means to provide for him. I, on the other hand, am stuck like the people of Pompeii perpetually fleeing from the wrath of Mt. Vesuvius. Giving my son up was supposed to afford me the opportunity to resume a normal life, learn and grow, but some essential part of me is missing, and Bill has come in to fill the void like the scientists who unearthed Pompeii, not with plaster casts like they used, but with his desires. He directs my every move, and I follow as though I have no will of my own.

Even if I could lift myself out of this funk, where would I go? I couldn't stay here at Shelby's. She has no room, has her hands full with Marnie, and her life is chaotic with people always coming and going. She and Daniel snipe at each other incessantly, too. My sisters are out. Mary Ruth is living in a college dorm, and Kathy is between apartments right now. Some young people in crisis go home to their parents. But Little Ma, formerly known as Wanda, is no longer legally responsible for my welfare and doesn't want to play a parental role in my life. She would welcome me in if I would agree to be her full-time caregiver, but while my feelings have softened toward her and she now shows kindness from time to time, I'm not about to get sucked into her world again. I'm sure being her live-in helper would be even more soul numbing than living with Bill.

I'm outwardly calm as I settle into the couch, but my tummy is all butterflies. When Bill and I arrived a short time ago, Shelby told me Michael will be here today. She sometimes includes news of Michael when she phones me, dropping tidbits in at the end of conversations, as though they hold less meaning for me than the weather. "Oh yeah, you know Michael's in Nepal now, trying to figure out how to set up some kind of import/export business. Why doesn't he just get a real job?" or "He's living in an unheated building in Toronto. It's so bizarre.

He doesn't even have a warm blanket." According to Shelby, Michael has never asked about me, not even when Daniel invited him over today. I'm always at a lost for words when she says stuff like that. I don't know if she's just insensitive or if she's down right cruel. I haven't seen Michael since we kissed goodbye on the porch of Holy Family Academy. I can't imagine what I'll do when I look into his eyes after all this time, more than four years. I also wonder whether Bill will be angry if I say more than a quick hello.

The day after we got hitched, Bill searched through my drawers for the gold and jade ring Michael gave me. I stopped wearing it around my neck after I moved into Bill's room at the org, but I kept it in a coin purse and would take it out every now and then when I was home and Bill wasn't. Bill found the ring, slipped it off the chain and onto his finger. "I'm your husband now. This ring should be mine. You have no business keeping it." A few weeks later, our apartment was burglarized. Thieves took our television and stereo—and Michael's ring, which Bill hadn't worn to work that day. Bill was livid. I kept mum, thinking it must have been a form of divine intervention.

People are always coming and going at Shelby and Daniel's, and I can barely return a hello when one of them greets me. Sometimes I'll take acid, sit still and stare at Shelby's evergreen hedge for hours. I don't want to be in a stupor when Michael arrives today though, so I refuse a tab Daniel offers me. Instead, I force myself to get up and step outside where the sun is shining. Marnie waves to me from her sandbox. Looking into her blue eyes, I wonder what my boy looks like now, whether his eyes are blue, brown or maybe even a dark greenish blend like mine.

I approach the rose bushes bordering the yard, lean in and take in a whiff of the sweet fragrance. I linger for some time at the hedge, feeling a stronger connection to the flowers and thorns than to anyone chatting nearby. When I turn around, I see Michael walking toward me, a tentative smile on his face. I feel a softening inside, a little glow. My pulse quickens. I want to run to him. But I stand in place, glancing from him, to the hedge, to the lawn, back to him, back to the hedge. When we are close enough to touch, he holds out his hands. My fingers meet his, and we pause inches apart. His eyes convey warmth, but not joy like they did the day we parted. We separate and walk in silence along the hedge. Finally he stops and asks, "Are you happy, Laura?"

I want to say I'm so far from happy, I don't have words to describe it. I want out of my life so bad it hurts like a polar bear tearing at my chest. But Shelby told me Michael came to town with a woman he lives with and will probably marry. Would he be willing to turn his back on her? Could I walk away from Bill? I am too chicken to find out. I just say, "Yeah, I guess I'm happy."

"I'm glad, then. I want that for you." I sense caring in his voice, maybe even love, but my mind is a traffic jam of thoughts. There are so many things I could say, I can't pick one thing and blurt it out. And since he's made no effort to contact me, except for one Christmas card long ago, what difference does it really make to him what I say?

Shelby steps into the yard. Bill comes out right behind her. She waves at Michael and me. I take Michael's hands in mine and say, "I hope you're having the best life ever." I let go and dash across the lush lawn to the porch, where Bill and Shelby are examining the barbecue chicken on the grill.

"So, that's the great, mysterious Michael," Bill says when I reach them.

I shrug and watch the sizzling meat in silence.

FORTY-SEVEN

July 1972

LA DONNA AND I CIRCLE CARSON PIRIE SCOTT'S furniture department. We are killing time before French class at the Loop branch of Chicago City College. La Donna and I met when she was a teller, and I was a clerk-typist at the bank. She liked her job, and I hated mine. She grew up in Cabrini Green, known to be one of the most violent public housing projects in Chicago, and I grew up in Hinsdale, one of the city's most affluent suburbs. But she invited me to take a coffee break with her my first day on the job, and we hit off. We started going to lunch together in the bank's cafeteria, which has provided free lunch for employees since the Great Depression. The laughs we shared are what made the job bearable. She calls me her conservative hippie because I love the *Whole Earth Catalog*, and my long hair now reaches to my elbows. I call her Isadora Duncan because she always keeps a long, colorful scarf handy, and when foot traffic is slow and no supervisors are looking, she waves the scarf in the air and dances out of her teller cage and down the hallway to the bathroom.

I left the bank about a year ago to work for a real estate developer of apartments for low- and moderate-income people. The developer's latest project is a new kind of community of sales and rental townhouses for people of all different incomes. My boss is a partner in the firm who is also a lawyer, so he takes care of the purchase agreements and all sorts of other legal aspects of housing development. I help with all his paperwork, but there's also a group of buyers who put down payments on units long before the project broke ground and a waiting list of families eager to buy a town home if one becomes available. They all have questions about the units under constructions, and they call the office frequently to get answers. The office is short-staffed, and nobody was returning their calls, so I learned how to read blueprints and consulted the architect for questions I couldn't figure out. Now I'm the go-to person for the project. And when a buyer grows impatient and backs out of the deal, I call the family at the top of the waiting list. We meet at the site; I take them on a tour, prepare their contracts and get them to sign. It's a lot more interesting than typing at the bank ever was.

La Donna still likes her job, though. She joined a management-training program, and the bank's going to pay for her schooling all the way through a master's degree in some area of finance. I have no idea what I want to major in, definitely not finance, though. A guidance counselor in high school said my language aptitude test scores were so high I should study foreign languages and become an interpreter. I don't know why that idea has never grabbed me. I seem only to feel strongly about what I don't want and can never get a picture of what I want. Going to school at night is good for me, though. I'm meeting people my own age who have so much energy they seem to sparkle with fairy dust. Bill lets me go to class only begrudgingly and picks me up every evening in an orange Karman Ghia we just bought. If I'm talking with any male classmates when he pulls up to the curb, veins are popping out at his temples when I slide into the passenger seat.

La Donna and I often meet at Carson's before class to browse the domestic vignettes. They are perfect, three-dimensional still lifes we can step into, imagining what it would be like to own a butter-soft tan suede couch and matching stuffed chairs or a queen-size bed with teak headboard, a reading light on each side, and a little shelf for books or knickknacks. Each time I brush my hands across the brocade of an ottoman or take a seat at a dining room table large enough for a boarding house, the fantasy of having a different life consumes me. In my daydreams, I don't live with Bill in a rundown apartment decorated in what I call Early Modern Woolworth's—our end tables fashioned from floor tiles glued to cardboard, our tattered couch, table and chairs culled from dumpsters and damp basements.

Today, La Donna and I settle into a pair of straight-backed chairs at a cherry-wood dining table. I concentrate on an oil painting of cherubs dancing around a tree.

"What is it, Laura?" La Donna asks. "You're even more quiet than usual."

"I don't know. Just feeling down, I guess. "

"Come dancing with me and Hal tonight after class. That'll pep you up. We can drive you home, too."

"That's way out of your way."

"Sometimes a drive up the lake shore is just the thing to set the stage for romance," she says.

"Nah, Bill's picking me up, like always. Besides, your romance doesn't need staging."

Hal is La Donna's third husband. At her wedding reception she said three is the charm, and she kept trying until she found the right man, the one who makes her happy in every way. She emphasized "every" in a Mae West tone, one eyebrow raised.

A saleswoman in a black pantsuit approaches. Her nametag says Carole. "May I help you?" she asks.

"No thanks, Carole. We're just looking," La Donna says.

We get up and walk the department's perimeter in silence before sitting again, this time on a trundle bed, made up with sheets, comforter, and pillow cases in bold, primary colors. A fake window on the wall has matching curtains. I wonder what it would have been like to say the "Now I lay me down to sleep" prayer in such a room, a haven someone had decorated just for me.

"I don't love him." I look down at my comfy burgundy leather shoes with rounded toes and one-inch heels.

La Donna takes my hand and pats it several times. Her salmon-hued nail polish complements her light brown skin. "You're saying you don't love Bill. Bill, your husband of what—two years now?"

"Two years, two months. Seems like an eternity."

"Look at me, girl." She lifts my chin. Her big brown eyes hold compassion and humor. "This is true, really, true that you don't love him?"

"Most mornings I wake up and I fantasize about him dying." I turn my head away.

"And you're married to him?"

"Married, and about to move with him to Lansing, Michigan. He's getting transferred there, unless he dies first, of course." I crack a nervous smile.

"Girl, I don't know what's going on in that head of yours. But if you don't love him, then you can't go to Michigan with him. You gotta leave him."

"It is sick, isn't it, wishing him dead. I'm just a wreck, a ruin, I guess."

"You're not the first person who's ever wished that," she says. "It's just a message from you to you is all. You've gotta ask yourself, do you want to wake up ten years from now in the same fix?

"Definitely not, not at all, but I'm wrecked, a ruin. I don't know what to do."

"You might feel like a ruin now, but mark my words, my friend, you're resilient, too."

"A resilient ruin, is that it?"

She laughs. "Girl, you crack me up."

I see Carole making a beeline toward us. "Hey, look, there's our gal, zeroing in again. Let's split before she gets here."

La Donna and I scramble off the trundle bed and bolt toward the escalator. As we descend, she says, "You know I'm here for you, don't you?"

"Yeah, but, see, I'm not here for me. I don't know if I ever will be."

"You're making things way too complicated. Life's too short for that shit."

We reach the ground floor. "How 'bout we try out some perfume." I look at a nearby display. "I want something fancy, from Paris maybe."

"I know just the one." La Donna steps ahead and motions for me to follow, which I do, wishing perfume could cast a magic spell, one that would make me more like La Donna and less like myself.

FORTY-EIGHT

September 1972

DRESSED FOR WORK IN BLUE SHIRT and beige slacks, Bill opens our front door, but instead of stepping out of the Lansing apartment we now call home, he turns away from the threshold, points a finger at me and says, "If I find out you're fucking Steve, I'll kill you both."

I shiver by the dining room table. "This is because I went with him to buy wine yesterday?" I ask.

It seemed like a harmless outing to me when Bill's long-time friend Steve asked if I'd ride along with him to pick up more booze for a party he threw to welcome Bill and me to Michigan. It didn't occur to me Bill would mind. I now realize he must have stewed all night about what he imagined Steve and I must have done in all of twenty minutes away from him.

"You two are up to something. I know it, and I swear you'll both be dead if I catch you." He slams the door on his way out.

His threat hangs in the air as I dash to the window, pull aside the sheet, a temporary curtain, and see a parking lot, gravel, a field of tall grass stretching to the horizon, a little road recently paved a thick, gooey black. Bill emerges from the building and saunters through the Indian summer morning to our orange Karman Ghia—stupid stick-shift car I never learned to drive. It didn't help that Bill yelled at me for not releasing the clutch smoothly enough during the one lesson he gave me. There can be no jerky shifting around Bill, just like there can never be one thing out of place, not a magazine on the kitchen table, not a tissue left overnight in a wastebasket, not one shoe knocked out of its neat little row in the closet. But I can't blame him for my driving problems. All of my troubles started long before I met him.

Bill towers over the car, thinning hair on top of his head resembling an old shirt shredded at the elbows. He opens the door, scrunches his spindly frame inside, starts the engine and backs out of the space. He doesn't look up before turning onto the road and zooming out of sight. I sit for a few minutes to make sure he doesn't return. Then I call Kathy in Chicago.

"Hello?" she says.

"Kathy, it's me. Bill just threatened to kill me."

"Really? Oh, Laur."

"I don't know if he would really do it."

"That man is a loser."

"I don't love him."

"I know. I know."

"I don't like being stuck here in Lansing either."

"Listen, I'll take the day off and come get you."

"You don't have to. I could take the bus or something."

"Nonsense. This is what sisters do, you know."

"Okay, okay ... Kathy?"

"Yeah?"

"You're a peach."

"Just sit tight. It'll be okay."

I go to the kitchen to make some Lopsang Souchong tea, craving its smoky, bitter taste. I think about the last time I tried to leave Bill just over a year ago. I stayed in an apartment Mary Ruth rented with some friends. She was back in town to earn some cash before heading to law school in California. Venturing out with her in the evenings,

I started to laugh again. Colors everywhere looked brighter. But then I saw Bill walking toward me in Lincoln Park one Saturday. I hadn't considered the possibility of encountering him, even though we were living only four blocks apart. I panicked and stopped. The sight of him caused all of my optimism to go into hiding.

"Can we talk?" he asked.

"Okay."

We found a bench and sat down.

"How've you been?" His voice cracked, and his words snapped in around me, clicking me into a place I didn't want to go. I wanted to get up and run away, but my body wouldn't move.

"I've been fine." I looked across the path at pigeons pecking in the grass.

"Laura, I can't live without you. And you can't live without me. It's only a matter of time before you fall apart. You'll overeat, get fat. You have to stop this nonsense and come home."

The happiness I'd felt just moments before vanished, as though a malevolent wizard had waved a magic wand. Negativity rose from within and snuffed out my fledgling dreams. My forays into a new life seemed utterly false, a fantasy.

He reached for my hand. I let him take it. "Come back to me," he begged.

I tried not to feel sorry for him, but I did. And I felt not a shred of compassion for myself, certain I'd been a fool to dream of a better life. I agreed to return to him.

Now, I hope I'll be able to break away for good. I finish my tea and flit around, a clumsy ballerina leaping and spinning to the very real thought of escape. The apartment is flooded with late summer's light, making it seem like a happier home than it is, especially since it's a new building with no memories oozing from the walls, no secrets whispering through creaking furnaces and rusting pipes. I turn on the radio, and *Good Morning, Starshine* from the musical *Hair*, comes on. What a joyous song. I try to sing along, but my throat tightens, no sound comes. Still, the song's optimism lifts my mood. I spin around the apartment, surveying each room for things I need to take with me. One bedroom, one bathroom. A narrow kitchen, more of an alcove, really, and an open L-shaped living and dining area. A few closets. Pretty sparce. We moved here only three weeks ago when Bill's employer transferred him from Chicago. It doesn't feel at all like home.

Kathy drives a VW bug these days, so there's scant room for cargo. I slide open the bedroom closet door and pull out a handful of work dresses and throw them on the bed. I add a trio of blouses with open collars and puffy sleeves that were on sale at Casual Corner, my favorite long brown skirt, and a purple dress Mary Ruth mailed to me because she saw it in New York and thought it was perfect for me. I open a dresser drawer and yank a favorite pair of jeans that I've patched, appliquéd and embroidered to perfection. I add them to the heap, along with corduroy Levis, white hot pants, a few T-shirts, a fuchsia bikini and a couple of sweaters. I add underwear and nighties, a few scarves, a bright pink hat Kathy crocheted for me, a pair of wool gloves, and a little box of jewelry. I stuff all of that into a blue American Tourister suitcase. In a paper bag, I drop two pairs of shoes, winter boots, two macramé belts Kathy and I made together, and toiletries from the bathroom. Across the suitcase, I drape a jacket and a full-length wool coat. That's it. I'm done in ten minutes. The dishes I'll leave with the furniture. I don't want to be reminded of eating with Bill when I go.

It takes about four hours to drive from Chicago to Lansing. That gives me plenty of time to think about how I went so terribly wrong. I turned twenty-three last week, and I've spent almost all of my adult life with a man I don't love. This has been a time when America has opened up and exploded. People my age are so full of energy, so enthusiastic about being part of some great unknown, but certain to be better future. My peers have flocked to protest the Vietnam War, swoon at music festivals, break bread at communes, witness bra burnings, get arrested at sit-ins on university campuses. They've hitchhiked across Europe, fallen in love and moved to homesteads in the country, trekked to South America and the Far East. They've been growing in experience, growing in confidence, growing in possibilities.

I've done nothing but shrink. I wish I could erase the last five or six years of my life, live them over, the way I think they were supposed to be. It's like I took a detour into someone else's life. How could the person I've been all these years really be me? I take a yellow legal pad and ballpoint pen from a desk drawer, return to the window and sit down. I want to write Bill a farewell note but don't know where to begin.

FORTY–NINE

September 1972

AFTER DUMPING USED PAPER PLATES, PLASTIC utensils and Arby's sandwich wrappers into the trash, Kathy picks up our stepmother's bright yellow phone and dials Mary Ruth in California. I wipe down the dining room table before joining the woman who poisoned my childhood, who, much like she used to do, is issuing complaints from her recliner in the living room. My sisters and I call her Little Ma now, though no form of "mother" describes what she is to us. It's just a name we came upon that embraces her but also keeps her at a distance with a touch of humor.

I thought when I graduated from Holy Family Academy and flew to Boston that I was out of her clutches at last. And in a way, that was true. Feeble in mind and body, she commands nothing these days. I can't help but have pity for her. I don't know quite when it happened, but somewhere along the line I realized as long as I don't expect her to love me like a parent would, I can spend limited amounts of time with her. My sisters, each in her own time and way, came to a similar conclusion. And there's something comforting about returning to the home my father and uncle built long ago with so much hope hammered into every nail.

I sit on the floor by Little Ma's recliner, surrounded by stacks of *Women's Day, Good Housekeeping* and *Better Homes and Gardens.* She bumps the end table with her wrist, sending a clutter of prescription pill vials to my lap. I return the medicines to the table and begin massaging her tiny feet, size four and a half. Her parakeet, Murphy, chatters nearby, a blue and white cacophony bobbing his head up and down as he careens sideways along his perch, batting millet sprigs as he goes by. Seeds spray all over the wall-to-wall carpet. Someone will vacuum them, but not me.

Kathy enters and hands Little Ma the phone. "Mary Ruth wants to say hello," she says.

Little Ma bites her fever-blistered lips. Everything about her is going haywire. Her eyes, clouded with glaucoma, no longer express the rage that has ravaged her for decades. Next time I visit, she may only see a blur when I kiss her clammy forehead in greeting. She won't guess my name. She'll wait for clues because she has never been good at distinguishing my voice from my sisters'. In fundamental ways, we have all been the same to her, each girl a corner of a triad attached to the man she loved, the man who died and left her to scratch her elbows and spew obscenities until she could push us out her door without losing face among her friends and neighbors.

A few moments ago, while chewing her roast beef sandwich, she asked me to move in with her. She wants to conscript my future as she stumbles toward death. But after spending only an hour in her home, I feel as though I owe her the world when I know I owe her nothing. I must stumble toward life instead.

"Well, I don't like it—Laura gallivanting off to see you. It's not like she's in school or anything," Little Ma says into the phone. "Get her head together? That's a bunch of hooey. ... She could stay right here and do some good for me for a change. ... All right. ... No. Don't say that. ... You don't give a damn; you've never cared a rat's ass about me, none of you do. ... Nonsense. ... You didn't have to invite her to California. ... You just had to go to some fancy-schmancy school all the way across the country, didn't you. ... I may as well be dead for all you care. ... Fine. Yes, yes, then goodbye. ... Don't bother."

Little Ma hands the phone back to Kathy, who almost trips on the extra long cord as she returns to the dining room. She regains her balance and fills Mary Ruth in on my itinerary before hanging up. I'll be flying from Chicago to San Francisco. No return ticket. Mary Ruth shares a ranch house with three roommates in a place called Menlo Park. It's near Stanford, where she's in law school. They decided I can stay in their spare bedroom as long as I like unless I turn out to be someone who eats goldfish, walks around the house in her underwear and a boa, or something else weird like that. They're all second-year law students. I wonder if I'll even be able to talk to them.

I squeeze out some Jergen's lotion and breathe in its familiar almond aroma. I rub the balm into Little Ma's heels. They're rough and cracked, just like her mind. Then I put white crew socks on her feet, followed by the open-toe, strap-back, black canvas wedgie shoes she's worn forever. Similar shoes are in fashion now. I laughed when I saw them selling for twenty dollars at Chandler's. I don't care how popular or in vogue they become; no wedgies will ever be seen on my feet.

"I guess it's time to get going." Kathy leans against the wall near Little Ma's chair.

"Sure, sure, back to the city where life is so much better than it is here with an old bat like me." Little Ma sniffs several short breaths through her nose, then tightens her lips before opening her mouth to let out a long belch that permeates the air with a faint smell of onion.

It's useless to argue with her, as always. Even ordinary conversation is not possible. Growing up with her, I couldn't see how far gone she was, how truly disconnected from reality. Now I can tell there is a person trapped inside of her who comes out in rare bursts of lucidity, like when I called her from the hospital after my son's birth. Her kindness shocked me. The person I hope she really is deep down peeked out. Most of the time, however, it's like she is merely running a series of recordings that have taken her over. With my sisters and me, she's most often spouting a familiar litany of vitriol; when she switches to her charming mode, she talks in a jumble of clichés from movies and TV. I pat her tiny feet, thinking I've never known her and probably never will.

"So long for now." I stand up and reach for my purse on the chair across from her.

"Take one of those umbrellas, there." Little Ma points to a corner near the chair. "I got three for a dollar at Ben Franklin the other day."

"Um, it's not raining." I recall with embarrassment the many trips with her to that store during my childhood.

She sniffs and folds her arms across her chest. "Well, suit yourself, but into every life, as they say, and don't look a gift horse, you know."

"Okay, you've convinced me," I say, realizing it's her way of trying to wish me well. "Thanks." I pick up the umbrella.

"Don't let the door hit you in the ass on your way out." She chortles, picks up the remote and turns on the TV.

I bend down and give her a good-bye peck on the cheek. Kathy does the same. Once outside, I open the umbrella, put it over my shoulder and twirl it, then I hold it out at arm's length and spin around on my way to the car. "Into every life ..." I say.

Kathy leaps out of the umbrella's path, laughing. "Don't look a gift horse ..." she says.

I catch my breath at Kathy's VW door and survey the block where I spent endless hours dreaming up games to push away the sadness that permeated every crevice of my childhood. It's just a quiet suburban street like countless others across the country. But the trees turning from green to shades of red, orange and brown; the houses with new coats of paint; the cars fresh off the assembly line and pulled into tidy garages; the neighbors still peeping from curtains, looking for secrets unfolding—all of it fills me with anxiety. I close the umbrella and crunch into the passenger seat, relieved I won't ever again have to call this place home. Kathy starts up the engine and backs out of the driveway.

"So, it's off on an adventure for you in the morning," Kathy says. "That's good. If you stayed with me in Chicago, Bill might drive down and try to get you back, but he won't buy a plane ticket to pursue you."

"Remember when he said he wouldn't spend two dollars to see Jesus Christ?"

"Yeah, but it's all over now. You're free. You can travel. You can go back to school full time. You can do anything."

"That reminds me of something." I dig through my purse and pull out *What Color Is Your Parachute?*, a book I plan to read on the plane. I flip through the pages, find a bookmark and hold it up. "Shelby sent me this. It says, 'Today is the first day of the rest of your life.' I've been seeing that everywhere lately."

"Me too," Kathy replies. "There's always some truth in those clever little sayings people glom onto."

"Yeah, but I want to figure out how to make this one really mean something."

"You will, dear. I know you will." Kathy eases the car along the streets we used to walk as children. Soon we'll be speeding east along the freeway toward Kathy's New Town apartment.

I turn on the radio. The Eagles' *Take it Easy* fills the car. Kathy sings along. Reveling in her strong, clear voice, I join in, faltering, barely audible. The days when I belted out every tune that blasted from my transistor radio come to mind. Music once gave me energy, life, connected me to my peers. Now it's barely on the periphery. I haven't been able to sing since I gave my son away.

"That's good, Laur. Keep it up; keep it up. We'll be harmonizing in no time," Kathy says.

As she merges the Beetle onto the freeway, I envision Little Ma's and Bill's claims on me melting like snow during a January thaw. This brings forth a little smile, not an ear-to-ear, teeth-showing, joyous smile, but a quiet smile coming from hope birthing deep within. I have demons lurking inside, too; there will be no clean slate for me, no miracles. Whatever follows once I board the plane for California tomorrow won't be easy. But I hope to persevere, to muster the courage to dive back into the pool after belly flops so big I feel I'll never breathe again. Thinking about my life so far I feel like a jellyfish forever drifting alone in the ocean, but I realize I've never truly been alone. Kathy and Mary Ruth, Gramma, Uncle John, Uncle Thomas, Mrs. Henderson, the Sisters at Holy Family Academy, many friends along the way, and sometimes even strangers, have all pulled for me at different times and in different ways. I hope someday to become a source of happiness for them, not worry; to stop punishing myself for a past I cannot undo; to face forward and take small, solid steps toward a better life.

Epilogue

I'LL BEGIN WITH AN ADVENTURE FROM February 1973, five months after I boarded a plane to visit Mary Ruth in California. The story was published in 2015 in the *My Gutsy Story 2* anthology.

The Icelandair flight taxis down the runway. I peer out the window, a brown suede shoulder bag clutched to my chest. Moments later, the jet lifts off and zooms toward the clouds. New York City shrinks, the North American continent recedes, and it hits me: we're crossing the Atlantic; there's no turning back.

I open my bag to affirm the travelers checks, passport and open-ended return ticket are tucked where I last saw them—about a minute ago. Also inside is a note with the address of a friend of a friend in Switzerland, along with a list of Youth Hostels in Europe.

It's 1973. I am twenty-three years old and feel like my adult life so far has been a great big zero. No, scratch that. It's been a negative number. I just left a man thirteen years older than I am. A man I met when I was eighteen and confused. A man I didn't love but married anyway because I thought I'd never be able to leave him. A man who recently threatened to kill me. That jolted me out the door, at last.

Now I am about to land in Luxembourg without a plan. I might be crazy; I don't know. I've attended night school, and I want to return to college full time. But when I think of sitting in a classroom with students several years younger than I am, I can't imagine what

I would say about myself. That I could have gone to college right out of high school, but I put it off, stumbled instead into things that ripped me apart and left me that way? That I allowed myself to be so completely controlled by someone that I often couldn't even speak? That I don't know if I deserve to have any hopes at all? Not exactly good ice-breaker material.

I want to create a new life, a different me. Flying to a continent where I don't know a soul may be foolhardy. But I've heard that young people from all over the world hitchhike and ride trains throughout Europe, and the people there welcome them. I thought I'd give it a try.

I nap during the flight and then delve into *The Teachings of Don Juan* before the plane lands for a stopover in Reykjavik, Iceland. It's 11 a.m. and pitch black when the other passengers and I deplane to explore the wares on sale in the airport store. I admire a brown lopapeysa-style sweater with a yoke of brown white and tan. A woman who looks about my age approaches and says, "Nice, huh." The lenses of her wire-rimmed glasses are tinted pink.

"Sure is, but it's probably way too expensive for me," I say.

"Me, too. Dan–the guy over there; he's my boyfriend." She points to a tall man with long, wavy brown hair. He's wearing a green parka and looking at a jewelry display. "We have about four hundred dollars to last us our whole trip."

"I've got less than that, but there's only one of me." We both laugh.

"I'm Mags." She extends her hand.

"Laura." I reach out, too, and we shake.

"Where are you headed when we land?" she asks.

"The Youth Hostel."

"That's where we're going; let's go together."

"Sounds good to me."

Dan looks up and motions for Mags to come over. "Oh, my guy's up to something. I'll see you later," she says.

After we arrive in Luxembourg, Mags introduces me to Dan and three other young travelers she's just met. We all pick up our backpacks and duffel bags and share a ride to the city, marveling at the breathtaking bridges we pass. Once we're on the street, I find the address of the local Youth Hostel. Dan studies his map and picks a route. We march off but are soon lost.

"We should ask for directions. Anyone speak French?" Mags asks.

I know a little French, but I'm sure someone in the group is more fluent than I am. After a long pause, I say, "I can try."

I approach a tall woman with black hair and smiling eyes, "*Excusez-moi, s'il vous plaît. Où est 'l'auberge de jeunessse?*"

She replies with such speed I cannot understand her. I ask her to please speak slowly. She laughs and then drags out, "*Allez tout droit pour un bloc, puis tournez à droite et il sera là.*

I thank her and tell the group, we're just a block away.

Mags grabs my hand and says, "You're handy to have around." She pulls me, skipping, toward the hostel. I feel a little blush of pride.

In the morning, all those who bunked in the dorms gather over café au lait to talk about where we've been and where we're going next. Mags and Dan are headed for Amsterdam. Two guys from Ohio are meeting friends in Paris. They ask me to join them. I recall staring at posters of Sacré Coeur and Montmartre during French class when I was in junior high. I opt for Paris.

The Ohioans and I become siblings for a few days. We buy croque monsieur sandwiches from street vendors, tour the Louvre, Musée d'Orsay, and all the landmarks I used to dream about as a child. We talk over French bread, cheese and wine long into the nights in our *pension*. Then, with different destinations calling to us, we part ways. They board a train to Marseilles, and I catch a ride with a Canadian family bound for Madrid. As I settle into a spot in the back of their VW van, a blue eyed preschooler offers me a bag of trail mix, "Wan' some?" he asks.

"Sure." I say.

The van lurches forward. The boy tosses a roasted nut into my mouth. I toss a raisin into his. We continue our game as the van bounces along, and I realize my new life has begun.

And what a wonderful life it has turned out to be. I almost want to end right there and say, see you in the next book, but it seems my projects pick me rather than the other way around, and another book-length memoir isn't calling to me just yet. So, since early readers of this book wanted to know how I've fared since my youth, I will attempt to tell you without repeating the epilogue to my childhood memoir, *Reversible Skirt*.

Perhaps the most important thing I did in terms of recovering from the harmful decisions I made in my youth was to not become enmeshed romantically for a long time while I figured out what I was interested in and what I wanted in life outside of a mutually loving, life-long romance. I did have relationships, but I kept my distance from the men I dated. Looking back now, I see they were a learning tool for me to study what kind of person I was attracted to (charming but emotionally aloof or abusive and not interested in my needs) and why (they reminded me of my father in various ways), what I expected from the people I dated (to have qualities they didn't possess), and how I reacted to the way they treated me (total scaredy pants if I was beginning to care about them).

My relationships gradually became healthier, and I became clearer about what I needed and whether a potential partner was a good fit. I met my future husband, Jim, through a mutual friend in 1984, and we've been together since our first date (Paula Poundstone at The Other Café in San Francisco's Cole Valley, for those who were in the city back then). Our relationship isn't perfect, of course, but it is supportive, committed and solid. Jim's approach to the big challenges he has faced, as well as the ongoing support he gives to people on the road to recovery from addiction, is an inspiration to me.

I am content (most of the time), live in beautiful Sonoma County, California, work full time as an editor, and always have a writing project in some phrase of development. In addition to having a devoted husband, I have two stepsons and one daughter (all three bring me joy), and recently became a grandmother to a beautiful baby girl whose enthusiasm for life is contagious. I often post pictures of her on Facebook, www.facebook.com/laura.mchale.holland.

My sisters, Kathy and Mary Ruth, and I all migrated to California in the 1970s and live within 100 miles of each other. They are my life-long best friends. They are the ones who have propped me up when I've felt like I couldn't keep going and who show up without fail no matter what's going on. Without them, both in the abusive home environment where we grew up and later, in the aftermath and recovery, my road to the kind of equilibrium I enjoy today would have been far more difficult, if not impossible. Their encouraging words, along with those of my daughter, continue to lift my spirits, which is a precious gift.

In the early days of my "new life," I stewed a lot and wished I could delete the years from my sixteenth to twenty-third birthdays. I knew this was impossible, but I still wished for it. I could not come to terms with that period in my life and would rarely talk about it. I was able, however, to talk about my early years, the ones covered in my first memoir, and through gradually opening up about the trauma of my mother's suicide, the subsequent void where information about her should have been, my father's death at a young age, and my stepmother's abuse, I was able to find and reconnect with the lost little girl in me who, it turns out, had much to say once I started to listen.

I pursued various forms of healing, the most significant of which was a form of peer counseling that gave me a safe place to experience and release whatever emotions I was feeling. I was able to break through a maze of negative thoughts and self-judgments long enough to get a peek at who I am down deep. It gave me some distance from the mess of thoughts running through my mind, too, which enabled me to see that my feelings don't necessarily correspond to reality, that is, I might feel like I'm to blame for certain situations or that I don't deserve to live, but that doesn't mean it's true. This was a major step forward. In my youth, when I had negative feelings about myself, I thought they were the truth. Now, they still enter my mind, but I no longer believe them to be true.

Through the years, no brilliant epiphanies have lifted me to a sustained new level of awareness or functionality, but neither have I experienced anything like the downward spiral of my youth. In addition to peer counseling, I've been lucky to have used many resources that were not available to my mother: meditation, healing spiritual retreats, self-help books aplenty, yoga and other movement classes, acupuncture, Chinese medicinal herbs, Shiatsu massage, and more. I also returned to school and earned a degree in interdisciplinary creative arts from San Francisco State University. I have derived much satisfaction from creative writing and live storytelling in particular. Both have enriched my friendships and strengthened my awareness of who I really am rather than who I think I should be.

After I married Jim and became immersed in parenting, I remained dissatisfied with myself and was focused on fixing certain things: the way I cave when there's even a hint of conflict, my eating habits, my moods, the times I get nervous, the times I give up. I wanted to transform, transform, transform. One evening when I was in my mid forties, I realized that after twenty years of hard, consistent work, I was still trying and not succeeding at self-improvement. I asked myself if I wanted to still be doing this in another twenty years. And, no, I didn't. In that moment, I accepted that there were things I'd likely never be able to change, and that I should stop trying so hard.

I have since found that if you focus on what's good, it will grow stronger, and the weak or undesirable things will occupy less space. I also came to realize it's essential to focus on what you want, not what you don't want. This is still a challenge for me. For the longest time I felt like I didn't deserve to have any goals. I expect people who were seriously abused in their formative years will understand this well; others might find it unfathomable.

Shortly after the period covered in this memoir, I learned from a priest in the family that on his deathbed, my maternal grandfather berated himself because he liked to play the horses. Some of my happiest childhood memories are of going to the racetrack with him, betting two dollars, and watching the horses speed so gracefully by. My grandfather gambled only small amounts. He never bet his home or money for household expenses or savings. He never went into debt. He provided for his family and, in the end, had a little money left after his final hospital bills were paid. The priest was saddened that my grandfather couldn't see the totality of his life and what a good person he was. Since my grandfather made these statements as part of ordinary conversation, not as part of a sacrament, the priest told my sisters and me about them because he thought it would help us in understanding our family dynamics. Sometimes I think this tendency toward self-blame could be a family curse passed on to some of us, including my mother—who committed suicide when I was two years old—and me.

When I was a young adult seeking information about my family, I heard from a few folks willing to talk about my mother that many people loved and respected her—from childhood friends who recalled her extraordinary kindness to students she inspired to try a little harder, to family members who cherished every memory of her. Yet she obviously didn't see her worth on the day she chose to end her life.

I can't imagine she had an inkling of the long-term effects her suicide would have on her children. I also do not believe my stepmother had bad intentions when she married my father. She was not evil; she was just a terrible parent. For reasons I will never know, raising children brought out the very worst in her. She was overbearing and sadistic with my sisters and me, but I expect these qualities took her by surprise when they surfaced in the privacy of our home. She was also a positive force in the lives of several friends who cherished her all the way to the end of their lives.

As an adult, I let go of any expectation that my stepmother would ever mother me and had numerous amicable interactions with her over the years. And today, while my feelings for both of my mothers are complex, the overriding one I have for each of them is love. If you want to know what it was like for me as a young child trying to make sense of things after my mother's suicide, my first memoir, *Reversible Skirt*, will fill you in. Not to worry, though. I now have a wonderfully imperfect life that is full of blessings, not the least of which is the abundant love I share with family and friends—the most important thing, after all.

So as we all carry on in this complex, troubling yet miraculous world of ours, I'll share thoughts that help me point in a positive direction:

Relish every breath, every day, knowing you have a right to live.

Do your best and forgive your failings.

Love who you are, not who you think you should be.

Seek out people who help you feel, not repress, your emotions—and vice versa.

Tell your loved ones often how magnificent they are.

Remember your kindness is powerful, and words do work magic.

Focus on what's good in you, in others and in the world.

Know that you have a right to articulate what you want and pursue your dreams.

Rejoice in the spirit that connects us all.

I hope you have compassion for the struggles you've had in life and that my words inspire and encourage you. And if you've taken wrong turns in life, I hope you think of them as learning experiences and face each morning with a hopeful, peaceful heart.

With all good wishes,
Laura McHale Holland

Acknowledgements

ALWAYS, I GIVE THANKS TO MY blessed family for loving me through the years: my husband, Jim; daughter, Moira; stepsons, Ryan and Jackson; sisters Kathy and Mary Ruth; and Uncle John, who turned 96 in July 2016.

Surrealist poet Nanos Valaoritis, who encouraged me when I was a student at San Francisco State University, will always have a place in my heart, as will Ruth Stotter, who opened the world of live storytelling to me and continues to inspire me today.

I also want to give a shout out to the astute readers who gave me feedback when this memoir was nearing completion: Cath Bore, Susan Callis, Lysle Catron, D.A. Hickman, Nancy Pogue LaTurner, Jennie (Shi) Marima, Chris Predick, Tanya Savko and Joanell Serra. In addition, I am grateful to Skye Blaine, Patrice Garrett and Marie Judson-Rosier who, week after week, offered insightful questions and comments as I worked on bringing this story to life; Ana Manwaring for her enthusiasm and excellent editorial feedback; Karen Batchelor, who welcomed me to the Sonoma County writing community almost a decade ago; and Claire Blotter, poet extraordinaire, who asks difficult questions that rattle my assumptions.

And I cannot end without thanking the people who read my childhood memoir, *Reversible Skirt*, recommended the book to their friends, posted reviews on Amazon and other online sites, and took time to send me notes of appreciation. I am grateful for every comment and question, big and small.

About the Author

WHETHER PENNING A MEMOIR, WRITING FLASH fiction and poetry, or telling stories live, Laura McHale Holland's aim as an artist is to engage people and touch them in ways that matter. *Resilient Ruin* is Laura's fourth published book.

Previously, she released a childhood memoir, *Reversible Skirt*; *The Ice Cream Vendor's Song*, a collection of flash fiction; and *Sisters Born, Sisters Found*, an anthology featuring seventy-six writers from across the globe. Laura's writing has also appeared in several anthologies, magazines and newspapers; her short plays have been produced in Sonoma County, where she lives with her husband and their two tiny, rambunctious dogs.

To connect with Laura and learn more about her work, stop by http://lauramchaleholland.com, and receive the free ebook *Have You Noticed?* for subscribing to her newsletter.

Free ebook created exclusively for newsletter subscribers.

Please take a moment to write a review

DID YOU KNOW THAT THE MORE reviews a book has, the more booksell-
ers like Amazon will spotlight it for potential readers? If you share
an honest review with others who love to read, you will contribute
significantly to this book's success, and I will be most grateful. Here's a
link to my Amazon Author Page, where you'll find links to this book
and the three other books I've published: http://www.amazon.com/
Laura-McHale-Holland/e/B004U8GYNK. Reviews don't need to
be long. Even just a couple of sentences will do.

Thank you so much for reading *Resilient Ruin: A memoir of
hopes dashed and reclaimed*. If you want to contact me directly, hop
over to http://lauramchaleholland.com and send me a note via the
Contact form.

CPSIA information can be obtained
at www.ICGtesting.com
Printed in the USA
FSOW02n0704291016
26684FS

9 780982 936573